D1365318

State Policies
and the Aging

State Policies and the Aging

Sources, Trends and Options

William W. Lammers
University of Southern California
David Klingman
The George Washington
University

LexingtonBooks
D.C. Heath and Company
Lexington, Massachusetts
Toronto

Library of Congress Cataloging in Publication Data
Lammers, William W

State policies and the aging.

  Includes bibliographical references and index.
    1. Aged—Government policy—United States—States.
2. Old age assistance—United States—States.   3. Inter-
governmental fiscal relations—United States.
I. Klingman, David, joint author. II. Title.
HV1461.L35 1984   362.6'042   83–48673
ISBN 0–669–07342–3 (alk. paper)

Copyright © 1984 by D. C. Heath and Company

Published simultaneously in Canada

Printed in the United States of America on acid-free paper

International Standard Book Number: 0–669–07342–3

Library of Congress Catalog Card Number: 83–48673

Contents

Figure and Tables

viii   State Policies and the Aging

Preface and Acknowledgments

Recent events have intensified interest in state policies as they affect the aging in the United States. How does one best explain the changes in state commitments? What do the changing economic fortunes of various regions suggest regarding capacities for effective policy responses? To what extent have past federal policies helped achieve the dual goals of expanded effort and greater nationwide uniformity of policy benefits? Can the states be counted upon to use proposed new latitude in ways that would enhance their commitments to the aging? Given past experiences, how should proposals for significant modifications in federal-state relations be viewed?

An adequate awareness of major questions on the current national agenda requires attention to recent trends and to the forces that have shaped those responses. The impact of factors such as differing population characteristics, economic conditions, and political cultures needs to be considered, along with differing lobbying efforts and leadership roles, in looking toward potential future state policies for the aging. In providing an assessment of state responses, it is important to consider policies in areas such as health and long-term care, income maintenance, social services, and consumer protection. The options that the states now confront can best be explored with a firm awareness of the differing characteristics of those policy areas and their differing potential for political support. We hope that an exploration of these and related issues will help the reader in both understanding—and helping to shape—state policy efforts for the aging.

In addressing basic questions regarding state policies and the aging, we have drawn heavily upon a research project funded by the National Institute on Aging (National Institutes of Health), grant number R01AG01408. It is a pleasure to express our appreciation of that support. We also express our deepest gratitude to all the individuals, too numerous to list here, who contributed to the research that is summarized in this book. These include officials of various government agencies and private organizations at the national, state, and local levels who graciously furnished information or identified sources of information, both published and personal, and present and past officials of state and local agencies and organizations who participated in our case study interviews. We are also indebted to colleagues both around the nation and at the Andrus Center who contributed wise counsel. Particularly deserving of mention among the latter are Neal Cutler and

David Mangen. We thank, in particular, those individuals who worked directly on the project: Mary Deming, Thomas Gillaspy, Marjorie Grace, Rebecca Gronvold, Amy Masters, Robert Myrtle, Marie Perna, Janice Ragsdale, David Samuels, Joann Slead, Raymond Steinberg, Carol Taylor, Michael White, and Eugene Wisnoski. The contribution by Robert Myrtle to our assessment of nursing home regulation was particularly extensive, and we acknowledge his role as a collaborator on that section of chapter 4.

The cooperation and support of our respective families has constituted a vitally important contribution to our research endeavors. Mary, Linda, and Caroline Lammers and Charlotte, Jeffrey, and Justin Klingman deserve far greater expressions of gratitude than are possible in this passage. Our parents, Claude and Lorraine Lammers, and Robert and Lois Klingman, also deserve our deepest expressions of appreciation for their longstanding encouragement of our respective scholarly pursuits. With love and appreciation, we dedicate this book to these very special persons.

State Policies
and the Aging

1 Introduction

The actions of state governments have a major impact on the lives of the aging in the United States. The scope, characteristics, and periodic innovations in Medicaid and social services programs, for example, are influenced to a marked degree by decisions made at the state level. Similarly, the nature of income maintenance policies that supplement Social Security and regulatory policies ranging from life-line utility rates to funeral industry controls are often substantially and even exclusively determined by state governments. In a pattern that parallels the evolution of federal and state responsibilities generally in the last three decades, the federal government has become more important financially, particularly with the growth of Social Security and Medicare, but questions surrounding the design and implementation of expanded federal programs have produced a growing role for state governments.

The importance of state actions on aging-related policies, coupled with the expansion in federal financial commitments, produces a continuing and important debate over the manner in which those dual responsibilities are best shared. In the recurring discussions of possible reform in the nation's federal system, aging-related policies such as Medicaid, social services under Title XX of the Social Security Act, and the regulation of long-term care facilities have had a major place on the nation's reform agenda (see Reagan and Sanzone 1981; Feder and Holahan 1980; Walker 1981). The continuing interest in modifying the federal system—with repeated definitions of a new, New Federalism—underscores both the importance and the uncertainty surrounding existing patterns of federal-state relations. In these discussions, it becomes important to assess issues such as the impact of recent federal policies on the overall level of state effort and the extent to which greater uniformity in the handling of cases in different policy areas may be occurring throughout the country. To evaluate prospects for future state action and the appropriateness of various reform strategies, it is essential to understand the forces that have been shaping those state responses and the magnitude and characteristics of past state efforts.

Basic Issues

The expansion of state policy roles raises critical questions of interest to both policy analysts and participants in policy formation for the

1

aging. Issues involving socioeconomic influences on policy development and the varying nature and significance of key political roles
clearly deserve attention. In terms of socioeconomic influences, for
example, it is important to consider the extent to which state policies
are being shaped by the relative size and well-being of aging populations in the states. With projections of future populations in a number
of states beginning to rival Florida's present 17 percent for those 65
and over, the indications of potential influence stemming from basic
demographic changes have an obvious importance. In examining the
characteristics of the older population, questions also arise surrounding
more specific conditions and their impacts. Do changes on dimensions
such as the proportion of elderly that is over age 75 make a difference
in policy outcomes? Does the number of widows or the number living
alone have an impact on the development of social services policies?

Socioeconomic conditions are also important as potential influences on overall policy development. Does the level of urbanization
and industrialization lead to more substantial policy responses irre-
spective of other political considerations? More generally, to what extent does the level of economic well-being in a state shape policy
responses for the aging? Because of the strong interest in separate
agencies and separate advocacy networks for the aging that has emerged
in the past two decades, the question of the relative uniqueness of
aging policy is of major importance. Do states that are more liberal
than others in their policy responses for various clientele groups also
do more for the aging, and does this occur regardless of specific aspects
of political organization?

An assessment of the impact of political behavior and institutional
relationships is also essential. Are there indications that the aging network of policy specialists and advocates makes a difference in state
policy development? More generally, regarding administrative structures, do different patterns of organization in the human services area
make a difference in the nature of policy outcomes? In turn, do the
increasing levels of aging-based interest group activity show a discern-
ible influence? Turning to the roles of various governmental policy-
makers, governors have often been looked to as a source of political
influence in state politics, especially for people who lack significant
political resources of their own. One must ask if governors make a
difference in policy development for the aging. Finally, the increasing
professionalization of state legislatures, with the greater use of full-
time personnel, longer legislative sessions, higher salaries, and greater
staff assistance, raises the question of possible increases in the level of
legislative influence in policy development. The growing debate over
the sources of state policy development, coupled with the increased

interest in modifying present federal-state relations, underscores the importance of an expanded understanding of state policymaking for the aging.

Previous Studies

The increasing interest in state policy efforts for the aging has produced a growing literature in several related research areas. These include, first, an increasing literature on aging-based interest groups. The impact of comparative approaches in state politics in recent years has produced a second major research thrust: systematic studies of differences in state policy responses. The increased use of federal policy initiatives in an effort to modify state actions has generated a third area of expanded research: aging-related studies of intergovernmental relations. A brief review of major studies in these three areas gives an indication of existing understandings and current research issues.

Aging-Based Interest Groups

The study of interest group activity by the aging has moved from a primary emphasis on nationally focused organizations to an examination of both state and nationally focused organizations. Major early works include those of Holtzman (1963) and Pratt (1976). Both studies give important indications of issues involved in interpreting the role of interest groups in the development of public policy. Neither of these assessments, however, gives extensive attention to the role of such groups at the state level.

State-level interest groups are also now producing major studies. One indication of an emerging interest in the analysis of state-level interest group activities came with the study of California's pension movement by Putnam (1970). After carefully describing the position of the California interest groups since the 1920s, Putnam attributes major importance to their actions in fostering California's relatively strong policy response in the 1950s. California's development is important but quite unique, since most states were doing very little for the aging in the 1950s. More recently, Bruner (1978) undertook a lengthy analysis of aging-based interest groups in Iowa. In his study, those groups in the mid-1970s were judged to have a significant role as issue raisers but were not viewed as major forces in the shaping of overall policy responses. In a study of the role of the Silver-Haired Legislature in Florida, however, Matura (1981) attributes greater im-

portance to aging-based lobby efforts. Each of these state studies points
to differing levels of importance that can be found in different states
and in different configurations of leadership styles and key issues.

To date, the most systematic analysis of state interest group activity
on behalf of the aging has been undertaken by Dobson and Karns
(1979). In that study, legislators, lobbyists, and rank-and-file members
of the National Council of Senior Citizens (NCSC) were surveyed in
some 27 different states. Overall, the authors see substantial limitations
on the roles of aging-based interest groups in their efforts to influence
state legislators. Besides the importance of those conclusions, this study
also underscores the importance and feasibility of examining state interest group activity in a comparative context.

Policy-Oriented Studies

A major set of writings on state politics and the aging has focused on
specific policies, with an increasing interest in comparative analysis.
The first significant set of analyses of state policy outcomes came with
the efforts of the Council of State Governments in the 1950s and the
activities leading to the 1961 White House Conference on Aging. Each
of the states produced a report surveying existing policies, and some
projects produced book-length volumes—for example, the work on
Washington by Hopkins (1961) and on Minnesota by Rose (1963).
These reports provided valuable background on existing policies but
did not involve a systematic attempt to explain the differing levels of
state policy effort.

The first systematic comparisons of state policy efforts for the aging
were undertaken by Dye (1966) and Sharkansky (1968), who studied
state Old Age Assistance (OAA) policies. As frequently occurred in
early writing on state policy, economic factors showed a greater influence than political factors in explaining policy differences. Sharkansky's analysis was limited in terms of the time period being studied and
statistically did not go beyond partial correlation analysis. Nonetheless,
the issues raised, and the usefulness of comparative analysis, were
clearly revealed in that initial study.

The 1970s have seen an increasing variety of policy studies using
systematic comparative approaches. In the area of health care, Dunlop
(1979), Davidson (1980), Buchanan (1981), and Bovbjerg and Holahan
(1982) have made significant contributions. In Dunlop's analysis, the
growth of nursing home bed supply is examined with both a fifty-state
comparison and case studies of ten states. In that analysis, the importance of examining both socioeconomic factors and federal policy

changes in explaining changes in state-level responses is dramatically underscored. With this approach, Dunlop is able to show that bed supply was responding to changing demographic conditions and had started to increase substantially several years prior to the passage of Medicaid in 1965. Davidson's (1980) analysis of Medicaid effectively shows the importance and usefulness of comparative analysis that measures policy effort on the basis of not only dollars but also scope of services and the liberalness of eligibility requirements. The studies of Medicaid reimbursement rates and policies by Buchanan (1981) and Bovbjerg and Holahan (1982) similarly show the importance of analyzing policy in a given area on the basis of multiple dimensions. The evolution of policy-oriented studies has thus clearly been toward more systematic comparisons, comparisons that include a range of policy responses.

Federal-State Relations

The changing nature of federal-state relations has also attracted scholarly interest. In a comprehensive study of responses in Massachusetts, Derthick (1970) was able to demonstrate the impact of greater federal commitments for OAA programs on important dimensions such as uniformity of coverage and administrative efficiency. The work by Harbert (1976) constitutes a major contribution in this area. In her analysis, the impacts of different federal strategies vis-à-vis the states are examined in the three policy areas of (1) OAA, (2) Older Americans Act funding for Title III programs, and (3) Vocational Rehabilitation Services. From a fifty-state comparison, Harbert draws two major conclusions. First, the grant system manifested in these three programs is not producing a major equalization effort in terms of dollars spent among the states. Second, the determinants of state performance in the grant system include demographic, economic, and political factors, with the latter playing an important role. These two conclusions, drawn from three policy areas, show the importance of examining issues such as equalization and levels of effort in the study of state policy responses for the aging within a federal system.

The development of social services programs and the operations of the Older Americans Act have also produced several studies of differing state responses. The work of Gilbert and Specht (1979, 1982) has focused on differing state practices for the targeting of social services funds for the neediest groups in the population, as well as the division of support between aging and nonaging recipients. Regarding the Older Americans Act, analysts like Steinberg (1977) have examined differing responses in the initial establishment of organizational structures being promoted by the Older Americans Act. The most forceful evaluation of those responses has been in the work of Estes (1979). The author develops a critical evaluation of the Older Americans Act on the basis of several of the goals being expressed during its enactment in 1965. In terms of the tendencies for the new structures to produce a pooling of resources for the aging, the existing responses are seen as distinctly limited. In turn, the fragmentation of service programs that is exacerbated by the operations of the Older Americans Act is seen as a means of producing symbolic rewards more than a significant, coordinated set of social services. The Estes critique thus forcefully underscores basic issues regarding the performance of the states under the Older Americans Act.

The recent proposals calling for greater flexibility in federal approaches toward state policy for the aging (and other clientele groups) have also produced an important debate (see Estes et al. 1983). Representative of this emerging debate is the assessment by Hudson (1981). In that review, the author questions a number of the claims being raised surrounding the New Federalism while suggesting that there are some advantages for the aging in the present set of role relationships between the federal and state governments. In particular, Hudson is concerned with the possibility that a shift to greater reliance upon the states may produce a reduced tendency to aid the most disadvantaged among the aging population. Regardless of the outcome of the proposals launched by the Reagan administration for a New Federalism, it seems likely that the 1980s will produce an intensified debate over the appropriate federal and state roles in various policy areas that affect the aging.

Research Approaches

The study of state policy formation has undergone considerable expansion in the 1970s. The initial debate over the relative impact of politics or economics has been replaced by more focused questions (see Dye and Gray 1980). Expanding research methodologies now include greater sophistication in the use of statistical techniques and greater integration of case studies and quantitative measures. While issues of measurement and interpretation understandably remain, the study of state policy for the aging can build from an increasingly substantial set of research activities. The following discussion thus focuses on key issues and findings as they relate to the expanding research opportunities.

Policy Characteristics

Students of state politics have increasingly begun to explore opportunities for comparative analysis that looks specifically at different types of policies. Perhaps the first dimension to gain recognition was the distinction between policies that involved significant direct financial outlays and those that were primarily regulatory in nature. The importance of this distinction has been demonstrated by studies in recent years that have given considerable attention to regulatory practices such as consumer protection (see Sigelman and Smith 1980) and environmental protection (see Perry 1981). Since these studies have not directly compared regulatory and expenditure-based policies in the same framework and with the same variables, the degree of systematic comparison is limited. Nonetheless, initial findings like those by Perry (1981), which stress the importance of the legislative role in environmental protection responses, forcefully underscore the need to study nonfiscal state policies. Fortunately, because policy efforts for the aging do include both expenditure-intensive and regulatory policies, several opportunities for comparison are readily available.

A second form of comparison has received growing attention since the publication of the major work of Fry and Winters (1970) on the degree of redistribution in state policy efforts. The central issue raised in that work and in more recent analyses by, among others, Sullivan (1972), is the extent to which the net operation of state politics (including taxing and spending) produces an increase in the after-tax income of the lowest income groups in the states. Despite measurement limitations with this policy dimension, the findings from recent studies have given an indication that the degree of redistribution in overall policy commitments constitutes an important line of inquiry. Similarly, analyses in specific policy areas point to the importance of considering policy responses on the basis of the degree of redistribution that is achieved. Clearly, the use of analytic concepts like levels of redistribution in assessing policy characteristics stands as an important development in the emerging approaches to the study of comparative state policy.

A third distinction that is important in the literature on public policy has received limited attention in the comparative state politics literature. This distinction involves differences between direct and indirect policy designs. Discussions of strategies for combating poverty have often focused on the appropriateness of direct financial assistance versus services and in-kind assistance (see, for example, the discussions by Garfinkel and Skidmore 1978, and Garfinkel 1982). Less attention has been directed, however, toward the question of the extent to which various policy strategies, in specific political environments, are apt to draw differing levels of support. State policies for the aging, with their wide range of direct and indirect approaches, constitute an important arena for an examination of this issue. In the development of a research strategy, it is important to pursue potentials for comparison among policy characteristics, including in-kind versus cash policies, differing degrees of redistributive impact, and regulatory versus expenditure-based policies.

Differing Federal-State Relations

It has become increasingly apparent in recent years that students of state policy must pay close attention to the differing requirements and incentives that surround state policy efforts in different policy areas. The development of a single index of state innovativeness in the pioneering work by Walker (1969) has produced, for example, subsequent interest in subdividing those policy areas, as reported by Gray (1973), and some concern, as expressed by Rose (1973), that the innovation indexes are not sufficiently sensitive to the differing degree of federal control in respective policy areas.

More generally, as discussed in our review of aging-related policies in the area of federal-state relations, interest in the extent to which different federal policies will contribute to varying levels of state response has increased. Thus, federal-state relationships, along with concepts differentiating state policies, emerge as important future directions for studies of state policies for the aging.

Changes over Time

Following, in part, the lead of studies of policy formation among different nations, students of state policy have sought to increase the number of analyses that trace policy responses over substantial periods of time. There are important opportunities in longitudinal analysis for measuring the impact of different forces on state politics without being confined to a single period within the overall flow of politics in the nation; that is, cross-sectional studies show responses in terms of different levels of development but within the context of national policies at a single point in time.

Diffusion of Policy Innovations

The study of state policy has also begun to include different patterns in the diffusion of policy innovations among the states. State innova-

tiveness, or the tendency to adopt new policy programs and procedures, was initially viewed in the classic work by Walker (1969) as a
dependent variable that needed to be explained by other factors that
were influencing state responses. More recently, however, innovativeness has also been employed as an independent variable in attempts
to explain the adoption or nonadoption of programs in a variety of
substantive policy areas (see Glick 1981). In the more extensive literature treating policy innovation as a dependent variable, the major
issue has been the extent to which innovativeness can be considered a
consistent and enduring trait of state governments. Although Walker's
original measure was intended to tap a general dimension of state
policy that is stable across time and type of program, several subsequent studies have suggested that innovativeness is not a general and
stable characteristic of states but is instead specific to particular policy
issue areas and time periods (see Canon and Baum 1981). In contrast,
by employing a more sophisticated measure of overall innovativeness,
Savage (1978) did uncover some evidence that certain states were consistently lower than others in innovativeness over time. Clearly, the
key issue of possible general differences in innovative tendencies warrants attention in subsequent studies.

Two related issues in the literature on state policy innovativeness
have also emerged: first, the extent to which policies have diffused in
regional patterns and, second, the extent to which actions of the federal
government influence state policy effort and innovativeness. Although
Walker (1969, 1971) found evidence of national as well as regional
networks of specialized communication among state officials, the same
studies that found little relationship within or between policy areas in
state and local innovation also found little evidence of regional patterns
of diffusion, except within certain narrow policy areas (Bingham 1977).
In the most direct investigation of the issue of regional patterns of
innovation, however, Foster (1978) controlled for some of the systematic variables associated wtih region (population, urbanization, industrialization, and reapportionment) and still found significant differences
in innovativeness across regions.

The evidence concerning the homogenizing effect of federal influence and other nationalizing forces, in contrast, has been even more
mixed. For example, Welch and Thompson (1980) found that federal
involvement somewhat affected the rate of policy diffusion among the
states, and Savage (1978) detected some increase in similarity among
the states over time in their rates of adoption of new policies. However,
Kemp (1978) found evidence of the effects of diffusion in changes over
time in the across-region variation in state expenditures but no consistent nationalizing trends. These conflicting findings underscore the im-

portance of examining the diffusion of policy innovations in comparative state studies.

Political Culture

In the search for underlying social dimensions that help to explain different policy responses, researchers have directed increased attention to the importance of state political culture. The initial studies undertaken in the 1960s did not include specific cultural dimensions, in part because of the difficulty involved in developing specific measures. The judgmental analysis undertaken by Elazar (1972), and the modifications that have followed (see Kincaid 1982), have nonetheless produced a renewed research interest in the impact of state political cultures on state policy responses. It is important to note that studies in several different policy areas, as reviewed by Savage (1981), have found political culture to be a significant factor in shaping state policy.

Measures of Political Behavior

Due in considerable part to the limited measures of political behavior that were available in the 1960s, the initial assessments of the political dimensions of state policy formation emphasized formal dimensions of political structures such as legislative apportionment, the formal powers of the governor, and the length of legislative sessions. Voter turnout and levels of party competition, while capturing some aspects of political behavior, typically constituted the only dimensions being included in studies such as those by Dye (1966) and Sharkansky and Hofferbert (1969). The critique of these works by Uslaner (1978) emphasizes that the political dimensions of policy formation can only be captured effectively with the development of more refined measures.

Case Studies

An increasing number of state policy formation studies have shown the importance of including case study analyses with fifty-state comparative analyses. In studies involving aspects of public policy affecting the aging, this approach has been exemplified by Dunlop (1979), Dobson and Karns (1979), and Vladeck (1980). The use of both case studies and fifty-state comparisons by Morehouse (1980) constitutes a forceful example of the advantages involved with the inclusion of case-study interpretations. The effectiveness of case studies of states has emerged, in particular, in assessments that have utilized a careful sampling strategy for the choice of states warranting intense examination.

Summary

The emerging research directions in the comparative study of state policy formation provide a number of suggestions for approaches to the study of aging-related policy development. Policies need to be examined through the use of analytic concepts, and variations among states over time in federal-state relationships deserve careful attention. In addition, important leads have emerged surrounding the study of change over time, diffusion patterns, and the impact of political culture. Finally, in the pursuit of complete explanations, it has become increasingly evident that it is essential to consider behavioral dimensions of political processes and to seek linkages between case studies and empirically based comparisons. Given the increasing importance of state policies for the aging, it is gratifying to find an expanding range of techniques and approaches available for use in comparative state research.

The Research Design

This study of state policy development for the aging builds upon existng studies in several respects. State efforts are statistically examined for a twenty-year time period (1955–1975) to facilitate an assessment of change over time. In this aggregate-level portion of the analysis, measures of state policy efforts in the areas of income maintenance, health and long-term care, social services, and regulatory protection are used as dependent variables to be analyzed with the use of socioeconomic and political variables as potential predictors of different state responses. To focus that initial aggregate-level analysis on key underlying issues, a basic analytical framework is employed. The examination of policy process characteristics has in turn been pursued through a series of case studies in eight states. These states were chosen on the basis of preliminary results of the initial aggregate-level analysis to enhance the significance of the case-study findings. To confront the policy issues being raised in the 1980s, the initial findings regarding different patterns of policy effort and support have been evaluated regarding indications of potential support for different policy areas and policy designs. The following discussion reviews major aspects of each of those approaches.

Aggregate-Level Analysis

The model depicted in figure 1–1 serves as an initial organizing framework for the large number of variables included in the aggregate-level analysis.[1] Despite the absence of extensive theory in some areas of comparative state research, it is possible to bring together existing studies into a basic framework for analysis. That basic model includes, as potential explanatory factors, sets of relationships in the areas of political capacity, political openness, lobbying efforts for the aging, general policy liberalism, tax capacity, characteristics of the older population, and basic socioeconomic aspects of each state.

Turning first to the political aspects of the model, a state's level of overall policy effort in the area of aging is conceptualized as being a direct function of three interrelated characteristics: (1) the state's *fiscal capacity*—that is, ability to generate revenue; (2) its *general policy liberalism* (Klingman and Lammers 1984), or its predisposition to respond through the public sector in areas related to aging (for example, social welfare, health, and civil rights); and (3) its level of *aging advocacy,* or the extent of lobbying activity at the state level on behalf of the aging.

The relative importance of each of these concepts in explaining the cross-state variance in state aging policy effort is by no means obvious. Indeed, it is not clear that a high score on each of them is a necessary condition for a high level of aging policy effort, but one or more of them may be sufficient. Thus, states with extremely high fiscal capacity may generate substantial efforts for the aging regardless of the other three characteristics, simply because they can afford such policy commitments. Similarly, states with a generally liberal track record in other policy areas may also make a stronger effort in the area of aging, even without strong pressure on behalf of the aging. Even in the absence of large amounts of revenue, a state can make substantial regulatory efforts to benefit the aging. It is less clear, however, whether a state with strong advocacy by and for the aging can make substantial policy efforts on their behalf if the state lacks either the fiscal capacity or the general predisposition to do so—or worse, both.

In any event, general policy liberalism and fiscal capacity are seen as being mutually reinforcing, in that states with greater fiscal capacity can afford to make more substantial policy efforts, and more active states are more likely to seek additional sources of revenue. In turn,

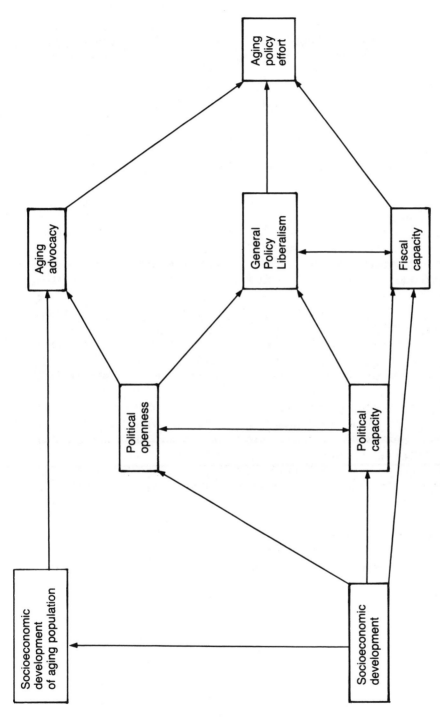

Figure 1–1. Conceptual Model of the State Aging Policy Process

each of these two concepts is further conceptualized as being dependent on the state's *political capacity*—that is, the level of development of its policymaking institutions, primarily the governor and the legislature; thus, states with more powerful and successful governors (Schlesinger 1971) and more professional legislatures (Grumm 1971) than those in other states are more likely to make substantial policy efforts in a variety of areas, to seek the sources of revenue to underwrite those efforts, and to develop strong bureaucracies to implement those efforts.

The aging advocacy component is seen as being dependent on the size and socioeconomic status of the state's aging population since a larger, wealthier, and more educated aging population might be more likely to generate demands for actions benefiting that clientele. Both aging advocacy and general policy liberalism are seen as being a function of the state's overall degree of *political openness*—that is, the level of political participation, interparty competition, and legislative apportionment in representing the diverse interests in the state. Political openness is also seen as having a reciprocal, mutually reinforcing relationship with the concept of political capacity; that is, participation, competition, and representation foster not only greater lobbying activity by diverse interests but also greater pressure for the development of stronger policymaking institutions. Strong institutions, at the same time, may also invite, facilitate, and even promote greater political openness.

Finally, aging population, political openness, political capacity, and fiscal capacity are conceptualized as being dependent on the state's level of *socioeconomic development*—that is, industrialization, urbanization, wealth, and size. Previous research in comparative state politics (see Dye and Gray 1980) has clearly shown the importance of such development in the production of state policy in a variety of substantive areas. But that literature has failed to specify the intervening steps that transmit socioeconomic influences through the political and policymaking processes of a state (see Stonecash 1980). The model depicted in figure 1–1 shows those influences contributing to the development of political activity on the part of a greater number of diverse interests and hence greater participation, competition, and representation. Socioeconomic conditions also directly shape the characteristics of the state's older population through basic demographic processes. Socioeconomic forces, in conjunction with political openness, also generate the need for stronger policymaking institutions as the state's society and economy become more complex and demanding of direction. Finally, the capacity of the state's economy, along with the capacity of its policymaking institutions, determines the extent of its revenue sources and its government's willingness to extract those revenues.

Not depicted in this model is the pervasive influence of policy efforts by the federal government in shaping state socioeconomic, political, and public policy characteristics. Federal activity clearly affects each of the major concepts depicted in the model to varying degrees. That influence cannot be directly incorporated in a cross-sectional model, however, because no single indicator or set of indicators exists to represent the differential impact of federal activity in each state, even in a fairly narrow policy area like aging. General measures such as total federal aid per capita to each state or the net flow of expenditures and revenues between the federal government and each state do not fully capture the variety of federal actions that influences state characteristics and actions. Instead, in a successive cross-section design, the influence of the federal government must be inferred from changes in the cross-state patterns of variation from one time period to the next and from the results of findings from case studies.

To fulfill the need for analysis over time, while at the same time keeping the size of the data set manageable, each of the variables (when available) is measured at five successive time points: 1955, 1960, 1965, 1970, and 1975. These respective time points thus enable us to measure the nature of state responses in distinctly different periods of national politics. As of 1955, state governments were doing very little in the area of aging, with the exception of a fairly strong effort in California and some stirring of activity in a few of the progressive states. The 1960 time point captures the level of state effort as the major debate over Medicare and Medicaid was beginning in Congress and in presidential politics. The 1965 time point measures the level of effort just prior to the beginning of the Older Americans Act programs and Medicaid. The 1970 period in turn taps the initial responses to those program efforts along with the instigation of a new group of social service efforts in some states. Similarly, the 1970 time point captures the degree of state regulatory effort in areas like nursing homes prior to the stronger federal role imposed after 1972. Finally, the 1975 time point measures the level of state activity in the context of an expanding set of responses by both federal and state governments in the 1970s. Although some individual policy measures were available after that date and have been included in the overall analysis, the absence of 1980 census data during the initial file creation period prevented a systematic inclusion of the 1980 time point. Since the case

studies were conducted in 1980, however, the case study interpretations also reflect events that occurred in the last half of the 1970s.

The Variables

The conceptual model of the state aging policy process presented in
figure 1–1 can serve as an organizing framework for a discussion of
the variables used in the fifty-state aggregate analysis for this project.
Most of the variables are by now standard in the literature on comparative state politics, but several were developed specifically for the
project. Many of the specially developed variables are conceptually
similar to indicators widely employed in the literature, but others were
designed to measure new concepts, especially regulatory policies in the
area of aging. The more familiar variables were available from standard sources such as various publications of the Census Bureau, the
Social Security Administration, and the Council of State Governments'
biennial *Book of the States,* plus various published tables and figures
in the literature on comparative state politics. The specialized measures
were usually gleaned from those same types of sources or more specialized publications of the federal government or reports issued by
private associations and institutes and university-affiliated research organizations. In all, the project data set contains approximately 200 raw
variables, over 500 including transformed variables, many with up to
six time points (1950 as well as the other five). To facilitate both the
understanding of these variables and their use in relation to presen-
tations in subsequent chapters, we have emphasized in this presentation the conceptual manner in which the measures are being employed
and have then included specific definitions, with sources, in the appendix. For convenience, although the variables were not always available for the exact quinquennial time point, they will be referred to as
representing either 1955, 1960, 1965, 1970, or 1975.

Aging Policy Effort. The dependent variables of the study consist of a
variety of single indicators and composite factors (see note 1) measuring state policy effort for the aging in four major substantive policy
areas: (1) income maintenance, (2) health and long-term care,
(3) regulatory protection, and (4) social services. In the area of *income
maintenance,* two single indicators served as the principal measures of
state policy effort for the aging in all five time periods. Both indicators
involve the federal-state formula matching grant program of OAA prior
to 1975 and optional state supplements to the federal program of Supplemental Security Income for the elderly (SSI-Aged) for 1975. The

two indicators are the average monthly payment for OAA-SSI and the number of recipients of those payments as a percentage of the elderly population of the state. The third measure of aging income mainte-nance effort is a composite factor available only for 1975, representing the following five variables: average dollar amount of tax relief (both property and income combined) for the elderly and four features of state supplemental payments under SSI-Aged: monthly payment limits for individuals, monthly payment limits for couples, the ratio of state supplement recipients to federal payment recipients, and state supple-ment recipients as a percentage of all aged poor.

A substantially larger number of indicators and factors were em-ployed in the area of *health and long-term care*. Two dichotomous dimensions serve to classify these numerous variables. Substantively, the variables represent either state Medicaid program characteristics or state provisions for nursing home regulation. Methodologically, they are either expenditure-based or nonfiscal (usually regulatory) mea-sures. All of the nursing home regulation variables are nonfiscal in nature, usually measuring the scope and stringency of state regulatory provisions. Some of the Medicaid variables are also nonfiscal in nature, measuring the scope and generosity of requirements and services, but many of the Medicaid variables are expenditure based, measuring the amount of money spent for various services.

The expenditure-based Medicaid variables available for both 1970 and 1975 include state expenditures per elderly person for skilled nurs-ing care, dental care, and total for aging recipients. Expenditures for skilled nursing, home health, dental, and total correlated sufficiently with the previously discussed income maintenance factor to warrant creation of a broader factor spanning the two policy areas of income maintenance and health care, labeled the *aging health and welfare pol-icy factor*. As with the income maintenance factor, this factor was also available only for 1975. However, data were available for 1965 on the number of recipients and total state and local expenditures per elderly person under Medicaid's predecessor, the Kerr-Mills program of Med-ical Assistance to the Aged (MAA). Also available for that period were four indicators of state medical provisions under the OAA pro-gram: (1) medical expenditures as a percentage of total OAA expen-ditures, (2) average monthly medical payment per recipient of OAA (state and federal combined), (3) total number of dental services avail-able to recipients of OAA, and (4) number of years since first partic-ipation in a medical vendor payment program for nursing home patients. One indicator of the early years of the Medicaid program, the number of years since establishment of a Medicaid program, successfully com-bined with all the listed measures of health policy in 1965 except the

MAA recipients measure to form what was labeled the *early aging health policy factor*.

The nonfiscal measures of state Medicaid policy included some that were available for both 1970 and 1975 and some that were available for only 1975. Those available for both time points included number of optional medical services available to recipients of Medicaid, method of reimbursement for health-care providers, extent of inclusion of medically needy persons (that is, those who would be impoverished by medical bills), extent of program limitations, and an index of the overall scope of the Medicaid program (Davidson 1978). Variables available only for 1975 included mechanisms for payment, profits, and depreciation for health care providers; cost basis for such providers; cost control provisions; occupancy requirements; ease of admission to nursing homes; income limits; and arrangements for recipients of SSI. The measures of payment mechanism, cost basis, and occupancy requirements successfully formed a composite factor labeled the *cost control factor*. Because of their relevance for nursing home care, this factor and the other measures of regulation of health care providers could appropriately be included under nursing home regulation rather than Medicaid characteristics. The cost control factor henceforth will be so classified.

As for the various nonfiscal measures of nursing home regulations other than those arising from the Medicaid program, some were available for 1970 and others for 1975, but none was available for both time periods. The indicators available for 1970 included number of fire safety regulations, number of patient care regulations, status of the chairmanship of the board of examiners of nursing home administrators, composition of those boards, number of years since first adoption of a Certificate of Need program, and number of years since agreement on cost containment under Section 1122 of the Social Security Act. In addition to the cost control factor as discussed, the following variables were available for 1975: home health agency coverage under the Certificate of Need program, type of civil remedy utilized to enforce nursing home standards, extent of use of temporary licensure for noncompliance with nursing home regulations, extent of legal services provided by the attorney general's office to the state agency that licenses nursing homes, the degree of specificity of nursing home regulations, extent of recent changes in nursing home regulations, organizational placement of nursing home licensing activity within the state bureaucracy, organizational structure of licensure programs of the state nursing home regulatory body, number of nursing home consulting staff per 1,000 nursing home beds, number of nursing home survey staff per 1,000 nursing home beds, and average number of inspection visits to long-term care facilities by the nursing home regulatory body. No composite factors were successfully created from these various indicators of nursing home regulation.

In addition to these numerous measures of nursing home regulation for 1970 and 1975, two indicators were available for 1955: (1) number of years since first adoption of nursing home regulations and (2) stringency of relative responsibility requirements under OAA. Also, a large number of variables measuring the characteristics of nursing homes and other health care facilities, including number of institutions in various size categories (number of beds), total bed supply, increase in the number of facilities and beds, and cost of added facilities, were available for various time periods as independent variables in the analysis of cross-state variation in nursing home regulation (see chapter 4). Finally, the number of physicians and the number of hospital beds per 100,000 persons were used as indicators of overall health care capacity in each state.

The policy area of *regulatory protection* included nonfiscal measures of state regulation of age discrimination in employment, generic drug substitution, hearing aid sales, funeral home practices, and public guardianship arrangements. These measures were available for only 1975 except for overall scope of regulation (that is, the number of provisions favoring older workers) of age discrimination in employment, which was available for 1955, 1965, and 1975. The number of years since adoption of age discrimination legislation was another measure available for that area. A mail survey of state agencies charged with enforcing age discrimination regulations was intended to produce measures of the number of successful prosecutions of violators, but it yielded only the number of complaints filed and was fraught with missing data. In the area of generic drug substitution, similar measures were available, but only for 1975: overall scope of regulation (that is, the number of provisions facilitating substitution at the pharmacist's discretion) and number of years since adoption of such regulation. Similar measures were also available for hearing aid regulation as of 1975: overall scope of regulation (that is, the number of provisions protecting the consumer and prohibiting fraudulent sales practices) and number of years since adoption of such regulation. In addition, a measure of the composition of the state hearing aid regulatory board (that is, the proportion of consumer as opposed to dealer representatives) was also employed. In the area of funeral home regulation, only a measure of overall scope of regulation (that is, the number of provisions outlawing predatory sales practices) and regulatory board composition (again, consumer versus industry representation) were employed, again only for 1975. Finally, a measure of overall scope of regulation of public guardianship (that is, the number of provisions protecting the interests of the incapacitated person) was available, once again for 1975. As with nursing home regulation, no composite factors were successfully created for these various indicators of regulatory protection.

The final policy area, *social services,* was represented primarily by indicators of the characteristics of the State Unit on Aging (SUA), or the government agency in each state designated to serve as the focal point for funds distributed under the Older Americans Act. These indicators were all available only for 1975, except for the scope of organization of the SUA (that is, the total number of points assigned for features like paid staff), which was available for earlier state aging offices as of 1955 as well. The following indicators for 1975 successfully formed a composite factor labeled the *SUA size factor:* total SUA budget, SUA administrative budget, number of SUA staff personnel, and number of Area Agencies on Aging (AAAs) in the state. The following variables for 1975 successfully formed a composite factor labeled the *SUA status factor:* level of administrative placement within the state government, location of the SUA in an umbrella agency, and administrative status of the director of the SUA (appointed versus merit). The following indicators for 1975 successfully formed a composite factor labeled the *social services factor:* amount of state funds in the SUA budget per capita, amount of state funds in the SUA administrative budget per capita, and percentage of federal funds distributed under Title III of the Older Americans Act that the state allocates to actual social services rather than to administration and so forth. Finally, the following single indicators were also employed for 1975: total SUA budget per 1,000 elderly persons, percentage of Comprehensive Annual Service Program (CASP) social services allocated for elderly persons, and percentage of Title XX social services expenditures for the aged going to aged persons receiving SSI payments.

Aging Advocacy. The second major concept in the model depicted in figure 1–1 is aging advocacy, which represents the extent of lobbying activity at the state level on behalf of the elderly. This conceptual area would be measured ideally by indicators such as numbers of lobbyists and amounts of money spent lobbying on behalf of the elderly. Unfortunately, such data simply are not available from even the most cooperative of the aging interest groups. Instead, aging advocacy in this study was measured by a variety of indirect indicators that we hope reflect to some extent the overall level of interest group activity on behalf of the elderly at the state level. Fortunately, at least the indirect measures that were available were occasionally available for multiple time points.

The most extensive data for this area were generously supplied by the American Association of Retired Persons (AARP). The variables here included total state membership in AARP as a percentage of the state's elderly population, number of years since establishment of the state's AARP chapter, number of bills promoted by the state chapter, number of promoted bills enacted, and for analysis as an independent variable in the area of nursing home regulation, number of references to nursing home regulation and related topics in the state AARP chapter's publications. For the other national, aging-based interest group with state-level organizations, the NCSC, the only available measure was a subjective rating of each chapter's lobbying effort, as judged by a knowledgeable member of the NCSC national staff. These measures were available only for 1975, except AARP membership, which was also available for 1970.

A set of indirect measures of the overall level of aging-based interest group activity in each state that we were able to develop for 1965, 1970, and 1975 was the number of state and local organizations in general and, more specifically, the number of senior organizations in the state represented by witnesses at hearings of the U.S. Senate Special Committee on Aging. Similar, but only for 1950, was the number of registrants from the state at the 1950 White House Conference on Aging. In addition to total number, those registrants were classified as public sector, private sector, or academic. Finally, also available for 1950 was the number of active Townsend clubs in the state, representing the remnants of the nationwide pension movement that peaked in the late 1930s.

General Policy Liberalism. As might be expected, a vast array of indicators would theoretically be available to measure the state's general policy liberalism, or its track record of overall policy effort in areas related to aging, such as social welfare, health, and civil rights. For this project, a seemingly representative sample of such indicators was selected as potential sources of partial explanation for state aging policy effort. Many of them were available for multiple time points; others were available for only single, but different, time points. Probably the broadest measure in terms of both time and substance is Walker's (1969) index of overall policy innovativeness, which measures earliness of adoption of policy innovations in 88 substantive areas dating from the nineteenth century. Another measure of innovation, reported also by Walker, was the number of times the state was cited as the source of legislation proposed in the 1970 program of model legislation sponsored by the Advisory Commission on Intergovernmental Relations (ACIR).

Several more specific measures of state policy effort in policy areas similar to aging were also utilized. First, three measures of state policies under the federal-state program of Aid to Families with Dependent Children (AFDC) were available for various time periods: average monthly payment per recipient, for all five time points; state and local percentage of total expenditures, for 1955, 1960, and 1966; and overall scope of eligibility requirements, for 1960 and 1970. Second, average monthly payment per recipient and state-local funds as a percentage of total expenditures were measured for both Aid to the Blind (SSI-Blind in 1975) and Aid to the Disabled (SSI-Disabled in 1975) for all five time points. Third, for the parallel area of general social services, the percentage of federal Title XX funds for social services actually spent by the state was available for 1975. Total state expenditures for vocational rehabilitation programs were available for 1965, 1970, and 1975. Finally, an index of the regressivity of the state's tax burden was available for 1970 and 1975.

Nonfiscal measures of the state's general policy liberalism, all available only for 1975 unless otherwise noted, included number of professions for which there are continuing education requirements, number of consumer-oriented provisions, an index of the liberalism of provisions for voter initiatives (1965), an index of the scope of civil rights (antidiscrimination) legislation (1961), and two measures of the state's position on the Equal Rights Amendment (ERA): number of years since ratification and an index of the ease of ratification. Finally, six of these variables, both expenditure-based and nonfiscal in nature and spanning an extensive time period, successfully formed a composite factor labeled the *general policy liberalism factor:* the index of overall policy innovativeness, the index of antidiscrimination provisions, average monthly payment for AFDC, number of years since ratification of the ERA, number of consumer-oriented enactments, and percentage utilization of Title XX social services funds. (For a more extensive discussion, see Klingman and Lammers 1984.)

Fiscal Capacity. For the third major explanatory concept in the model of the state aging policy process depicted in figure 1–1, state fiscal capacity, or ability to generate revenue, once again a large number of measures were available for potential use. The concept encompasses the overall level of development of the state government, including administrative capacity as well as fiscal capacity. In essence, the concept reflects the scope of the state's public sector relative to its private sector and of the state government relative to the state's local governments. Accordingly, various revenue measures were derived from figures available for all five time points, not only on revenue from each level of government's own sources but also on intergovernmental transfers, including funds from the federal government. The resulting revenue measures thus represented each combination of the following dichotomies: state-only versus state-local, derived from own sources versus available for own purposes, and per capita versus percentage of state personal income. In addition to revenue measures, data on government employment were also employed to measure the scope of the state's public sector. The employment measures similarly represented each combination of the following dichotomies: state only versus state local and per capita versus percentage of labor force. Fortunately, most of these derived measures of both revenue and employment contributed to the formation of two composite factors: a scope of state government factor and a scope of state-local government factor.

Additional single indicators, available for all five time points unless otherwise noted, were employed to represent other aspects of the concept of state fiscal capacity, including state government expenditure as a percentage of state-local government expenditure (a measure of centralization); state government employment as a percentage of state-local government employment (another measure of centralization); a ranking of the states based on a similar index of centralization (Perry 1976) for 1970; percentage of state-local revenue derived from taxes (a measure of the state's willingness to extract revenue), plus similar measures for each type of tax (personal income, corporate income, general sales, selective sales, and property); and two measures of the related concept of tax effort: state-local tax revenue per $1,000 of state personal income and state-local tax revenue actually extracted relative to the amount of tax revenue available to be extracted from the state's economy, available for all but 1955.

Political Capacity. The concept of political capacity depicted in figure 1–1 represents the level of development of the state's policymaking institutions—notably, the governor and the legislature. Three measures of the characteristics of the state's governors were used for all five time points: the Schlesinger (1971) index of the formal powers of the governor, an index of the office-seeking activity by the state's governors, and an index of the number of years in each five-year period during which the state had a governor rated as outstanding (Sabato 1978). (For coding values, see the appendix.) One composite factor was recreated from data in the *Book of the States* (Council of State Governments, biennial) for each time point using methods closely resembling those used by its originator: a legislative professionalism factor (Grumm 1971) consisting of length of legislative session, number of enactments per biennium, legislator salaries, expenditures for staff operations, and program review effort (Crane 1977), with the latter variable available only for 1975. Finally, a rating of the status of the state legislative committee on aging, if any, was available for 1975 only.

Political Openness. Only two single indicators and one composite factor were employed for each time period to measure the concept of political openness, or the degree of access of the public to the policymaking process. The first indicator was a measure of political participation—namely, voter turnout for president (not governor, due to the fewer votes cast for that office) in the nearest presidential election (for 1970, the average of 1968 and 1972). The second indicator was a measure of the degree of choice available to the electorate—namely, the Ranney (1976) index of interparty competition for the periods 1946–1963 (used for 1955 and 1960) and 1962–1973 (used for 1965, 1970, and 1975). Finally, the composite factor for the concept of political openness was recreated from data in the *Book of the States* (Council of State Governments, biennial) for each time point using methodology closely resembling that used by its originator: a legislative apportionment factor (Schubert 1965), measuring the magnitude of deviations from average district size of the least populous and most populous districts in both houses of the legislature. The indicators comprising the factor were first reflected (reversed) to make the factor a measure of positive apportionment rather than malapportionment.

Socioeconomic Development. As might be expected, a vast array of indicators was available to measure the level of socioeconomic development of the state. Fortunately, most of them were successfully combined into three composite factors representing the major socioeconomic dimensions of the state. Although missing years for some indicators had to be estimated through linear interpolation, all three factors were available for all five time periods. First was the socioeconomic need factor, measuring the magnitude of disadvantaged groups in the state, and composed of the following five indicators: percentage black, percentage nonwhite, ratio of the nonworking population to the working population, Gini index of income inequality, and percentage of families below the poverty level. Second was the socioeconomic status factor, measuring the magnitude of advantaged groups in the state, and composed of the following five indicators: percentage professional and managerial, percentage with high school education, median education, per capita income, and median family income. Third was the industrialization-urbanization factor, composed of the following six indicators: population density, percentage urban, percentage in Standard Metropolitan Statistical Areas (SMSAs), percentage not in agriculture, value added by manufacture, and percentage of nonagricultural population in labor unions. The latter indicator was also used separately in the analysis.

Other single indicators measuring additional dimensions of the socioeconomic characteristics of the state were also employed (all were available for all five time points, occasionally with the help of linear interpolation, unless otherwise indicated): total population size, interpreted as a measure of the degree of complexity of the state's society; the unemployment rate, reflecting the extent of stagnant economic conditions, often worse in the most advanced industrial states; life expectancy at birth, reflecting overall health conditions in the state; the net migration rate, or the number of in-migrants minus the number of out-migrants, divided by the total population; and two measures of the cultural characteristics of the state: the Sullivan (1973) index of cultural diversity and an index of the dominance of Elazar's (1972) three types of political cultures, with Moralistic states scoring high, Traditionalistic states scoring low, and Individualistic states scoring in the middle.

Finally, a few measures were derived from some of those discussed earlier. A hierarchical cluster analysis of the three socioeconomic factors for 1975 (status, industrialization-urbanization, and need) produced distinct groupings of states along a dimension reflecting socioeconomic development, and the index ranking those clusters was therefore labeled the development index. In addition, rates of change over the previous five years for each time period were calculated for total population and per capita income to distinguish growing and prospering states from declining and stagnating states.

Status of the Aging Population. The final concept in the model depicted in figure 1–1 involves various characteristics of the state's old-age population. Again, all the indicators were available for all five time points— occasionally with the help of linear interpolation—unless otherwise noted. It is significant that no composite factor could successfully be produced as an indicator of general need among a state's older population. Rather than showing a single underlying dimension, the various indicators of living arrangements, income, life expectancy, and so forth produced substantial variation. As a result, it was necessary to employ several individual indicators in this analysis. First, percentages of the total population for various age groups were available: ages 60 and over, 65 and over, and 75 and over. Data on other distinctive and particularly needy subgroups of the over-65 population were also employed: percentage female, percentage widowed, percentage in poverty, and percentage eligible for SSI. A measure similar in concept to these was the aged poor as a percentage of the total population. Finally, three key indicators of the status of the aging population were employed: median family income of families whose head is aged 65 or over, life expectancy at age 65, and elderly in-migrants as a percentage of the over-65 population of the state.

Summary. As might be expected, not all the indicators proved useful in the final analysis for this project. Preliminary correlation and regression analyses (see methods section, following) suggested that many of the indicators, especially those that seemed conceptually weaker or duplicative of other indicators, would not contribute substantially to the explanation of the cross-state variation in aging-policy effort. We have thus chosen to include in the specific variable list in the appendix only those variables that are being reported in the statistical analyses contained in the subsequent chapters.

Methods of Analysis

Exploring the interrelationships among all of these indicators required several modes of analysis, all of which utilized the computer program package known as Statistical Analysis System (SAS). As already mentioned, factor analysis (actually, principal components analysis) was employed to reduce some of the indicators into composite factor–score variables, using the principal components option in the SAS procedure FACTOR. Within each substantive policy area presented earlier, simple correlation analysis, using Pearson's *r* coefficients calculated by the SAS procedure CORR, was employed for each of the five time periods to examine the patterns of relationship among the dependent (policy) variables for that policy area, between each of those dependent variables and each of the independent variables or potential predictors, and finally among the various independent variables. Preliminary analysis of these correlation matrices, coupled with considerations of theoretical relevance and duplication among predictors, led to selection of a core set of predictors for each policy area, with considerable overlap from one set to the next. The analyses in subsequent chapters on each substantive policy area focus on the correlations among the dependent variables in each area, as well as correlations between those dependent variables and their pool of potential predictors. Correlations among the predictors are discussed only when deemed particularly relevant.

The third, and most important, mode of analysis was stepwise multiple regression, using the SAS procedure STEPWISE, which served to identify the best combination of predictors for explaining the cross-state variance in each dependent variable at each time point. The procedure (the MAXR option in SAS STEPWISE) selects predictors for inclusion in the regression equation (model) according to the maximum improvement in the variance accounted for (explained) in the dependent variable. In the analyses reported here, the only models considered acceptable were those in which the regression coefficient for each predictor included, as well as the overall F-test for the entire model, was significant at the .05 level or better. Furthermore, to guard against multicollinearity, models were rejected when the standard error of the regression coefficient for a predictor that had been included in a previous step increased substantially due to high correlation with the predictor just added in the subsequent step. The methods employed in this book for exploring the interrelationships among the numerous indicators gathered in the course of the project thus provide an extensive basis for identifying the characteristics that best explain state differences in aging policy effort.

Case Studies

Site visits to eight case study states comprised the second major component of the overall research project. Through case studies, patterns and influences that were not necessarily evident in the fifty-state comparison could be explored. At the same time, the relationships that emerged in the aggregate-level analysis could be assessed more fully through the field investigations. The selection of the eight case study states and the nature of the interview process require brief discussion.

State Selection. The selection of case study states was undertaken to provide maximum variation on three basic dimensions: (1) percent of aging population, (2) level of policy effort for the older population, and (3) general liberalism in overall policy responses. Since the states experienced some changes in their relative positions in the twenty-year period under study, it was decided to make the selection on the basis of the relative state positions as of the 1965 midpoint of the study. Because the state selection had to be undertaken fairly early in the project, the range of available indicators was somewhat limited. For the aging policy commitment, we used average monthly state payment for OAA along with rankings on the dates of passage of legislation protecting against age discrimination in employment and of the establishment of nursing home regulation. For general liberalness in a state's policy responses, we included two variables: the degree of progressiveness of a state's tax structure and the level of average monthly AFDC payments. The percentage of the population age 65 and over represented the third dimension. Average ranks were computed for each of the first two dimensions, and the three composite rankings were then dichotomized into high- and low-ranking categories. Each state was then classified into one of the eight cells formed by the combination of the high-low dichotomies on the three dimensions.

The initial classification of states on the three basic dimensions produced the results contained in table 1–1. With an eye toward regional balance, we then selected seven of the states: Minnesota, Iowa, California, North Carolina, Maine, Florida, and Ohio. Because Wash-

Table 1–1
Classifications of States on Three Policy Dimensions for Case-Study Selection

	(High) Percentage of Population over 65 (Low)		
(High)	Kans. Okla. / Mass. Oreg. / Minn. Vt. / N.Y. Wis. / N. Dak.	Alaska Hawaii / Calif. Mich. / Colo. N.J. / Conn.	(High)
(Low)	Iowa / Mont.	Ariz. N.C. / Del. S.C. / Idaho Utah / La.	

General policy liberalism

			(Low)
(High)	Maine / Nebr. / Pa. / R.I. / Wash.	Md. / Nev. / Va.	
(Low)	Ark. Mo. / Fla. N.H. / Ill. S. Dak. / Ind. W. Va. / Ky.	Ala. Ohio / Ga. Tenn. / Miss. Tex. / N.M. Wyo.	

Aging policy effort (High / Low)

ington was close to the break point on old age population, we moved that state into the category of low general liberalism, low old age pop- · ulation, and high policy effort to achieve greater regional balance. Although some of the states as examined in the field did not entirely fit all aspects of their initial classification, they did provide wide and analytically useful variation on the dimensions used in the initial sampling process.

The Interviews. The individuals to be interviewed in each state were selected on the basis of a so-called snowball sampling technique in which a number of initially suggested or known contacts were used as sources of additional names. An effort was made in each state to examine key relationshps from a variety of perspectives and with individuals who represented a multiple set of referrals rather than a single chain of informants. As shown in table 1–2, individuals were interviewed from different categories including governors and their staffs, legislators and staff members, administrative officials, lobbyists, and outside experts. Those interviews were usually at least an hour in length, and many lasted substantially longer. Since individuals were promised anonymity, the list of interviewees has been combined by general position for each state.

The interviews were conducted between April and October 1980. Besides questions raised concerning the 1955–1975 time period, a number of the discussions also included a consideration of more recent developments. In California and Florida, the interviews were conducted by both authors jointly, with each author subsequently visiting three states individually. To maximize the comparability of interpretations, each interviewer carefully reviewed interview notes and background reports from the other states, and an informal set of rankings and evaluations was then developed through extensive discussions.

Policy Analysis

The analysis of public policy can proceed in several ways. (For a recent classification of various approaches to policy analysis, see Dunn 1981.) In some discussions, the primary emphasis is on evaluations of impacts of policies. A second approach focuses on the choices among different policy strategies and designs. A third approach combines interests in policy design with a strong emphasis on the nature of political support that tends to emerge for different types of policies. In our analysis, we

Table 1-2
State Interviews

Group	Calif.	Fla.	Minn.	Iowa	Ohio	Maine	Wash.	N.C.
Legislators (N = 26)	6	1	3	3	4	4	3	2
Legislative staff (N = 29)	8	2	4	3	5	2	3	2
Governors and staffers (N = 8)	—	—	2	3	—	1	1	1
Aging network (state and local) (N = 37)	6	4	4	2	4	5	5	7
Related agency officials (N = 29)	6	3	4	2	3	2	4	5
Interest group leaders (N = 27)	3	4	6	2	4	2	4	2
Outside experts (N = 36)	6	3	8	5	2	4	3	5
Total (N = 192)	35	17	31	20	22	20	23	24

have drawn upon several types of materials but have focused upon policy design and political support questions.

Several basic questions emerge from a focus on policy design and political support. Are there differences, first, in the nature of the support that states tend to show for different types of policies, like in-kind versus cash assistance, or those with universal eligibility versus means-tested programs? Comparing across policy areas, do the factors that lead to support in one area for a given state also produce strong efforts in other policy areas? How, in turn, have the various designs of federal policies for the states differed in their ability to achieve the desired state responses? Finally, in terms of political support, are there particular situations in which programs can be developed by strong actions that are not substantially tied to levels of socioeconomic development or a state's political culture?

To place the analysis of policy design and political support issues in a larger perspective, it is often useful to think in terms of a basic policy cycle approach. The policy cycle approach has become increasingly common in policy studies, as reflected in the work of Rosenbaum (1981), Cronin (1980), and the earlier formulations by Cobb and Elder (1972) and Jones (1975). In this approach, the basic components include issue raising, support building, policy design, bargaining (incuding the use of political resources to influence those outcomes), implementation, and oversight. Viewing actions in these terms, one might find, for example, that aging-based interest groups are important on issue raising and policy design issues but less important in specific bargaining processes. Similarly, governors may be involved with support building and bargaining but not with policy design and specific aspects of policy implementation. The policy cycle approach thus facilitates a comprehensive assessment of the role of key participants in the policy process.

The study of state policies for the aging is thus most effectively conducted by the combined use of policy analysis techniques as well as case studies and the quantitative assessment of changes in factors which can be shown to influence differing policy responses. To set the stage for that analysis, it is useful to consider at the outset some of the basic changes in socioeconomic and political characteristics of the American states in recent decades.

Note

1. The fact that each of the major constructs depicted in the model is represented by a large number of indicators necessitates some effort

at data reduction. Thus, principle components analysis (see the section on "Methods of Analysis" later in this chapter) was employed in an attempt to combine the multiple indicators for a given concept into one or more composite variables, thereby simplifying subsequent analyses of the interrelationships depicted in the model. It should be noted at the outset, however, that exact specification and formal testing of the model would have required simultaneous estimation procedures, like two-stage least squares, due to the presence of reciprocal relationships, which make it a nonrecursive model. Such procedures would have required successful creation of one or a very few composite factors for each concept depicted in the model, and present levels of measurement do not facilitate this degree of data manipulation.

2 The Changing States

Major changes have occurred in recent years in not only the nature of state policies for the aging but also state capacities for policy development and the distribution of key demographic characteristics. The states have become more important in the design and financing of health policies, the regulation of long-term care facilities, and the design of social services, while the financing of income maintenance policies has grown primarily at the federal level. The so-called quiet revolution of state government, with a growth in full-time legislatures, staff support for both governors and executives, and a younger, more professionally oriented group of state legislators, has profoundly altered the nature of policymaking activity in state capitals. The massive efforts in the South to achieve economic growth, coupled with the decline experienced in some of the nation's older industrial states, have at the same time sharply reduced disparities in economic resources among the states.

An examination of major changes, as well as areas of continuity, in state characteristics provides a helpful basis for subsequent analyses of specific policy areas and assessments of possible alternative strategies. In this chapter, we review major aspects of those changing characteristics and illustrate those changes by introducing several of the specific variables that are used in subsequent chapters.

Major Policy Efforts

The changing magnitude and scope of state policy efforts for the aging can be assessed in several different ways. If one looks at total expenditures, there has clearly been a substantial increase. In the 1950s, state spending for the aging was primarily in the area of OAA. As of 1956, the $800 million that state and local governments were contributing to OAA overshadowed all other state commitments. Only a few states were making significant use of the opportunities for vendor payments as a basis for medical care. In the area of social services, the embryonic state efforts involved primarily the development of commissions. They were largely viewed as promoting devices and usually had budgets of only a few thousand dollars. Conversely, by 1981 total Medicaid expenditures for the aging had reached almost $10 billion (Estes et al. 1983, p. 164), and the states were contributing over $4 billion to that total. In actual dollar amounts, the states by the 1980s were clearly doing substantially more for the elderly than in previous decades.

Comparisons of state effort on the basis of dollar amounts must also be considered in several other contexts. If viewed as a percentage of a state's budget or in terms of spending in constant (non-inflated) dollars then the record of state spending increases is substantially less impressive. Although total Medicaid expenditures have often been viewed as an area of uniquely rapid growth in state spending, Davidson (1980, p. 23) shows that, between 1965 and 1977, state and local Medicaid expenditures actually increased at approximately the level at which state highway expenditures were increasing. Furthermore, the increase in state Medicaid expenditures was occurring at only about one-fourth the rate of state increases in educational expenditures during the same period.

In assessing changes in total state effort for the aging, several other program efforts need to be examined. In the area of income maintenance, the increase in Social Security coverage plus the enactment of SSI have reduced state expenditures on that program for both federal- and state-administered supplements to a sum of under $150 million as of 1980. In 1955, the states had been spending over $700 million as their share of OAA benefits for the elderly (Council of State Governments 1955). State contributions to direct income maintenance programs have thus fallen in constant as well as current dollar amounts in the past quarter-century. The states did also expand forms of indirect income support, however, through tax assistance for both income and property tax liabilities, and with the provision of a variety of free or reduced cost services, varying from educational programs to park admissions and bus fares. The estimates of total tax relief for the aging are quite impressive. The elderly were receiving some $140 million in homestead exemptions, and circuit-breaker forms of assistance were giving them $108 million in relief in programs based solely on age, plus a substantial amount in programs that did not contain an age limit (figures calculated from U.S. Department of Housing and Urban Development 1975). Finally, in terms of social services, the states were certainly spending more in the 1970s than in earlier decades, but their total direct supplements were quite modest (Estes 1979).

The record in financial terms can be summarized as follows. The states have been spending substantially more of their own revenues on programs for the aging in the 1980s than in earlier years when one simply looks at budget amounts. When examined in terms of noninflated dollars, however, that increase has been much less substantial.

Medicaid expenditures have increased in both current and constant dollars, but payments for OAA-SSI have declined in constant dollars. Finally, as a proportion of state budgets, Medicaid has been growing, but not as rapidly as state educational expenditures between the mid-1960s and the late 1970s. As a consequence, if one looks at the combined spending of state and local governments in 1955 and 1980 (which is necessary because of the interrelated subnational roles in the earlier period), spending for the aging has fallen as a percentage of revenues received from own sources. This is based on expenditures of approximately $0.8 billion on the aging out of state and local government own-source revenues of $22 billion in 1955, compared with spending of roughly $5 billion out of state and local government own-source revenues of $264 billion in 1980. (For recent budget figures, see Bureau of the Census 1981, p. 285, and Advisory Commission on Intergovernmental Relations 1982.)

Financial commitments nonetheless give an incomplete picture of state policy roles. Key aspects of program development, program implementation, and regulatory policy changes also require consideration. State policies for the aging mirror changes throughout the federal system in the past two decades in which the growth of personnel has been at the state and local level rather than at the federal level. The implementation of both Medicaid and the programs being funded under the Older Americans Act uses state and local rather than federal government employees. As Feder and Holahan (1980) and Vladeck (1980) have stressed, there has been a tendency for the federal government to rely upon the states to try to resolve some of the difficult administrative decisions that program development has entailed. As we shall see in considering aspects of Medicaid, for example, the states have often exercised substantial discretion in the design of programs in which they are receiving extensive financial assistance from the federal government. State government roles in designing and implementing programs for the elderly create a final impact that goes well beyond their basic financial commitment.

As a final dimension of the changing state role, the expanding regulatory efforts need to be considered. As of the 1950s, a number of the states were interested in job discrimination issues, but they extensively debated few other regulatory matters. Similarly, in the 1960s, while job discrimination issues continued in the states, regulatory policies were not a highly salient issue.

The 1970s and 1980s have produced a very different regulatory response. The sharply increasing interest in regulatory policy was encouraged to some extent by the consumer movement in general as well as by specific lobbying efforts by groups representing the aging. Efforts by Ralph Nader and the public interest group movement had a strong impact on policies affecting the elderly. In the 1970s, widely debated regulatory efforts included generic drug substitution laws, hearing aid industry regulation, and reform of funeral industry regulation. In the 1980s, there were major discussions and state government actions on regulatory issues such as provisions for the use of reverse annuity mortgages, life-line utility rates, provisions in zoning codes that allowed for the use of so-called granny flats in residential neighborhoods, and sanctions against elder abuse. Clearly, the states have come to play a significant regulatory policy role. Furthermore, with the resistance to regulatory policies that emerged in Washington, D.C., in the early 1980s, this role seemed likely to continue and possibly expand.

The nature of the state policy efforts for the aging as of the 1980s reflects some financial expansion over previous decades in constant dollar amounts but, in particular, a growth in state roles involving policy design and implementation. Many of the policy efforts that have taken place over a number of years have been included in our specific assessment of the sources of state policy effort. To illustrate further the changes that have occurred in those efforts and to introduce major variables being used in this book, the following discussion presents state rankings on several measures of expenditure-based and regulatory policy efforts.

The data and rankings presented in table 2-1 and 2-2 provide a description of the manner in which the states have responded to the income maintenance needs of their older populations. It should be noted in evaluating table 2-1 that the shift from OAA to SSI in 1974 made a major difference in the incentives that were being offered to the states and in the nature of the state responses. Several points nonetheless stand out from those data. As of the 1950s, the states that had the highest average monthly payments were the larger, more industrial states with a generally liberal political tradition. By 1970 and 1975, however, the characteristics of high-effort states were less pronounced. That decline in readily apparent groupings, as discussed in chapter 6, is also evident in the statistical analyses. Conversely, in assessing the lower rankings, there is some indication by 1970, and a clear indication by 1975, that the southern states are not as predominantly clustered at the bottom as they had been in earlier years.

The data in table 2-2 provide an indication of overall state efforts as of the 1970s on two major factors: income maintenance and health and welfare combined. Those two rankings provide an opportunity for comparison of income-oriented policy efforts, plus the more general health and welfare factor, which includes both Medicaid and SSI components. Although these factors are very highly correlated, it is im-

Table 2–1
OAA Average Monthly Payments (State-Local Portion)

Rank	1955 State	Amount	1960 State	Amount	1965 State	Amount	1970 State	Amount	1975 State	Amount
1	Colo.	51	Colo.	58	Calif.	56	Calif.	52	N.C.	115
2	Conn.	50	Calif.	50	Wis.	53	N.H.	47	Calif.	95
3	Mass.	48	Wash.	49	Colo.	46	Conn.	47	Ariz.	94
4	N.Y.	45	N.Y.	48	N.H.	44	N.Y.	44	Mass.	89
5	N.J.	36	N.J.	48	Mich.	44	Alaska	44	Ky.	85
6	Calif.	35	Mass.	46	N.Y.	40	Iowa	44	Iowa	75
7	Minn.	35	Minn.	46	Alaska	40	Hawaii	41	Conn.	74
8	Oreg.	33	N.Dak.	43	Minn.	40	Mass.	36	S.C.	72
9	Kans.	33	Wis.	42	Mass.	39	Kans.	33	Mont.	67
10	Wis.	33	Conn.	40	Ill.	39	Colo.	33	Ill.	66
11	N.Dak.	31	Oreg.	39	R.I.	38	Wis.	29	Alaska	61
12	Alaska	31	R.I.	37	Conn.	37	Pa.	29	Wis.	57
13	Wash.	31	Iowa	37	Nebr.	37	N.J.	29	Nev.	55
14	R.I.	28	N.H.	36	Ohio	37	Wyo.	28	N.Y.	54
15	N.H.	28	Kans.	35	Kans.	36	Minn.	27	Va.	49
16	Ill.	28	Ohio	34	Okla.	35	N.Dak.	25	Kans.	43
17	Utah	27	Ill.	34	Iowa	35	Mich.	24	Ohio	43
18	Okla.	27	Mich.	34	Nev.	34	Nev.	23	Ala.	40
19	Wyo.	27	Nev.	33	N.J.	34	Wash.	23	Mich.	39
20	Mont.	26	Okla.	32	Ind.	32	Ind.	23	Minn.	38
21	Ohio	26	Wyo.	31	N.Dak.	31	Vt.	23	Vt.	37
22	Iowa	26	Hawaii	27	Wyo.	31	Mo.	23	Mo.	37
23	Mich.	24	Pa.	27	Wash.	31	Idaho	22	Colo.	36
24	Nev.	24	Nebr.	26	Pa.	29	Va.	21	Hawaii	35
25	Idaho	24	Idaho	26	Vt.	28	Ohio	20	Idaho	33
26	Ga.	24	Alaska	25	S.Dak.	28	Okla.	19	N.H.	33
27	Ariz.	23	Ind.	24	Md.	25	Oreg.	19	Nebr.	33
28	Ind.	21	La.	24	Maine	24	N.C.	19	R.I.	31
29	Nebr.	20	Utah	24	La.	24	S.Dak.	19	Ind.	30
30	La.	19	Md.	23	Oreg.	23	La.	18	Fla.	29

Table 2–1 continued

Rank	1955 State	1955 Amount	1960 State	1960 Amount	1965 State	1965 Amount	1970 State	1970 Amount	1975 State	1975 Amount
31	Pa.	18	Mont.	22	Del.	23	Del.	18	N.Dak.	29
32	Hawaii	18	Mo.	21	Mont.	23	Mont.	18	S.Dak.	28
33	Mo.	18	N.M.	21	Hawaii	22	Ill.	18	Wash.	28
34	Md.	17	Vt.	20	Mo.	22	W.Va.	18	N.J.	28
35	Maine	16	Maine	20	Idaho	20	Md.	17	Okla.	24
36	S.Dak.	15	S.Dak.	19	Utah	19	Nebr.	16	La.	24
37	Vt.	15	Fla.	18	Tex.	18	Tex.	15	Ga.	23
38	Del.	13	Del.	17	N.M.	17	Ala.	15	Tenn.	23
39	Tex.	12	Ariz.	17	Ariz.	17	Maine	14	Del.	23
40	N.M.	12	Tex.	15	Ala.	17	Ariz.	13	Oreg.	21
41	Fla.	12	Ala.	15	Fla.	16	R.I.	12	Wyo.	21
42	Ky.	10	Va.	15	Va.	16	Tenn.	12	Pa.	21
43	Tenn.	10	Ark.	14	N.C.	15	Fla.	12	N.M.	21
44	Ark.	10	Ky.	13	Ark.	15	Ark.	11	Maine	21
45	Ala.	9	Ga.	13	S.C.	14	N.M.	11	Ark.	13
46	S.C.	9	S.C.	12	Ky.	14	Utah	11	Miss.	11
47	Va.	9	N.C.	12	Ga.	14	Ky.	11	Utah	4
48	N.C.	9	Tenn.	11	Tenn.	13	S.C.	11	W.Va.	0
49	W.Va.	7	W.Va.	10	W.Va.	11	Ga.	10	Tex.	0
50	Miss.	7	Miss.	8	Miss.	8	Miss.	7	Md.	—

Table 2–2
State Rankings on Income Maintenance and Health and Welfare Factors, 1975

State	Income Maintenance	Health and Welfare	State	Income Maintenance	Health and Welfare
Ala.	26	20	Mont.	42	22
Alaska	—	—	Nebr.	8	12
Ariz.	37	42	Nev.	—	—
Ark.	30	24	N.H.	22	14
Calif.	2	2	N.J.	12	9
Colo.	5	—	N.M.	45	41
Conn.	6	—	N.Y.	4	—
Del.	23	29	N.C.	31	25
Fla.	35	37	N.Dak.	40	21
Ga.	39	16	Ohio	25	19
Hawaii	7	4	Okla.	16	15
Idaho	18	17	Oreg.	19	18
Ill.	20	13	Pa.	14	8
Ind.	34	27	R.I.	11	—
Iowa	28	30	S.C.	33	32
Kans.	24	36	S.Dak.	38	35
Ky.	27	26	Tenn.	36	40
La.	32	33	Tex.	46	31
Maine	10	11	Utah	43	38
Md.	—	—	Vt.	15	10
Mass.	1	1	Va.	41	34
Mich.	9	6	Wash.	13	5
Minn.	17	7	W.Va.	—	—
Miss.	29	28	Wis.	3	3
Mo.	21	23	Wyo.	44	39

portant to note that in a few instances states do significantly better on one factor than on the other. Montana, Texas, and North Dakota are among the notable examples of that phenomenon, with each of these states scoring substantially higher on combined health and welfare efforts than on the income maintenance factor alone.

Differing levels of state health policy effort are presented in table 2–3. The early health factor reflects the pre-1965 efforts on the program initiatives that preceded Medicaid. That factor suggests several interesting issues for analysis, including the low performance of some large industrial states such as New York and New Jersey, along with the strong showings for some states without general traditions as high effort states, such as North Dakota and New Hampshire. The other two measures both indicate more recent efforts directed toward the control of nursing home supply and reimbursement. Again, as with the early health factor, a number of the top states are no particular surprise, but some unexpected results are also revealed. The unexpected performances include, for example, the high ranking on Certificate of Need program development for Nevada and South Carolina and the rather low ranking on both dimensions for Pennsylvania. Combined with the performance data in table 2–2, these rankings underscore the differing levels of effort that states at points have manifested within the overall area of health and long-term care.

The final examples of relative levels of state policy effort to be illustrated involve social services and regulatory protection. On the social services factor score rankings, presented in table 2–4, the results differ quite substantially from those found with health and income maintenance policies. Once spending is divided by population size to give a per capita measure, there is a tendency for smaller states to have the higher scores. Nonetheless, there are both a number of confirming indications of the relationship between this factor and one's intuitive expectation regarding different states, as well as some interesting results that are addressed in chapter 5. Among the larger, more industrial states, Pennsylvania scores fairly high, with New York and California displaying lower rankings. While both of the latter two states have put substantial amounts of money into Medicaid, their social services allocations under the Older Americans Act have been quite limited. At the same time, states with relatively large older populations, such as Arkansas and Florida, emerge with substantially higher scores in this area than on the other factors. Given these differences, the search for explanations of the social services factor, as well as other measures of social services policy efforts, would appear to be particularly intriguing.

Turning to the area of regulatory protection, table 2–4 includes two columns that show the extent to which such efforts have not been

Table 2–3
State Rankings on Health Policy Performance

Rank	Early Health Factor	Certificate of Need Requirement	Cost Control Factor
1	Mass.	N.Y.	N.Y.
2	N.Dak.	Md.	Calif.
3	Wis.	R.I.	Ind.
4	Minn.	Calif.	Minn.
5	Wash.	Conn.	Conn.
6	Ill.	Nev.	Wyo.
7	Conn.	Minn.	N.J.
8	N.H.	S.C.	Mo.
9	Oreg.	N.J.	Colo.
10	R.I.	Mass.	Oreg.
11	Calif.	N.Dak.	Ala.
12	Utah	Okla.	Va.
13	Mich.	Ariz.	Mass.
14	Nebr.	Wash.	Ohio
15	Ohio	Oreg.	Wash.
16	N.M.	Ky.	N.M.
17	W.Va.	S.Dak.	S.C.
18	Pa.	Miss.	N.Dak.
19	Hawaii	Kans.	Tenn.
20	Okla.	Fla.	R.I.
21	Iowa	Colo.	Mich.
22	Kans.	Va.	Ga.
23	Nev.	Tenn.	W.Va.
24	Maine	Ill.	N.C.
25	Md.	Hawaii	Maine
26	Idaho	Ga.	Mont.
27	Colo.	Mont.	Idaho
28	Vt.	Tex.	Vt.
29	Mo.	Ohio	S.Dak.
30	Wyo.	Ark.	Md.
31	Tex.	Ala.	Hawaii
32	Ark.	Wyo.	Nev.
33	Del.	Alaska	Del.
34	Ky.	Wis.	Fla.
35	N.C.	W.Va.	Wis.
36	S.Dak.	Iowa	Ky.
37	La.	Maine	N.H.
38	S.C.	Ind.	Kans.
39	Fla.	Mo.	Iowa
40	Tenn.	Miss.	Ill.
41	Ga.	N.C.	Pa.
42	Ala.	Utah	Tex.
43	Miss.	La.	Utah
44	Alaska	Pa.	Ariz.
45	N.Y.	Vt.	La.
46	N.J.	Nebr.	Okla.
47	Ind.	N.H.	Alaska
48	Ariz.	Idaho	Ark.
49	Va.	N.M.	Nebr.
50	Mont.	Del.	Miss.

Table 2–4
Social Services and Regulatory Protection Performance

State	Social Services Factor Rank	ADEA Year of Adoption	Generic Drugs Year of Adoption
Ala.	49	none	1979
Alaska	1	1960	1976
Ariz.	45	none	1978
Ark.	9	none	1975
Calif.	47	1961	1975
Colo.	30	1903	1976
Conn.	24	1959	1976
Del.	4	1960	1976
Fla.	17	1969	1974
Ga.	38	1971	1977
Hawaii	5	1964	none
Idaho	28	1965	1978
Ill.	36	1967	1977
Ind.	41	1965	none
Iowa	31	1972	1976
Kans.	43	none	1978
Ky.	22	1972	1972
La.	25	1934	none
Maine	12	1965	1975
Md.	7	1970	1977
Mass.	19	1937	1976
Mich.	32	1965	1975
Minn.	26	1977	1974
Miss.	27	none	1977
Mo.	40	none	1978
Mont.	18	1974	1977
Nebr.	14	1963	1977
Nev.	2	1973	1979
N.H.	15	1971	1973
N.J.	23	1967	1977
N.M.	20	1969	1976
N.Y.	46	1958	1977
N.C.	39	1975	1979
N.Dak.	10	1965	1979
Ohio	44	1961	1977
Okla.	42	1974	none
Oreg.	34	1959	1975
Pa.	8	1955	1976
R.I.	3	1956	1976
S.C.	35	1972	1978
S.Dak.	11	1974	1978
Tenn.	37	none	1977
Tex.	50	1967	none
Utah	6	1975	1977
Vt.	21	none	1978
Va.	48	none	1977
Wash.	29	1961	1977
W.Va.	16	1971	1978
Wis.	33	1959	1976
Wyo.	13	none	1979

occurring earlier in the states that one might intuitively expect to be the leaders in these areas. The first measure, the date of enactment of a state's age discrimination in employment law, does show a number of the states that are innovative in other policy areas also emerging as earlier adopters of legislation in this area. The second regulatory measure, however, the scope of generic drug legislation, shows a rather intriguing distribution of early adopters, which would seem to defy obvious bases for explanation. These indications that regulatory policy may have a set of explanatory forces somewhat distinct from expenditure-based policies underscore the importance of analyzing both types of policies in looking at the changing patterns of state policy effort for the aging. Given the importance of federal-state relations in many of these areas, it is useful next to consider the manner in which these policy efforts relate to changing patterns of state interaction with the federal government.

The Federal Role

The evolution of state policy efforts for the aging has been taking place in the context of a series of changes affecting all aspects of federal-state relations. This includes the extent of federal support, major changes in the areas of assistance, and shifts in the form of assistance. The following review highlights aspects of those overall changes, with the design of specific aging-related programs being presented as they are analyzed in subsequent chapters.

The magnitude of federal support for subnational governments has increased as both a percentage of overall revenue for those governments and in absolute dollar amounts. The portion of total revenue that state and local governments were receiving from the federal government in the 1950s hovered around 15 percent. The dollar flow grew from approximately $3 billion in 1950 to $7 billion in 1960 (Mosher and Poland 1964). During the late 1960s and 1970s, that percentage figure grew to just over 25 percent, and the dollar figure reached $91 billion by 1980 (U.S. Office of Management and Budget 1983, p. H-20).

Federal aid to state and local governments became a major target for budget cutting in 1981. Although constituting less than 15 percent of the total federal budget, those aid programs received more than a third of the cuts that President Reagan achieved in summer 1981. Supporters of retrenchment emphasized the rapid growth that had occurred in the 1970s, as federal grants grew at a level substantially exceeding the growth in the overall budget. Critics, in turn, pointed to the concentration of those cuts in the state and local government area. In part because of a resistance to further cuts on the part of Congress in 1982, the projected figures for aid to state and local governments as of 1983 again began to show slight increases, with a projected dollar level of $102 billion by 1986 (U.S. Office of Management and Budget 1983, p. H-20).

The growth in federal aid to state and local governments in recent years has occurred along with a major shift in the policy areas receiving primary assistance. As of 1960, the largest single category of federal funds (43 percent) was for transportation—a reflection of the commitment to highway building in this period. Income security received a significant proportion, some 38 percent of those federal funds (including OAA), and health care received only 3 percent. By 1982, the mix of expenditures had changed dramatically. Transportation assistance was down to 14 percent, and income maintenance reflected the more direct federal role (through Social Security's direct payments to individuals) with a drop to 25 percent. Health expenditures, reflecting the growth of Medicaid, had risen to some 21 percent of all federal commitments to subnational governments. Thus, by the early 1980s, the nature of federal assistance was not only larger but also substantially more oriented toward health care programs (U.S. Office of Management and Budget 1983, pp. H-14–H-15).

The manner in which federal assistance was being provided also changed considerably. The system of assistance employed in the 1950s was dominated by categorical grants in which the federal government sought to promote programs in such areas as OAA and AFDC. Many of these programs were designed with matching formulas that sought to compensate for the differences in economic resources among the states. Whereas wealthy states might receive less than half of the total costs of a given program, the poorest states in some instances received 80 percent or more of total program costs from the federal government.

The 1960s began a period of major experimentation with the nature of federal-state relations that has continued, with few interruptions, into the 1980s. Initially, the Kennedy and Johnson administrations were interested in using federal programs to promote more diverse objectives. With the programs of the War on Poverty (centralized in the Office of Economic Opportunity), cities were given a larger role and there was greater interest in using federal initiatives to help promote participation by various clientele groups (Lee and Benjamin 1983; Reagan and Sanzone 1981). The Older Americans Act, passed in 1965, paralleled aspects of the War on Poverty programs with the emphasis on advisory councils. It is significant that among those program efforts of the mid-1960s, organizational provisions of the Older American's

Act have been the major survivor because programs within the Office of Economic Opportunity and the Model Cities programs have lost their initial organizational characteristics.

The 1960s also saw the introduction of a substantially larger group of programs designed as demonstrations. Often, these took the form of program grants in which a state or local government had to initiate interest in a project and demonstrate a likely capacity for successful implementation. For the elderly, the demonstration programs used for nursing home ombudsmen constitute a typical example of this approach. The growth in program grants, along with the expansion in total number of federal grant programs, contributed to the series of new reform efforts beginning in the early 1970s.

The major reform efforts of the 1970s involved revenue sharing and the use of block grants. The Nixon administration promoted general revenue sharing as a major aspect of domestic policy reform along with a greater federal role for basic welfare programs (including OAA). In 1972, Congress passed the State and Local Fiscal Assistance Act that made an annual sum of approximately $5 billion available for local government use by 1975 (Hale and Palley 1981). Despite the initial enthusiasm, however, the funding for general revenue sharing did not grow as rapidly as support for more specific approaches in the remainder of the 1970s. Block grants were also instigated to give state and local governments greater discretion in specific program areas. The design of the Comprehensive Employment Training Act of 1973 (CETA), with its funds to be used for a broad range of job-creating activities, exemplified this approach. Similarly, the design of programs under Title XX of the Social Security Act in 1974, while not technically a block grant, exhibited aspects of the interest in allowing the states greater flexibility in designing their social services programs.

The series of proposals instigated by the Reagan administration beginning in 1981 and 1982 constituted another round of potential change in the nature of federal-state relations. These proposals seemed, in the eyes of many state government officials, to offer something of a Hobbesian choice (Peterson 1982; Schechter 1983); state officials were interested in being granted greater flexibility but were extremely concerned with the decrease in funding that was associated with those proposals. Strong critics like Walker (1981) felt that the present system was lacking in accountability, equity, and efficiency. For other analysts, Lovell (1983), for example, the present system is viewed with considerably greater sympathy. In her assessment, a division in the financing, design, and implementation of public programs represents an important recognition that these three basic activities do not all have to be undertaken by the same level of government.

The overall changes in the nature of federal-state roles in the past quarter-century and the continuing debate over possible reforms thus raise fundamental issues for those focusing on policies affecting the aging. Programs that involve the aging, such as Medicaid, social services, and many regulatory policies, have been central to the nation's debate over the appropriate form of federal-state relations. In confronting that debate, as well as in interpreting the nature of state responses more generally, it is essential to consider the manner in which key political characteristics of the states have been changing during the same period.

Political Characteristics

The states have experienced major changes in their capacities for developing policy in the past two decades. This is sometimes referred to as a quiet revolution, since many of the changes occurred without major public notice. For close observers of state governments, these changes have involved major changes affecting legislatures, the potential for gubernatorial leadership, and the general scope of state government operations. In addition, a dimension of importance for those exploring federal-state relations has been the growth in the capacity for the states to represent themselves in Washington, D.C.

The change in the characteristics and policymaking capacities of the state legislatures has been one of the transformations affecting state government in the past two decades. This has occurred in part as a group of younger and somewhat more career-oriented legislators has replaced the part-time legislators of an earlier era (Congressional Quarterly 1983). This development has had considerable significance for aging-related policymaking since it has been fairly common to find relatively young legislators developing strong interests in policies for the elderly. As a less encouraging development, however, it was also being noted in the early 1980s that the rapid turnover of legislators was adversely affecting the expertise that could be developed since a significant number of individuals either concluded that legislative roles in the face of mounting budget pressures was not a satisfying experience and voluntarily retired, or else they moved to another office (Rosenthal 1981).

Along with the changes in the characteristics of state legislators has come a substantial increase in professional staff support. This now includes professional staff assistance for committees and, in some instances, the availability of professional staff for individual legislators. In the site visits for this project, for example, we found several of the states employing individuals in legislative staff positions with professional training in various aspects of public policy and the aging. Some who generally support staff expansion, like Rosenthal (1981, p. 231), have offered a word of caution, stressing that in some contexts a legislator may end up being overly insulated from constituency pressures. Nonetheless, the growth in staff is widely viewed as giving the legislature a more substantial opportunity than before for participating in policy development. Because of the importance that has been attached to the change in legislative characteristics, we have been anxious to include that dimension in our analysis. The standings of the states as of 1975 on legislative professionalism are presented in table 2–5. It is important to emphasize from that ranking that the growth in legislative professionalism has not occurred only in the progressive states where it might be most expected. In reviewing the rankings, while California and New York not unexpectedly lead the rankings, the top states include Texas (tenth), Florida (twelfth), Virginia (thirteenth), and North Carolina (fifteenth).

Recent students of the governors have also stressed the emergence of a more serious group of chief executives and an expanded capacity for policy development as a result of staff expansion. For Sabato (1983), the change in the background characteristics of the governors since 1950 is reflected in the title of his book, *Goodbye to Goodtime Charlie*. Similarly, Ransone (1982) has argued that the governors have emerged as a significant group in the development of state policy. Although his account is essentially very favorable, he nonetheless stresses that the increase in the costs of campaigns has to be recognized as a troublesome aspect of the recent changes in the nature of governors' leadership potential. Governors, along with the legislators, have been increasing their staff support. In large states, it is not uncommon to have an individual in the governor's office who is interested in aging-related policies in terms of both policy design and the political opportunities and constraints involved.

As a development being promoted by both governors and state legislatures, significant activities are now involved in the representation of states both individually and collectively in Washington, D.C. By 1980, some three-fifths of the states had individual offices representing their interests in Washington, D.C. (Sabato 1983). For purposes of collective action, the National Governors' Association (formerly the National Governors' Conference) was used as a focal point for research on proposals affecting the states and as a focal point for an expression of state concerns over recently proposed changes in federal-state relations. The National Conference of State Legislatures also expanded its policy evaluation operations and continued to serve as a focal point

Table 2–5
State Rankings on Key Political Variables

State	Party Competition, 1973	Legislative Professionalism, 1975	Turnout, 1976
Ala.	50	25	47
Alaska	15	16	42
Ariz.	11	30	41
Ark.	44	44	32
Calif.	20	1	34
Colo.	26	28	17
Conn.	12	23	9
Del.	2	31	21
Fla.	39	12	33
Ga.	45	22	49
Hawaii	38	14	43
Idaho	25	38	12
Ill.	13	3	16
Ind.	16	27	15
Iowa	17	35	8
Kans.	27	24	20
Ky.	34	40	40
La.	49	17	37
Maine	19	29	5
Md.	42	9	36
Mass.	30	6	11
Mich.	4	4	19
Minn.	1	21	1
Miss.	48	18	39
Mo.	35	36	25
Mont.	10	32	7
Nebr.	5	43	27
Nev.	21	45	45
N.H.	23	47	18
N.J.	9	7	22
N.M.	36	49	31
N.Y.	18	2	35
N.C.	43	15	48
N.Dak.	24	41	3
Ohio	22	8	29
Okla.	37	34	28
Oreg.	3	33	10
Pa.	6	5	30
R.I.	32	37	13
S.C.	47	20	50
S.Dak.	28	39	6
Tenn.	40	19	38
Tex.	46	10	46
Utah	7	46	2
Vt.	29	48	26
Va.	41	13	44
Wash.	8	26	14
W.Va.	33	42	23
Wis.	14	11	4
Wyo.	31	50	24

for those interested in disseminating information on new policy ideas. Thus, in their relationships with Washington, D.C., as well as in their state-oriented policymaking activities, the states were clearly taking on an expanded role.

Important developments have also occurred in relationships we have categorized as representing political openness. Two of the rankings presented in table 2–5 provide an overview of relative state positions on that dimension. On party competition, the results, not surprisingly, find the southern states still predominating among the less competitive states. It should be noted, however, that their levels of interparty competition have substantially increased since the 1950s (see Bass and DeVries 1976, p. 512). On the turnout measure, it is essential to notice that the large, industrial states have scored rather poorly, while the more sparsely populated and less urban states have produced voting levels that often place them near the top of the list. Thus, while Utah and North Dakota rank second and third respectively (following Minnesota) at the top of the voter turnout ranking, California and New York stand at a low thirty-fourth and thirty-fifth respectively. In terms of political openness measures, these rankings thus suggest that neither party competition nor voter turnout is linked as tightly to general measures of state industrialization and urbanization as might be expected.

The states have also shown changes over time in their willingness to use the public sector. One key measure of that growing commitment in the states has involved the decision to levy increased taxes. In the 1960s and 1970s there was a general willingness to expand the scope of tax effort quite substantially. Income taxes were expanded in both number and scope, with sales taxes also displaying a gradual growth. Beginning with the tax revolt in California via Proposition 13 in 1978, however, a strong effort was made in a variety of states to grant additional tax concessions to various groups and to limit the overall growth of state government taxation (see Estes et al. 1983; Peterson 1982).

There have also been important changes in the distribution of tax effort among the states. As one general indicator, the measure of tax levels in relationship to economic capacity developed by Halstead (1978) presents important findings. On that measure, the states have shifted considerably, but not so that the less developed states have increased their tax efforts relative to the other states. Rather, with an expansion in their economies, the more rapidly developing states (often in the South) have been able to increase their average expenditures on various programs, but in many cases their ranking in terms of the utilization of tax capacity has actually fallen. Thus, in reviewing table 2–6, the states that have fallen at least five ranks from 1960 to 1975 include over half of the eleven southern states, while a comparable list

Table 2–6
Tax Effort Performance, 1960 and 1975

State	1960		1975	
	Rank	Score	Rank	Score
Ala.	36	91	44	79
Alaska	6	116	38	84
Ariz.	18	104	10	109
Ark.	38	90	46	79
Calif.	13	109	6	120
Colo.	21	100	24	92
Conn.	28	94	20	95
Del.	42	87	34	86
Fla.	37	90	45	79
Ga.	19	102	32	87
Hawaii	1	155	4	120
Idaho	39	89	23	93
Ill.	40	88	17	97
Ind.	41	87	25	92
Iowa	33	91	21	95
Kans.	25	96	33	87
Ky.	46	80	41	81
La.	15	106	39	82
Maine	4	126	7	118
Md.	14	106	12	104
Mass.	5	121	2	131
Mich.	12	110	11	105
Minn.	17	105	9	115
Miss.	9	113	16	97
Mo.	47	76	37	85
Mont.	43	86	19	96
Nebr.	49	72	35	86
Nev.	30	93	49	79
N.H.	27	95	42	80
N.J.	23	97	15	99
N.M.	45	84	30	88
N.Y.	2	136	1	152
N.C.	26	96	28	88
N.Dak.	35	91	22	94
Ohio	34	91	43	80
Okla.	29	94	48	71
Oreg.	8	113	14	99
Pa.	24	96	18	96
R.I.	10	112	8	115
S.C.	16	106	31	87
S.Dak.	32	92	27	90
Tenn.	31	93	40	81
Tex.	50	67	50	68
Utah	22	98	26	91
Vt.	3	130	3	121
Va.	44	84	29	88
Wash.	7	114	13	101
W.Va.	20	101	36	85
Wis.	11	110	5	120
Wyo.	48	73	47	73

of states that have increased at least five ranks includes only Virginia among the southern states and includes eastern states such as Connecticut, New Jersey, and Pennsylvania, plus Indiana, Minnesota, and Wisconsin in the Midwest, and California.

The dynamic that was taking place on tax effort as of 1975 is thus quite evident. The economically expanding states had not been increasing their tax effort as rapidly as their economic growth would seem to allow, while the older industrial states, which had historically engaged in relatively higher tax efforts, had sustained a higher level of taxation because of either direct tax increases or a reluctance to reduce taxes in the face of more sluggish economic growth. That lack of responsiveness to economic change is dramatically apparent in the position of Texas as the state with the lowest tax effort in the nation in both 1960 and 1975, while Michigan maintained its high ranking over the same period.

The reluctance of the more recently prosperous states to expand their tax effort may be related in part to the nature of general political attitudes, or underlying political cultures, within the respective states. It is instructive, for example, to consider the distribution of states on what we have labeled their degree of general policy liberalism (see table 2–7).

The states that have been most likely to respond aggressively across a variety of policy areas are almost exclusively either nonsouthern coastal states or states in the Great Lakes region. The one exception among the top fifteen states is Colorado, which has a fairly distinct leadership position among the Rocky Mountain states. Thus, in conceptualizing the states that have had the greater tendency toward policy responsiveness in the 1960s and 1970s, it is useful to think of that distinct grouping of states as being nonsouthern coastal and Great Lakes states. Conversely, it should be noted that the southern states typically occupy the bottom positions on general policy liberalism, with interior (that is, land-locked) states occupying the middle positions. In terms of regional tendencies, the position of the New England states should also be noted, with the smaller states of New Hampshire, Vermont, and Maine joining the more industrial states of Massachusetts, Connecticut, and Rhode Island in the top half of the list. Despite the major changes that have occurred among the states in several key characteristics, there are clear suggestions that political culture constitutes a relatively slowly changing aspect of a state's politics.

As a final aspect of our review of changes in areas that are central to our analytical framework, it is useful to emphasize briefly the extent to which aging-based advocacy patterns have changed. Presently, it is sufficient to emphasize two basic changes. First, there is more activity

Table 2–7
General Policy Liberalism: State Factor Scores and Ranks

Rank	State	Score
1	N.Y.	1.862
2	Mass.	1.805
3	N.J.	1.518
4	Calif.	1.464
5	Conn.	1.453
6	Oreg.	1.436
7	Wis.	1.378
8	Minn.	1.227
9	Colo.	1.121
10	Mich.	1.100
11	Pa.	1.060
12	R.I.	.871
13	Wash.	.576
14	Ill.	.539
15	Md.	.393
16	N.H.	.386
17	Vt.	.352
18	Iowa	.303
19	Kans.	.207
20	Ohio	.145
21	Idaho	.138
22	Maine	.119
23	Mont.	.107
24	Del.	.090
25	Wyo.	− .081
26	N.Dak.	− .110
27	N.M.	− .146
28	Nebr.	− .251
29	Ky.	− .304
30	Tex.	− .389
31	Fla.	− .481
32	S.Dak.	− .582
33	Utah	− .584
34	W.Va.	− .608
35	Ind.	− .615
36	La.	− .668
37	Va.	− .738
38	Okla.	− .860
39	Mo.	− .895
40	N.C.	− .923
41	Ga.	− .933
42	Nev.	−1.170
43	Tenn.	−1.209
44	Ala.	−1.285
45	Ariz.	−1.403
46	S.C.	−1.491
47	Ark	−1.863
48	Miss.	−2.061

Source: David Klingman and William W. Lammers, "The 'General Policy Liberalism' Factor in American State Politics." *American Journal of Political Science* 28 (August 1984): forthcoming. Reprinted by permission.

Note: Alaska and Hawaii were omitted because of missing data.

than in earlier years, particularly in states that were virtually untouched by earlier advocacy efforts. Whereas a few states, such as California and New York, manifested fairly extensive efforts in the 1950s, today there is at least some activity in all the states. The participatory roles required by the Older Americans Act, while not always spawning extensive activities, have helped insure that there will be at least a modest amount of activity in each state.

As a second key development, there has been a tendency for the elderly to come forward more often as advocates for their own causes (Williamson et al. 1982). In the 1950s, the lobbying that did occur was very often undertaken by professional social workers and health officials, with the elderly themselves often having, at most, a very marginal role. The members of the 1950 Conference on Aging, for example, were overwhelmingly comprised of professional persons. Furthermore, where older persons were involved in interest group activities, these groups were often, as in California (Putnam 1970), characterized by leader domination and limited rank-and-file participation in key organizational decisions. Changes in advocacy patterns for the aging, along with the increased general capacity of state governments, stand as important aspects of the overall shifts occurring in state politics in recent decades.

Socioeconomic Dimensions

National trends and regional shifts among the states become apparent as one considers the changes that have occurred since the 1950s. There has been a major sharing in the growth of personal income and a nationwide trend toward higher levels of urbanization. Similarly, the growth in the nation's percentage of individuals age 65 and over has been substantially shared throughout the country. However, important regional shifts are also apparent. In general, the South is a less distinct region than it was in the early post–World War II years, and the differences in income between the South and other parts of the country have diminished. Reflecting a substantial southern success story, the states now show less variation on personal income measures than in earlier years. After adjusting for differences in cost of living, personal incomes in Atlanta and New York City were identical by the late 1970s (Moynihan 1980, p. 218). The position of the states on several of the variables being used in this book clearly illustrates several of those important shifts.

Socioeconomic Development

The relative positions of the states on the industrialization-urbanization factor are presented in table 2–8. Overall, those rankings emphasize a relative stability in state positions throughout the twenty-year period. In 1975, just as in 1955, the top positions are held (with the exception of California) by eastern or midwestern states. It is also important to note that some shifting has occurred in the position of the states. By 1975, a number of the southern states had moved up from the bottom ranks, with the last six positions all held by nonsouthern states. The least developed of the New England states (Maine, New Hampshire, and Vermont) have, at the same time, been falling continually on that basic factor. In analyzing policy responses in the 1970s, it is thus important to bear in mind that the group of states that clusters around the middle ranks includes not only Minnesota, Oregon, and Wisconsin but also Alabama, Arizona, Georgia, Louisiana, and Tennessee.

The importance of the changing position of the South is also underscored by the changing level of per capita income. Between 1950 and 1974, for example, the eleven southern states increased from 72.9 to 87.7 percent of the national average (see Bass and DeVries 1976, p. 21). As emphasized by Sharkansky (1972), the regional variation among the states has become less pronounced at a number of points as the South has undergone substantial economic development in the years since World War II.

The Aging Population

Changes in the distribution of the nation's older population also show several interesting patterns, evident in (table 2–9). In comparing 1955 and 1980, for example, a decline in the percentage of those age 65 and over was experienced only in Utah and Wyoming. The most dramatic increase, of course, was in Florida, which moved from a ranking of eleventh in 1955 to an undisputed first position by 1980. A number of the states that possess some of the highest percentages as of 1980, at the same time, continue to be the states with a high rate of out-migration of their younger population and/or those with particularly high rates of life expectancy. These include states following Florida in the list of high percentage of elderly such as Arkansas, Iowa, Missouri, Nebraska, Kansas, South Dakota, and Oklahoma. Migration by the aging has not normally been a significant factor in the development of these concentrations, although Arkansas has exprienced somewhat higher in-migration levels than one finds in the other states.

Table 2–8
State Rankings on the Industrialization-Urbanization Factor

Rank	1955	1965	1975
1	N.Y.	N.J.	N.J.
2	N.J.	N.Y.	N.Y.
3	R.I.	Mass.	R.I.
4	Mass.	R.I.	Calif.
5	Pa.	Calif.	Mass.
6	Conn.	Ill.	Ill.
7	Calif.	Ohio	Ohio
8	Ill.	Pa.	Mich.
9	Ohio	Mich.	Pa.
10	Mich.	Conn.	Conn.
11	Md.	Md.	Md.
12	Del.	Wash.	Hawaii
13	Fla.	Ind.	Ind.
14	Ind.	Hawaii	Wash.
15	Wash.	Mo.	Nev.
16	Utah	Nev.	Tex.
17	Mo.	Del.	Del.
18	Ariz.	Tex.	Mo.
19	Colo.	Colo.	Fla.
20	Tex.	Utah	Colo.
21	Wis.	Fla.	Utah
22	La.	Wis.	Wis.
23	Nev.	Oreg.	Ariz.
24	Oreg.	Ariz.	Va.
25	Va.	Minn.	Oreg.
26	N.H.	La.	Minn.
27	Minn.	Va.	Tenn.
28	Ga.	W.Va.	La.
29	Okla.	Tenn.	Ala.
30	Tenn.	Ala.	Ga.
31	N.M.	Okla.	Okla.
32	Ala.	N.H.	W.Va.
33	W.Va.	Ga.	Ky.
34	Maine	Kans.	Alaska
35	Kans.	N.M.	N.H.
36	Iowa	Ky.	Kans.
37	Ky.	Maine	N.M.
38	N.C.	Alaska	N.C.
39	Nebr.	Iowa	S.C.
40	S.C.	Mont.	Iowa
41	Wyo.	Nebr.	Ark.
42	Mont.	N.C.	Nebr.
43	Vt.	S.C.	Maine
44	Idaho	Ark.	Miss.
45	Ark.	Wyo.	Mont.
46	Miss.	Idaho	Wyo.
47	S.Dak.	Vt.	Idaho
48	N.Dak.	Miss.	Vt.
49	—	S.Dak.	N.Dak.
50	—	N.Dak.	S.Dak.

Note: Alaska and Hawaii are not included for 1955 because they had not yet achieved statehood.

Table 2–9
Distribution of Population Age 65 and Over

State	Rank	Percent	Rank	Percent	Rank	Percent
Ala.	34	7.4	25	10.5	23	11.3
Alaska	50	2.4	50	2.5	50	3.0
Ariz.	46	5.9	29	10.1	24	11.3
Ark.	10	10.1	2	12.8	2	13.6
Calif.	30	8.4	34	9.7	33	10.2
Colo.	28	8.5	43	8.3	45	8.5
Conn.	20	9.1	26	10.4	18	11.7
Del.	36	7.3	42	8.6	36	9.9
Fla.	11	9.9	1	16.3	1	17.3
Ga.	39	7.0	40	8.7	40	9.5
Hawaii	49	4.5	49	6.6	47	7.9
Idaho	26	8.7	33	9.7	35	10.0
Ill.	17	9.3	27	10.3	28	11.0
Ind.	21	9.1	31	10.0	31	10.7
Iowa	2	11.1	3	12.7	4	13.3
Kans.	9	10.2	6	12.5	8	12.9
Ky.	24	8.8	20	10.9	26	11.2
La.	41	6.8	37	9.1	38	9.6
Maine	4	10.8	10	11.8	11	12.5
Md.	42	6.7	44	8.2	41	9.4
Mass.	7	10.3	13	11.6	10	12.7
Mich.	37	7.2	38	8.9	37	9.9
Minn.	12	9.8	17	11.2	17	11.8
Miss.	31	8.2	21	10.8	20	11.5
Mo.	6	10.5	4	12.6	5	13.2
Mont.	15	9.6	30	10.1	29	10.8
Nebr.	5	10.5	5	12.6	7	13.1
Nev.	48	4.9	48	7.5	46	8.3
N.H.	3	11.0	22	10.7	27	11.2
N.J.	27	8.5	24	10.5	19	11.7
N.M.	47	5.3	46	7.9	44	8.9
N.Y.	23	8.9	16	11.2	13	12.3
N.C.	43	6.1	37	9.0	34	10.2
N.Dak.	29	8.5	14	11.5	14	12.3
Ohio	25	8.8	32	9.9	30	10.8
Okla.	8	10.2	8	12.3	12	12.4
Oreg.	19	9.1	15	11.3	21	11.5
Pa.	22	9.1	12	11.6	9	12.9
R.I.	16	9.4	9	12.1	3	13.4
S.C.	45	6.0	45	8.1	43	9.2
S.Dak.	13	9.6	7	12.5	6	13.2
Tenn.	33	7.8	23	10.6	25	11.3
Tex.	38	7.0	35	9.5	39	9.6
Utah	44	6.1	47	7.6	49	7.5
Vt.	1	11.5	19	11.0	22	11.4
Va.	40	6.9	41	8.7	42	9.4
Wash.	18	9.2	28	10.3	32	10.4
W.Va.	32	8.1	11	11.7	15	12.2
Wis.	14	9.6	18	11.2	16	12.0
Wyo.	35	7.4	39	8.8	48	7.9

It is important to recognize that despite fairly substantial in-migration in some instances, the sunbelt states, as of 1980, were still often among the lower-ranking states in terms of the concentrations of older persons in their populations. Thus, Arizona ranked twenty-fourth, California ranked thirty-third, New Mexico ranked forty-fourth, and Texas ranked thirty-ninth. It is important to recognize that as of 1980, neither the Southwest nor the South (with the important exceptions of Florida and Arkansas) included any of the states with the highest proportions of older persons in their populations.

In evaluating the impact of the older population on policy outcomes, it is also useful to recognize that the absolute number of older persons in many states is quite large. As of 1980, for example, approximately 45 percent of the aging resided in just seven states. Both California and New York had populations age 65 and over in excess of 2 million persons each, while Florida, Illinois, Ohio, Pennsylvania, and Texas each had aging populations in excess of 1 million. Conversely, while some of the plains states had high percentages, the number of older persons was quite small. Factors involving both population size and percentage thus need to be considered in evaluating the impact of the nation's increasing older population on state policy responses.

Summary

The states show a wide variety of changes, as well as major instances of continuity, as one reviews developments since the 1950s. The states are becoming involved to a greater extent with policy design and implementation issues, and they are pursuing those actions with political processes reflecting an expanded capacity for policy development. They reflect, at the same time, a substantial increase in overall income levels throughout the nation and a significant shift toward greater nationwide uniformity, at least insofar as statewide measures are used. In their use of those expanded resources, however, the states have shown substantial variation, and some reluctance on the part of the rapidly growing states, to move toward a strong use of the public sector. Specific state responses can now be examined in relationship to these changing national trends.

3 Policymaking in Eight States

The widespread variation in state characteristics and policy responses is dramatically apparent in the eight case-study states. Differences in size, levels of industrialization, political cultures, and capacities for policy development have contributed to marked variation in both expenditure-based and regulatory policies. To highlight those differences, table 3–1 summarizes major political characteristics, and table 3–2 reviews state rankings on major policies for the aging. In addition, table 3–3 lists the governors who have served in the 1955–1980 period in those states.

California

California has been a consistently high achiever on several major dimensions of policy effort for the aging. Since the 1950s, its income maintenance policies have achieved a ranking in the top half-dozen states on OAA, and both the income maintenance factor and the health and welfare factor found California ranking second in the nation. Regulatory policies, while not coming uniquely early, have found California at least among the middle ranks or higher. California has been weak, however, in the area of social services. Here, it is important to emphasize, the social services factor shows the large states doing poorly. California stands as a strikingly low forty-seventh on that measure. Its record was substantially better, however, in terms of the speed with which Title XX funds were utilized at the fully authorized level. Indeed, it was in part the actions in California, as discussed by Derthick (1975) that produced the federal decision to place a ceiling on federal funds in 1972.

Regarding the socioeconomic and political factors that have been identified as likely contributors to more extensive policy efforts, California has had high rankings in several areas of potential influence. The percentage of the older population, it should be noted, declined very rapidly after World War II, so that California ranked only thirtieth and thirty-fourth in 1955 and 1975 respectively. In its overall socioeconomic development, however, California had a strong, growing economy during most of the past three decades and emerged as one of the

Table 3–1
Rankings of Case-Study States on Major Political Factors

Factor	Calif.	Fla.	Iowa	Maine	Minn.	N.C.	Ohio	Wash.
Party Compet. 1973	20	39	17	19	1	43	22	8
Voter Turnout, 1976	34	33	8	5	1	48	29	14
General Lib. (N = 48)	4	31	18	22	8	40	20	13
Innovation	3	31	29	20	12	24	11	14
Gov. Power	12	40	26	38	7	49	10	37
Legis. Profess., 1975	1	12	35	29	21	15	8	26
Senior Orgs. 1975	2	7	9	15	11	48	16	35

Note: For descriptions of political measures, see chapter 1 and the appendix.

Table 3–2
Rankings of Case-Study States on Major Policy Efforts

Factor	Calif.	Fla.	Iowa	Maine	Minn.	N.C.	Ohio	Wash.
Early Health	11	39	21	24	4	35	15	5
Health/Welfare	2	37	30	11	7	25	19	5
Income Maint.	2	35	28	10	17	31	25	13
Social Services	47	17	31	12	26	39	44	29
OAA Payment								
1955	6	41	22	35	7	48	21	13
1960	2	37	13	35	7	47	16	3
1965	1	41	17	28	8	43	14	23
1970	1	43	6	39	15	28	25	19
SSI Aged Pay	2	30	6	44	20	1	17	33
Cost Control	2	34	39	25	4	24	14	15
ADEA Age	1961	1969	1972	1965	1977	1975	1961	1961
Generic Age	1975	1974	1976	1975	1974	1979	1977	1977

Note: For descriptions of policy measures, see chapter 1 and the appendix.

Table 3–3
Governors of Case-Study States, 1955–1980

California	Goodwin J. Knight (1954–1958)	Rep.
	Edmund G. Brown (1958–1966)	Dem.
	Ronald Reagan (1966–1974)	Rep.
	Edmund G. Brown, Jr. (1974–1982)	Dem.
	George Deukmejian (1982–)	Rep.
Florida	Charley E. Johns (1952–1956)	Dem.
	LeRoy Collins (1956–1960)	Dem.
	Farris Bryant (1960–1964)	Dem.
	Haydon Burns (1964–1966)	Dem.
	Claude R. Kirk, Jr. (1966–1970)	Rep.
	Reubin Askew (1970–1978)	Dem.
	Robert Graham (1978–)	Dem.
Iowa	Leo A. Hoegh (1954–1956)	Rep.
	Herschel C. Loveless (1956–1960)	Dem.
	Norman A. Erbe (1960–1962)	Rep.
	Harold E. Hughes (1962–1968)	Dem.
	Robert Ray (1968–1982)	Rep.
	Terry Branstad (1982–)	Rep.
Maine	Edmund S. Muskie (1954–1958)	Dem.
	Clinton A. Clauson (1958–1960)	Dem.
	John H. Reed (1960–1966)	Rep.
	Kenneth M. Curtis (1966–1974)	Dem.
	James Longley (1974–1978)	Ind.
	Joseph Brennan (1978–)	Dem.
Minnesota	Orville L. Freeman (1954–1960)	DFL.[a]
	Elmer L. Anderson (1960–1962)	Rep.
	Karl F. Rolvaag (1962–1966)	DFL.
	Harold LeVander (1966–1970)	Rep.
	Wendell R. Anderson (1970–1975)	DFL.
	Rudy Perpich (1975–1976)	DFL.
	Albert H. Quie (1976–1980)	Rep.
	Rudy Perpich (1980–)	DFL.
North Carolina	William B. Umstead (1952–1956)	Dem.
	Luther H. Hodges (1956–1960)	Dem.
	Terry Sanford (1960–1964)	Dem.
	Dan K. Moore (1964–1968)	Dem.
	Robert W. Scott (1968–1972)	Dem.
	James E. Holshouser (1972–1976)	Rep.
	James B. Hunt, Jr. (1976–)	Dem.
Ohio	Frank J. Lausche (1948–1956)	Dem.
	C. William O'Neill (1956–1958)	Rep.
	Michael V. DiSalle (1958–1962)	Dem.
	James A. Rhodes (1962–1970)	Rep.
	John J. Gilligan (1970–1974)	Dem.
	James A. Rhodes (1974–1982)	Rep.
	Richard F. Celeste (1982–)	Dem.

Table 3-3 continued

Washington	Arthur B. Langlie (1948–1956)	Rep.
	Albert D. Rosellini (1956–1964)	Dem.
	Daniel J. Evans (1964–1976)	Rep.
	Dixy Lee Ray (1976–1980)	Dem.
	John Spellman (1980–)	Rep.

[a]In Minnesota, the official name for the state's Democratic Party is the Democratic Farmer Labor Party (DFL).

top states on the industrialization-urbanization factor. Over the twenty-year period, California moved from seventh to fourth among the fifty states. California's level of tax effort has also been substantial, with the ranking increasing from thirteenth to sixth between 1960 and 1975. Finally, regarding major political variables, California stood in the middle on party competition, somewhat below the average rank on turnout, and, very importantly, in a strong first position on the legislative professionalism measure. Several of these factors are helpful in interpreting the nature of aging-related policymaking in California.

It is appropriate to begin the California assessment with the role of the legislature, since many of the interview respondents placed considerable emphasis on the importance of that role. By the early 1960s, several factors were contributing to a strengthening of the overall legislative role in California. The elimination of cross-filing in the primaries and then reapportionment contributed to the development, particularly in the assembly, of a large group of reform-oriented legislators. During this period, with the encouragement of Speaker Jesse Unruh, the assembly also began a pronounced process of staff development. A pattern was begun in that period in which the amount of staff assistance available to legislators was distinctly higher than that found in most other states. A reform-oriented legislature, supported by enthusiastic new staffers, could then work with Governor Edmund G. (Pat) Brown, who was supportive of the interests of the aging as part of his interest in the overall expansion of social programs, although he was not uniquely concerned with the special problems of the aging.

The legislative role was also important during the eight years of Ronald Reagan's tenure as governor. Reagan was interested in curtailing a number of welfare programs including some that affected the aging. One of his early proposals, for example, was that provisions for relative responsibility on OAA (which were being either abandoned or left without a serious enforcement effort in most other states) be restored. There was considerable legislative pressure at the same time, however, for an expansion of benefits. Thus, when it came time for the state to establish its supplements to SSI in 1973, the actions of a number of the legislators (particularly the Burton brothers, with Congressman Phil Burton calling frequently from Washington, D.C., and brother John having an important legislative role in Sacramento) resulted in a negotiation with a number of intense lobby groups. The resulting package of fairly generous benefits (at least when compared to other states) was thus worked out in the legislative arena.

In recent years, the importance of legislative action has again been apparent at several points. In part, the establishment of a standing Committee on Aging in the assembly, and the existence of continuity in staff leadership, have provided opportunities for legislative promotion of policy interest. The personal interest on the part of one of the speakers of the assembly, Leo McCarthy, also provided a point of influence on some policy efforts. Interestingly, however, the California legislature has not produced the type of clearly identified spokesmen for the aging that has occurred in some states. While individuals in several related areas of policy specialization have been supportive at key points, no one or two people has made aging his or her issue. This may reflect in part the size of constituencies in California, plus the range of issues competing for a legislator's attention in a large and highly diverse state. Nonetheless, the California case stands as an important example of the significance of both legislative professionalism and the legislative arena as an area in which the development of coalitions around policy advances for the aging can take place.

The role of governors and their staffs as policy developers for the aging in California has, with few exceptions, been fairly modest. During the 1950s, there were occasional manifestations of interest in aging issues on the part of Governors Warren and Knight, perhaps in part because the aging issue at that time included a significant emphasis on the changing family structure of rural areas in which the Republican party was also distinctly interested in pursuing electoral support. Governor Pat Brown, in turn, was supportive, though usually at a fairly general level. In comparing the number of recommendations in the annual messages of the governor, for example, Brown stands out among the governors who served in the entire 1950–1980 period in the number and scope of his legislative recommendations. He also gave several key administrative appointments to individuals who were interested in an expansion of social programs. In terms of personal involvement, Brown did meet directly on several occasions with George McLain, the leader of the state's major lobby group for the aging, regarding the developments that led to the passage of health legislation in the 1961–1964 period. There is little indication, however, of a sustained, direct interest in aging issues during Brown's years as governor.

Ronald Reagan's tenure as governor did not produce major changes in policies for the aging. Indeed, the impact, in some observers' eyes, was substantially negative, with Governor Reagan's lack of interest in areas like the development of social services acting to stifle program expansion. Reagan's proposals for welfare curtailment usually focused on AFDC recipients rather than programs affecting the aging. With the use of a concept like the recently discussed safety net, his administration used the concept of the truly needy to endorse a number of programs for the elderly. In terms of social services development, however, neither the Office on Aging nor the Commission on Aging was given much support, and they suffered in this period from a lack of continuity in leadership. It should be noted also that the promotion of tax assistance for the aging, which did emerge as a fairly substantial program in the early 1970s, was viewed as being compatible with the general objectives of the Reagan administration. Ultimately, perhaps the most important point to emphasize is the relative lack of change in the state's position during Reagan's years as governor. Because of the strong legislative interest in program expansion and the expanding revenue capacity the state was enjoying, California continued, as reviewed in table 3–1, with a high ranking in most major policy areas in both 1970 and 1975.

Governor Edmund G. (Jerry) Brown, Jr., did not emerge as a particularly significant figure in the evolution of policy efforts for the aging. Some nonmandatory retirement legislation was promoted, and his appointees had some significant roles in shaping responses to federal reform initiatives, but there has not been a particularly strong overall impact. Despite an interest in futuristic issues in some areas of advanced technology, the growth in the nation's older population never captured Brown's sustained attention. California's governors, then, have not been pivotal figures in the development of policy efforts for the aging.

Turning to the administrative agencies, the aging network in California was viewed by a number of our interviewees as filling a limited policy development role. In part, despite the early developments surrounding the Commission on Aging between 1956 and 1966, the agency appears to have languished during the Reagan administration and was in a poor position to respond vigorously as the Older Americans Act program opportunities and broader objectives began to emerge in the

1970s. Rivalries between the Department of Aging and the Commission on Aging were not helpful at times, and the Department of Aging simply lacked the organizational resources to play a coordinating or promotive role in relationship to vastly larger organizations like the Departments of Health Services and Social Services. The record of general promotion on the part of the California Department of Aging and the Commission on Aging does include, however, some involvement with a number of important issue developments in the state in the early 1970s, including interest in alternatives to institutionalization and, more recently, the evolution of adult day care programs. Finally, in terms of administrative roles, it should be emphasized that a number of departments, including those of Health Services and Social Services, have had important roles quite independent of the efforts within the Department of Aging in helping to shape aspects of California's program response. On nursing home reform, for example, important advocacy came from within the Department of Health Services. Agency roles have frequently been important, in sum, but often without the Department of Aging as the central coordinating or promoting unit.

The development of aging-based interest groups in California presents, in turn, a very unusual set of responses. Most states did very little in the 1950s and 1960s but showed more activity in the 1970s; for California, however, the record is reversed. In the 1950s and early 1960s, the California League of Senior Citizens, under the strong leadership of George McLain, played an important role in state politics. McLain was effective at points in using the ballot initiative to advantage and maintained an extensive set of political clubs throughout the state. While his organizational style and distinct personal leadership style and preferences for a centralized organization offended some, Putnam (1970) concluded that McLain's group did have a significant impact on policy efforts for the aging. McLain had already begun to decline in political influence by the early 1960s, however, and after his death in 1965, his organization waned.

The fifteen years after McLain's death saw remarkably limited new development of interest group activity in California. No organization filled a coordinating role at the state level, and there were few instances in which legislators were experiencing tough, sustained lobbying activities or the meaningful presence of aging-based electoral activity. Aging-based interest groups were involved with nursing home reform and with coalition efforts in support of SSI benefit expansion, but they were often judged to be fairly secondary components of those coalition efforts. In terms of geographic areas, it should be noted that San Francisco, which has had substantial concentrations of aging neighborhoods, including the district of legislative champion Leo McCarthy, produced a number of local groups and displayed more interest in aging issues than was found in Los Angeles or other parts of the state. Finally, in terms of more recent developments, it should be emphasized that there have been significant attempts, in part through the Advisory Commission, to produce a more active and coordinated set of advocacy activities in 1981 and 1982.

The relatively low level of interest group activity in California in the 1970s has several possible explanations. To some extent, the diversity of the state and its geographic distances would appear to have contributed to the difficulty in organizing statewide efforts. In addition, apprehension regarding the rise of a "new George McLain" has been voiced by some as a reason for the reluctance to work toward a centralized advocacy network. Perhaps even more fundamentally, however, California was simply not a state in which extensive lobbying activity was necessary to achieve substantial program developments in a number of policy areas. It does seem likely that a stronger lobby might have produced a stronger set of social services programs, but in highly visible program areas such as Medi-Cal (California's label for Medicaid) and SSI, strong lobbying by the aging was not a necessary condition for the development of strong benefit packages. California thus stood, as of 1980, as an important example of a state in which a relatively high performance in a number of policy areas has occurred despite rather limited lobbying efforts by the aging.

The relationships that stand out from the California case study support several factors postulated in our overall model. The general policy liberalism of the state has been important, along with the high tax capacity and the willingness to utilize (at least prior to the passage of Proposition 13 in 1978) that relatively high tax capacity. As a reflection of the importance of structural capacity in state government, some significant roles in policy development have come from a number of the major state departments involved with health and welfare policies. Overall capacity has also been very important, particularly in the legislature. In political terms, finally, a variety of coalitions and instances of legislative leadership have been important, along with occasional encouragement from the governor's office.

Washington

Washington manifests distinct political tensions between its periodic tendencies toward distinctly liberal responses and a lingering emphasis on a conservative, tax-avoiding orientation that can make program development for the aging quite difficult. Regarding its progressive tendencies, Washington stands thirteenth on our general policy liberalism measure, fourteenth on Walker's (1969) innovation index, and (in 1960) seventh in its willingness to use its tax capacity. Historically, that tendency toward progressiveness was promoted in part by the Washington Pension Union, a group which used the initiative process after World War II to promote a number of pension proposals and related reforms. Thus, in the 1950s, Washington was also fairly innovative on some of its programs for the aging, including a state medical program, and had relatively high levels of OAA.

Resistance toward public sector activities has nonetheless at points been quite pronounced. Some have mentioned an individualistic political culture in this regard, while others have suggested that the eastern section of the state constitutes a strong conservative influence in the state's political performance (see Bone 1978). Intertwined with those conservative tendencies has been a continuing reluctance to establish a state income tax. This has become an increasing anomaly for one of the more progressive states and, in turn, has an important impact on state politics. Our respondents in Washington seemed to center their answers to the changing conditions of the local economy more extensively than in other states. Thus, Boeing's major decline in airplane contracts in the early 1970s was viewed as a major factor in the shaping of state policy, particularly because of the lack of alternative resource options that a more diverse state tax structure might have made possible.

In reviewing Washington's policy responses for the aging since the fairly progressive days of the 1950s, the striking characteristic is the recent development of a stronger emphasis on social services. Overall, on our project measures, Washington did not do particularly well between 1960 and 1975. The health and welfare factor did achieve a fifth rank, but the responses in areas such as tax relief, OAA, job protection, and generic drugs were quite average. The passage in 1976 of a state social services program—which did occur despite the state's economic problems of that year—marked, at the same time, an important initial step in the development of a stronger emphasis on state support for social services programs.

Turning to political roles, the governor's office in Washington presents few instances of strong interest and promotion. In looking back to the 1950s and early 1960s, Governor Arthur Langlie was not characterized as a significant figure, and Governor Albert Rosellini was often described as primarily interested in the development of state institutions. The record of Governor Daniel Evans, who served from 1964 through 1976, shows within that twelve years the extent to which interest in aging was apt to evolve. In the 1960s, his primary focus was on issues such as the state's educational system and the reorganization

of state government. Governor Evans did become substantially involved with the reorganization effort and the subsequent hiring of
Charles Morris as the first director of the Department of Social and
Health Services. At the same time, the Bureau of Aging was not a
major consideration in that reorganization and remained in a low hierarchical position in the new Department of Social and Health Services. Governor Evans was interested in promoting volunteer roles for
seniors and was supportive of the initiative for social services in 1976.
There were, in addition, some attempts at promoting aging issues with
a study commission shortly before he left office.

With the election of Governor Dixy Lee Ray, Washington found
itself between 1976 and 1980 with a governor who was fairly interested
in the state's older population. During the course of that one-term
governorship, approaches to her by key spokesmen for the aging were
helpful in preventing program contraction. She was also interested in
promoting senior issues with both policy-oriented and social appear-
ances before senior groups. The evolution of gubernatorial involvement, then, has been toward greater interest in senior issues.

The Washington legislature, like a number of the other legislatures
in our case study states, began a period of increased interest in policy
development in the early 1970s—in particular, as of 1973. This change
involved an expansion in staff and an increased interest in both policy
initiation and policy oversight roles. Prior to that time, the most recognized leaders on aging issues were themselves quite elderly. In the
last several years there has been only a moderate development of new
legislative advocates. That fairly modest growth may have occurred in
part because of the distinctive role the Senior Lobby, as discussed later,
was having in the state in the late 1970s. Thus, while the legislature
has become increasingly involved with a number of aging-related issues, including in particular a divisive issue involving nursing home
regulation and reimbursement rates, there were not uniquely high levels of overall involvement in policy development.

The role of the Senior Lobby in Washington, at the same time,
has been quite unique. It should be noted that the development is
quite recent, with the major leader, Norm Schut, along with other
observers, seeing 1976 and 1977 as building years, with the 1979 legislative session the one in which the seniors really came into their own
as a force in the state legislature. The start of a more aggressive social
services program in 1976, then, predated the emergence of the Senior
Lobby.

Several resources have contributed to the strength of the Senior
Lobby in Washington. First, the dominant leader, Norm Schut, had
developed lobby skills over a period of more than twenty years in

Olympia and was no stranger to many key legislators. Second, there was an interest in developing grassroots lobbying techniques that involved extensive workshops in 1976 and 1977. Third, through a process of member questionnaires and decisions by the board of directors of the Senior Lobby, there was an attempt to focus lobbying efforts on a few key issues during each session. Fourth, the development of social services programs even prior to the emergence of the Senior Lobby has provided a base that can be used for promoting program expansion quite effectively. Thus, with these resources, the Senior Lobby, particularly in 1979, was instrumental in the expanded financial support of the Bureau of Aging and with the maintenance of funding for other aging programs at a time in which budget cutting was already becoming a common topic throughout Olympia.

Finally, in terms of administrative roles, there was quite widespread agreement among our interviewees that the integrated Department of Health and Social Services had not produced a particularly helpful leadership role for the emergence of programs for the aging. In part, budget retrenchment was an underlying issue, and there was also interest in de-emphasizing casework approaches throughout the department. As for the Bureau of Aging, a number of reviews have been quite favorable regarding its overall operations. These operations have involved, in part, an extensive, early emphasis on case management approaches in their overall program development. In terms of the advisory committee roles, there were major problems in the early years stemming in part from the large (80-member) structure and the lack of strong leadership. In recent years, the advisory council has had close relationships with the Senior Lobby, including Norm Schut's appointment in 1976 by Governor Evans to the Advisory Council. Through the close ties among the bureau, the Advisory Council, and the Senior Lobby, communication on issues occurs on an extensive basis.

The Washington case is important in terms of the manner in which political support can be developed for social services programs. The Senior Lobby has also emerged as an important example of the manner in which lobbying efforts can develop. The Washington case, perhaps more than many, seems also destined as of the early 1980s to illustrate the manner in which differing levels of economic performance tend to influence a state's overall policy responses for the aging.

Minnesota

The policy responses in the nation's most northern state (other than Alaska) have often been characterized as progressive, pragmatic, and innovative (see, for example, Fenton 1966, and a more questioning view by Gieske 1979). The measures developed for this project provide some support for Minnesota's progressive reputation, since it ranked eighth on the general policy liberalism factor, ninth in tax effort, and twelfth on Walker's innovation index. These actions have occurred in a moderately sized state, which ranks a middling twenty-sixth on our industrialization-urbanization factor and which has a median family income level (as of 1978) placing it thirteenth in the nation. The underlying reasons for Minnesota's public sector responsiveness, while outside the scope of the present discussion, would seem to involve aspects of political culture and the leadership provided by a series of strong figures within the Democratic Farmer Labor party.

Regarding overall policy responses for the aging, Minnesota's record is at the same time somewhat mixed. The record on several of the major policy areas was quite strong, as reflected by the seventh rank on the health and welfare factor and the fourth rank on tax relief. In contrast, however, the commitments to SSI tailed off (in part due to strong views on federalism issues on the part of a key legislator who aggressively supported other welfare legislation), the state was a surprisingly late adopter of some regulatory provisions, and the social services rank was only twenty-sixth.

To complete the picture of responsiveness to aging issues in Minnesota, it should be noted that a substantial amount of activity was also occurring outside the measures used in this project. In the area of housing, for example, the state moved quickly to put state funds into the Minnesota Housing Agency, with a total of some $123 million being used to supplement state programs between 1973 and 1980 for low income groups, including a major emphasis on housing for senior citizens. A variety of housing and home care programs were also being fostered through a combination of public and private efforts, including the housing programs of the Ebenezer Society, the limited care programs of the Wilder Foundation in St. Paul, and the extensive efforts at the Minneapolis Age and Opportunity Center to develop programs that help the aging to remain in their homes. In varying degrees, other states could point to innovative activities of this nature, but the Minnesota case seems to constitute a particularly strong example of the diverse ways in which responsiveness to aging issues was emerging in the past decade.

To begin our analysis of political actions with the governors, Minnesota presents an interesting example of the widely differing responses on aging issues that have come from the governor's office. In the 1950s, Governor Orville Freeman was a clear example of a governor with a strong interest in expanding social services programs in general and with interests in aging that were fairly pronounced, given the political milieu of the 1950s. Governor Freeman fought tenaciously with key members of the conservative-dominated Senate in his quest for welfare expansion, and with some success. On aging issues, he was fairly promotive in the establishment of the Commission on Aging and met at least monthly with its first director. Governor Freeman was also conscious of the electoral dimension of the aging, using visits to nursing homes and congratulatory notes to the state's most senior citizens on their birthdays. Freeman's successor, Elmer L. Anderson, served only two years but showed some interest in aging issues, though he often was unable to gain passage of his basic legislative initiatives due to resistance within the more conservative wing of his Republican party.

The record of gubernatorial leadership in Minnesota in the 1960s shows little emphasis on aging-related issues. There were occasional proposals, as indicated in the systematic review of all gubernatorial proposals by Williamson (1976), but little indication that governors were taking a significant interest in either the specific issues surrounding the Board on Aging or the more general expansion in benefits through the new federal programs. One interviewee, for example, thought the commission might well have been abandoned in the later 1960s if it had not been required by the Older Americans Act.

Gubernatorial leadership in the 1970s produced its strongest impact with Governor Wendell Anderson's strong role in developing tax relief for the aging. Anderson took a direct, personal interest in that issue and was in turn supported in his orientation by an expanded personal staff, an active role by the state Planning Commission, and a strong movement (particularly in 1973) for reform that was also emerging within the state legislature. Thus, the decision to freeze property taxes for all senior citizens clearly bears the mark of Anderson's personal decision, while the general movement for tax reform must be attributed to the simultaneous impact of a number of forces moving the state toward tax reform in the early 1970s.

To round out the picture of gubernatorial leadership, it should be noted that Anderson was also fairly active in supporting senior legislation in the 1975–1976 legislative session. On the highly controversial issue of Medicaid reimbursement rate reform during that period, however, the leadership role centered substantially in the legislative arena. Regarding the two governors to succeed Anderson, Governor Perpich (from the state's staunchly liberal Iron Range) normally promoted program expansion but had neither the time in office nor the political support within the legislature to carry out much significant change in his initial services as governor. With the election of Albert Quie in 1978, the leadership role in the governor's office turned to a former

U.S. congressman who had made education a specialty while in the House and whose campaign emphasis was on tax reduction rather than program expansion. In 1982, Minnesota's voters again selected Perpich as governor. Minnesota's policies for the aging have thus had, overall, quite uneven support from the governor's office.

Turning to the legislative arena, the development of leadership roles on aging issues was slow to emerge but ultimately very important. In the 1950s and 1960s, there was often sharp resistance, particularly in the Senate, to both social services programs and some of the responses to federal programs around OAA and MAA. Governor Freeman became so incensed at the resistance of one key legislator, for example, that he personally campaigned very hard for the legislator's defeat. The senior committee chairmen who maintained strong fiefdoms in the Senate were often more than mildly difficult to persuade on a variety of human services programs.

The legislature in the 1970s, however, became an important focal point in several instances for policy development on a number of aging-related issues. The emergence of a major conflict-of-interest scandal, involving several officials responsible for regulating nursing homes, provided one catalyst, along with the emergence of strong lobbying activity on this issue. A new group of legislators became involved with strong interests on urban issues, poverty issues, and to an increasing extent, the problems of the aging. The growth of the state legislative staff in the early 1970s, at the same time, provided an opportunity for the legislators to become involved with more issues, particularly of an oversight nature, than had previously been the case.

The combination of extensive efforts by a dominant legislative coalition and several initiatives by Governor Anderson and his staff produced the basis for concerted policy action in the early 1970s. Martin Sabo, the speaker of the House, was a particularly critical figure, along with Nicholas Coleman, the majority party (DFL) leader in the Senate. Sabo was not uniquely committed to policies for the elderly, but as a populist figure with a strong interest in new programs, his actions in such areas as Medicaid financing and eligibility requirements provided an important influence. The departure of Speaker Sabo to the U.S. House of Representatives, along with the death of Senator Coleman and a rapid turnover in the legislature in the late 1970s, reduced the extent to which the legislature would be an initiating force in aging-related policy development. Nonetheless, in their actions during the period of expansion between about 1973 and 1976, the legislature provided a period of extensive activity which interestingly resembled the strong legislative role we observed in California in the early 1960s. Just as in the California case, the legislative initiatives occurred in concert

with a general commitment to program expansion in state government
on the part of the governor and his key aides.

The policy formation roles of major agencies in Minnesota have at
points taken on major significance. In the controversies over nursing
home regulatory reform, a number of key figures within the Health
Department, if not always popular in the legislature, were instrumental
in the shaping of that final legislation. In a similar way, the Department
of Public Welfare, while not benefiting from strong leadership at the
top in recent years, did have individuals who were providing background information. In addition, the State Planning Agency at points
contributed to the shaping of the policy agenda. Historically in Minnesota, however, the role of department heads had not been particularly strong, perhaps in part because of the problems of recruitment in
a state government that often looked more toward the outlying counties than to the Twin Cities and that tended to pay its department
heads less than individuals in comparable positions within the Twin
Cities area.

The role of the Minnesota Board on Aging focused initially (in the
1950s and 1960s) on the development of private sector and local government responses and more recently on management roles surrounding basic programs under the Older Americans Act. In the evolution
of that role, there have been occasional successes with the legislature,
as illustrated by an increase in the state supplemental appropriation to
the federal nutrition funds that was promoted in 1976. The general
emphasis, however, has been on program management, with fairly
limited attention to advocacy activities. The Advisory Committee, while
gradually moving away from a strong interest in management issues,
has taken on a somewhat broader interest in promoting support for
aging programs. This interest has included, for example, orientation
sessions with legislators on aging programs and issues at the beginning
of new legislative sessions. Overall, however, the familiar constraints
posed by rapid turnover and elaborate concern with representation
have made it difficult for the Advisory Committee to excel in forceful
lobbying activity. In the eyes of the legislators, it is often difficult to
sense just what constituency they are speaking for.

The overall interest group record in Minnesota, it is important to
note, is again one of substantial change. Prior to 1970, as was the case
in so many states, advocacy activity was extremely limited. Beginning
in 1970, a major early reform effort was led by Daphne Krause. After
initial experiences with a model cities program in an older neighborhood close to downtown Minneapolis, she became a key figure in the
initial publicizing of problems with the state's nursing home industry.
Subsequently, the Minneapolis Age and Opportunity Center, under

her directorship, became a strong advocate of expanded home care programs.

The lobbying efforts for nursing home reform ultimately included a number of groups. Several religious organizations were involved, including a fairly broad-based coalition effort. There was also an active Patients' Rights group. In addition, in the midst of the controversy over nursing homes, the Metropolitan (and now Minnesota) Senior Federation was created as an independent organization with nursing home reform as one of its concerns.

The Minnesota Senior Federation, with a substantial set of offices near the state capitol, represents an important example of the forces that can contribute to the development of advocacy roles for the aging. Financial support at the outset was provided by the Presbyterian Church as an outgrowth of its concerns with urban problems in the late 1960s. Organized labor also contributed, including the work of a long-time labor lobbyist, Arthur Tobler, who was responsible for the lobby efforts with the legislature. In building membership, the Senior Federation also developed a number of interesting financial incentives. Besides the familiar method of negotiated insurance packages for members, the organization was also successful in negotiating with hospitals and dentists in the state to provide discounts to members with low incomes. Thus, in a manner that resembles Olson's (1971) emphasis on direct incentives, the Senior Federation was using such incentives as well as the interest in promoting legislation in its fairly successful effort to build a solid membership.

In terms of political influence, the actions of the Senior Federation came in part after the completion of our formal comparison, so the evidence of their influence has to be drawn indirectly. The list of legislative efforts for which they are given credit as an important contributor includes an experimental dental program for low income elderly, nursing home reform, and the expansion of social services. The federation is also seen by a number of observers as contributing to the movement for a variety of local government responses involving steps such as bus discounts and home repair programs.

The Minnesota response suggests basic conclusions about program development in a state that has typically been regarded as fairly progressive and innovative. The record has not been uniformly strong despite the existence of fairly progressive responses in a variety of policy areas. There was certainly no automatic translating of policy responses for the aging on the basis of the state's overall political culture. The political record underscores, in fact, the importance of specific political actions in developing policy responses for the aging. Legislators have been instrumental at points, particularly in the early

1970s, governors have on occasion had important roles, agency heads have helped to form particular policy thrusts, and more recently, interest groups have begun to develop increasingly recognized roles in overall policy development. Specific actions, then, have been instrumental in shaping the fairly strong responses Minnesota has been making to its support of the aging.

Iowa

Perhaps the most distinctive aspects of policy development for the aging in Iowa is the large percentage of older persons in the state's population. The phrase "every eighth Iowan" has come into use in an effort to underscore that distinctive aspect of Iowa's population structure. Iowa continually ranked near the top in its percentage of older persons and has a number of rural, southern counties in which the percentage of persons age 65 and over exceeds 20 percent.

Iowa ranks close to the middle in a number of other basic characteristics. On our industrialization-urbanization factor, Iowa ranked a somewhat deceptive fortieth, due to the tendency for industrial activities to be located to an unusual extent in relatively small communities. On median family income, Iowa was again in the middle. Iowa stands as a major example of the tendency (ably described by Bryan 1981) for uses of high technology to be found outside the nation's large, urban areas. The multiple dimensions of contemporary Iowa are vividly characterized by the proximity of the classic small, rural towns— Herbert Hoover's birthplace, West Branch, for example—to a state university with major advanced research interests, including a lengthy tradition of involvement in gerontological research.

Iowa's public policy record also usually reflects a middle position. It is important to note, for example, that Iowa ranked eighteenth on our measure of general policy liberalism, but twenty-ninth on the Walker (1969) measure of innovation, which focused more substantially on earlier state responses. In its overall tax effort, Iowa improved its position quite substantially between 1960 and 1975, moving its ranking from thirty-third to twenty-first (Halstead 1978).

The policy responses for the aging also reflect a middle position. Indeed, one finds at points a consciousness of this situation reflected in the phrase, "Iowa, never first but never last." Thus, on the early health factor Iowa stood twenty-first, but it dropped to twenty-eighth and thirtieth, respectively, on the income maintenance factor and the health and welfare factor. It is interesting that despite the major emphasis on tax reform in the early 1970s, Iowa also ranked only twenty-third in the amount of tax assistance going to the aging. Finally, in terms of regulatory issues, Iowa was not a leader in its move to adopt any of the measures we have studied, but it did have some legislative provisions in all of the established regulatory areas.

Turning to the political processes and key participants, Iowa has had only two governors during almost the entire period under study. The governors in the 1950s displayed some modest interest in the early efforts and on one occasion in fire regulations for nursing homes, but in no instance was aging perceived as a key issue to be pursued. The election of Governor Harold Hughes in 1962 and his resounding re-election in 1964 (with a margin outdistancing Lyndon Johnson's) marked, however, a major shift in Iowa's orientations in a number of program areas. Hughes was a major advocate of social services programs, and policies like expanded efforts around Medicaid in the mid-1960s were included in his messages to the state legislature. He also contributed to a general atmosphere of change in state politics and appears to have prompted some expanded interest in aging issues. He was supportive, but not directly involved, and did not make support for the aging a uniquely important aspect of his overall program.

Governor Robert Ray, elected in 1968, was a person with unusual durability in office. Ray won re-election every two years until his decision not to run for re-election in 1982. Property tax reform was a major issue during the first years of his governorship, with aid for the aging one of several issues including state-local fiscal relations and levels of support for the public schools. He also became quite substantially involved with organizational matters in the reorganization efforts surrounding the state's Department of Social Services. There was little perception, however, of Ray as having more than an average involvement with, or interest in, issues relating to the aging. His most substantial involvement with the SUA came in 1976, amid questions surrounding the use of outside consultants by that thinly staffed organization. Thus, in terms of gubernatorial impact, Iowa, through the 1970s, has not seen a pronounced impact on aging issues coming directly from the governor's office. The use of appointments and budget deliberations, as in other states, could at points allow for the shaping of priorities but without a distinctive emphasis on aging-related issues.

The Iowa legislature has had a fairly important role at points in the evolution of policy for the aging. This has included staff support on several key issues and an important involvement in some new social services legislation. The staff, for example, extensively examined nursing home issues and included individuals with a strong interest in social services programs for the aging. In the attempts at building support for new legislation, the legislature developed a distinct aging advocate in Gregory Cusak, a young member of the assembly from Davenport. Representative Cusak was a key initiator in 1977, for example, in the promotion of an in-home care bill that ultimately was passed into law to provide some $1.5 million in state funds for this program (see Bruner 1978).

The limitations on the legislative role, nonetheless, have also been substantial. There has been important advocacy coming from some key supporters, and it also seems clear that the legislators do not want to be in a position of having to vote against legislation providing new programs or benefit levels for the elderly. However, the legislature, through committee deliberations, could also function as a veto point for new initiatives. Thus, while the legislature did initiate actions on occasions, there were no indications of an overriding interest in changing policies for the aging, particularly if substantial sums of money were involved with those initiatives.

Turning to agency roles, Iowa represents another of the attempts at integration in the administrative organization of the state's social services programs. The creation of an integrated Department of Social Services has subsequently led to considerable turnover in leadership and a strong feeling in a number of quarters that the integrated approach has not lived up to its initial expectation. In terms of departmental support for aging issues, the Department of Health has more often been perceived as playing a significant role, particularly in the shaping of the state's response on nursing home regulations. In addition, on regulatory issues, particularly as they affect lower income individuals, the Legal Services Corporation has been a strong advocate of expanded protection for the aging.

The Commission on Aging in Iowa has a history of promotive activities that goes back to the mid-1950s and that includes a number of innovative efforts stemming in part from the efforts of key individuals like Dr. Woodward Morris at the University of Iowa. Growth in the organization came very slowly, however, even after the establishment of the Older Americans Act. As a result, the organization had difficulty assuming additional responsibilities in the early 1970s and generated a political issue because of the use of outside consultants. Prior to 1976, the commission worked to promote volunteer activities (in part as a reflection of its very limited budget) but clearly could not be seen as a major factor in policy development across the range of issues in state policy that were affecting the aging.

In recent years, there have been increased efforts to consolidate managerial practices surrounding basic Older Americans Act programs and to generate support for a somewhat broader range of policies. This has included, in part, a careful evaluation of the various funding sources that have been contributing to the total range of state programs available for the aging in Iowa. In terms of more direct political influence, some good efforts have been undertaken to use the aging network (including the local area agenices) to help build support for social services programs. But these activities would have to be characterized as involving a relatively small range of the issues affecting the aging in state policy and a limited range of political actions.

The overall picture of interest group roles in Iowa must also be characterized as one of quite limited action. New organizations have been attempted on occasion, but without great success, and the state chapters of the major national groups (AARP and NCSC) have been quite limited in their state-level advocacy. Organizational memberships have been small, and the amount of political activity has been largely confined to some monitoring of legislation and periodic efforts to bring some individuals to hearings and to organize letter-writing campaigns. Thus, in his assessment of the interest groups as of 1977, Bruner (1978) similarly concludes that they have been primarily serving as issue raisers and not as major participants in the bargaining processes that shape state policy.

In part because of the limited nature of Iowa's interest groups, there have been a number of efforts to build coalitions with other groups. These efforts have included some alliances with religious groups, labor organizations, and consumer groups. The policy issue around which the most sustained efforts were achieved was nursing home regulation, in which actions of some significance emerged in the mid-1970s. However, coalition efforts overall were fairly sporadic, tending to occur for a short time and on relatively few issues.

A review of the political roles that have emerged in Iowa thus reveals few forces that would move the state strongly toward innovative or uniquely extensive accomplishments in its policies for the aging. The large percentage of older persons is recognized politically, but it tends not to produce distinctive program responses. Legislative advocates and the aging network on occasion help with program developments, particularly in the area of social services, but they do not generate sufficient support to produce dramatic changes. Through this process Iowa has produced a respectable showing in comparison with other states, but certainly not a uniquely extensive one.

Ohio

With a population in excess of 10 million, Ohio is the second largest of our case study states. Perhaps more important is the fact that Ohio stands as a state with a striking range of diverse social and economic patterns. A strong rural sector continues in the state despite its relatively high level of industrialization and urbanization. At the same time, the existence of the Cincinnati, Cleveland, Columbus, Toledo, Akron, and Youngstown metropolitan areas, all with populations over a half-million residents, gives Ohio a unique pattern of multiple urban centers without a single dominant metropolitan area. Thus, it is not a coincidence that Ohio, with its many cross-cutting social cleavages, has often been looked to as a bellwether state regarding possible trends in national politics.

Ohio has been repeatedly characterized, and emerges in our analysis, as a state in which public expenditures have come with considerable reluctance. In terms of general policy liberalism, for example, Ohio stands behind Iowa at a rank of twentieth. Perhaps even more dramatically, on tax effort, Ohio stood at thirty-fourth in 1960 and fell to forty-third by 1975.

Perhaps it is not surprising that Ohio's policies for the aging have reflected the state's cautious approach to public spending. The early health programs did give Ohio a ranking of fifteenth in the nation in the mid-1960s. However, the rankings on the health and welfare factor (nineteenth) and the income maintenance factor (twenty-fifth) in 1975 have generally fallen into the middle range. SSI benefit levels as of 1975, however, did rank seventeenth. In terms of social services, there was a fairly limited commitment until the mid-1970s, with the state ranking forty-fourth on the social services factor as of 1975.

On regulatory policies, Ohio's response level has been in the middle in both the earliness and the scope of regulation. The question of nursing home regulation was clearly the most widely debated of the regulatory activities, considering the amount of controversy that was generated, and certain Ohio citizens made some important contributions to the national movement for nursing home reform in the early 1970s, as vividly described by Mendelson (1974).

Turning to the roles of political actors, the impact of the governors has centered primarily around the actions of James Rhodes. With a record of service that totaled some 16 years by 1982, Governor Rhodes has indeed been one of the more durable of the nation's governors. (Somewhat coincidentally, our case study states have produced individuals with the unique record of having served 12 or more years— not only in Ohio but also in Iowa and Washington.) In terms of the impact Governor Rhodes has had on aging policies, the response was quite different in his second two terms (1974–1982) than in his first two (1962–1970). In his first eight years, the strong emphasis was on highway construction (funded largely through bonds) and a willingness to keep taxes low, with limited commitments in other areas. However, during his second eight years, which began in 1975, there was substantially greater interest in aging issues, including a close personal relationship with the politically appointed director of the Ohio Commission on Aging, Martin Janis. As a senior citizen himself, Rhodes initiated and helped publicize, among other things, a statewide senior discount card, known as the Golden Buckeye Card. Discounts of up to 50 percent were advertised, with a study by the State Commission on Aging concluding that individual savings in the neighborhood of $400 a year could be realized through use of that card.

The interest in aging issues on the part of Governor Rhodes became quite substantial in his last years in office. However, it has also been alleged that Rhodes' interest was confined to largely symbolic and politically valuable programs requiring little actual public expenditure. Interest was slight in the 1960s, however, and in the 1971–1975 period, Governor John Gilligan, while anxious to promote an expansion in state services like secondary education, was neither particularly interested in aging issues nor very successful in pursuing his proposed tax increases with the state legislature. It is worth noting that Ohio saw more activity in the area of aging during the Republican administration of Governor Rhodes than during the previous Democratic administration. This increase may well reflect, at least in part, the general expansion of activity for the aging that was occurring in the 1970s.

Turning to the legislative arena, several points deserve emphasis. First, Ohio is one of the stronger examples of the development of a professionalized state legislature. It ranked eighth on legislative professionalism as of 1975, and the Legislative Service Commission was actively involved with quite extensive reports in a number of policy areas, including several in aging-related areas. Second, a number of legislators, including both junior and senior members, have taken a substantial interest in aging issues in recent years, and one young champion in particular, Representative John Begala, emerged in the late 1970s.

The Ohio legislature, nonetheless, has not experienced as pronounced a period of major new coalitions forming around basic social policy issues as we have seen in some of the other states. There are no indications of a period of legislatively led expansion as occurred, for example, in California in the early 1960s. The legislative leadership has also been known to oppose sharp expansion of aging programs. Thus, while the legislative arena has at points been important for the formation of compromises on specific pieces of legislation, there have not been periods of particularly decisive legislative leadership.

The administrative structures in Ohio include, overall, a number of individuals with substantial professional expertise in aging-related policy areas. These individuals have contributed to the development of some innovative program efforts in both state and local operations in recent years. The state's Commission on Aging, at the same time, became fairly active in the promotion of social services policy initiatives by the mid-1970s. The commission benefited greatly from the personal interest in aging issues shown by Governor Rhodes and from his long-term personal friendship with the commission's director, Martin Janis, a former legislator and state director of Mental Health and Corrections, with a strong reputation for administrative skill as well as influence with the governor, the legislature, and interest groups. The commission has also been able to develop some close working relationships with key legislators and interest group representatives.

Finally, Ohio has shown a fairly pronounced increase in interest group development throughout the 1970s, particularly at the local level in the larger cities (most notably, Cleveland). In the 1950s and 1960s, the activity that did occur was often promoted by professionals who sought to speak for the aging. Part of the thrust toward greater interest group activity came in the early 1970s, with the coalition activities that occurred surrounding nursing home regulation. Here, the interest groups were most definitely important as issue raisers, and they appear to have had a fairly significant voice in the evolution of the ultimate changes in the state's regulatory policies. Organized labor appears to have been a particularly supportive coalition partner in Ohio, as has the association of nonprofit nursing homes. The state has not, however, seen the development of a particularly strong network of groups focusing on aging issues. Both the AARP and NCSC do have fairly active chapters in Ohio, it should be noted, and do maintain organizations in a number of the larger cities. While these groups do not boast as extensive a set of organizational activities as was found in Minnesota and Washington, these organizations were clearly growing throughout the 1970s and have been capable of mobilizing some degree of activity such as generating mail and phone calls to legislators on controversial bills. Moreover, several individuals, both within those organizations and others, like the state's universities, have been active as advocates on behalf of the aging.

Overall, perhaps the most striking aspect of the developments in Ohio has been the increasing extent of interest shown in aging issues throughout the 1970s. When visited in 1980, the state commission, legislature, and interest groups displayed a level of activity that far surpassed the minimal levels evident in the 1960s. It remains to be seen, however, whether or not this increase in interest and activity would be translated into major new policy commitments in a state with only a modest degree of general liberalism and in which economic contraction was becoming increasingly severe.

Maine

As the most sparsely populated of our case study states, Maine has exhibited in its policymaking processes in the area of aging the same informal and personalized pattern that has been attributed to politics in that state by a variety of observers (see, for example, Lockard 1959). The Maine case also exemplifies policymaking in a state with distinctly higher than average concentrations of older persons (although the ranking fell from fifth to tenth between 1955 and 1975) and fairly modest economic resources, ranking thirty-seventh on our socioeconomic status factor in 1975. Despite its resource limitations, however, Maine did achieve a ranking of twenty-second on our general liberalism factor.

In its overall pattern of policies for the aging, Maine has produced a fairly wide range of responses. In 1975 the state was eleventh in the country in its ranking on our health and welfare factor, was the eighth state in the country to adopt property tax relief for the aging, and was among the top states in the country in the scope of its protection for older workers under age discrimination in employment statutes and for those desiring to purchase generic drugs. In addition, its level of social services effort was fairly substantial, producing a ranking on that factor of twelfth in the nation. Maine's contributions to OAA supplements remained quite low, however. Since our formal rankings are as of 1975, it is important to note that Maine also stands as an example of a state that seemed to have more substantial amounts of activity early in the 1970s than in later years.

More extensively than in most of our case study states, the activities being promoted by Maine's aging network in the late 1960s and early 1970s seem to have had a significant impact. This occurred in part through the cultivation of local groups and the emergence of a young champion in the legislature, Representative Kathleen Watson Goodwin. After a series of changes in personnel in the mid-1970s in both the SUA (Bureau of Maine's Elderly) and the legislature, however, the leadership impact became somewhat less pronounced. By the late 1970s, however, the new leadership of the SUA, notably its director, Ms. Patricia Riley, was beginning to re-establish its influence.

Lobby groups in Maine have tended to be quite locally based, without a consolidated set of statewide organizational activities. Because of the personalized nature of the political process, however, those local activities seem at points to have been fairly effective. A number of individuals within the more active local groups and at the state's universities have also been involved in shaping aging policy at the state as well as local level. Interestingly, key factors in aging policy have also included individuals associated with proprietary nursing home interests in Maine. In fact, the director of Maine's Nursing Home Association was a member of the state's powerful Executive Council, or cabinet, from 1966 to 1972 and served as its chair from 1968 to 1972.

The legislative impact in Maine came primarily with the actions of a few individuals; the legislature as an institution is quite nonprofessional: mostly part-time, underpaid, and understaffed. Turnover was a problem in maintaining the role of a strong advocate, and there appeared to be somewhat less intense legislative leadership in the late 1970s. There were also some expressions of resentment toward the aging within the legislature, with some representatives taking the view that the aging "have had their day." The legislature has at points been important, then, with the actions of a few key individuals being the predominant mode of influence rather than a set of broadly based legislative coalitions.

It needs to be emphasized, finally, that the expansion in the early 1970s occurred in the context of the overall impact of Governor Kenneth Curtis on the scope of state government activities. His administration was expansive in a number of areas, and some support for the aging came directly from the governor's office. A major conference on the aging that was held in 1970, for example, served to help activate some interest in program development. At least in part that very expansion in overall state activity helped facilitate the election of an Independent governor in 1974, much to the surprise of virtually everyone in the state. The victory of Governor James Longley, who for two years had headed a task force studying management issues in the state, marked the introduction of an Independent leader with strong desires to curtail the overall growth of state government in Maine. The tone of that administration, as well as the leadership changes within the legislature and the aging network, appears to have contributed to the reduction in attention given to aging issues in Maine after the mid-1970s. It should also be emphasized that until 1976 the influence of Maine's governors was limited by the power of the state's independently elected Executive Council.

The nature of Maine's overall response to the aging has been fairly strong in relationship to the resources of the state. The process through which that development has occurred, at the same time, reflects the more personalized nature of politics in Maine. The concept of an aging network may be somewhat easier to develop, in short, in a relatively small state with fairly progressive traditions than in states that lack one or more of those attributes. Nonetheless, the development of an aging network under these conditions can also be somewhat difficult to sustain in the face of discouragement from major elected officials and difficulties with turnover in personnel within the aging network.

North Carolina

Differing interpretations of North Carolina have been a continuing aspect of the literature on comparative state politics (for a general review, see Beyle and Black 1975.) The simplest things to say are that North Carolina is relatively large geographically and in population size (ranking tenth in the country), that it remains ranked only thirty-eighth on industrialization-urbanization, and that (as is common among southern states other than Florida and Arkansas) the aging make up a distinctly smaller than average segment of the state's total population. As for its political culture, the evidence and interpretations are quite mixed. North Carolina, befitting the emphasis on its progressiveness, did rank twenty-fourth (and more highly than other southern states) on the Walker (1969) index of innovation. However, in terms of the general policy liberalism factor generated for this book, North Carolina ranked only fortieth, despite its reputation as being quite liberal, at least for a southern state. In its level of tax effort, North Carolina was twenty-eighth in 1975 and stood higher than its neighboring states of South Carolina, Virginia (which ranked twenty-ninth), and Florida. Among the southern states, only Mississippi ranked higher in its willingness to utilize its tax potential.

The record on programs for the aging is also mixed. In its commitment to OAA, North Carolina ranked no higher than forty-third in any of the rankings prior to 1970, at which time it had a rank of twenty-eighth. Then in 1975, with the change in program design under SSI, North Carolina emerged with a surprisingly strong position of first in the nation in terms of average supplemental payment under SSI. There was also some interest in home care programs.

Turning to potential sources of influence in the development of aging-related policies, one finds the governor's role in North Carolina manifesting only limited indications of overall importance. Because of the constitutional limitations on tenure, only recently abolished, North Carolina has had more governors than most of our case study states.

Yet few of those governors, as indicated by our overall rating of gubernatorial ambition and success, have become strong, long-term political figures in the state—even nationally renowned governors like Terry Sanford. There were also few indications that the governors provided direct acts of leadership in the area of aging to any degree beyond trying to have some impact through the budgetary process and through the use of appointments to influence the development of major state agencies. By the late 1970s, however, gubernatorial interest in aging-related issues did begin to increase with the election of James B. Hunt, Jr., in 1976 and his successful re-election (following a constitutional amendment making re-election possible) in 1980. More than any of his recent predecessors, Governor Hunt has displayed a distinct interest in the aging as part of his electoral concerns and in at least some of his administrative actions and appointments.

Interest in aging issues in North Carolina has been, until recently, primarily confined to a relatively small group of professionals, with Dr. Ellen Winston, former U.S. commissioner of welfare, being the most prominent in that group. Dr. Winston was identified by a number of our interview respondents as being a particularly influential force shaping aging policy in North Carolina. While there were advisory councils and fledgling efforts at establishing an SUA prior to 1976, the overall level of interest and support was quite modest. By the mid-1970s that activity did begin to expand somewhat—however, primarily with a greater interest in developing specific programs under the Older Americans Act.

Lobbying activity has also been quite modest. The AARP chapter has done some work in connection with the SUA but has not been a strong force in electoral politics or in legislative advocacy. Some observers allege, in fact, that the aging network of the SUA and interest groups is used primarily to generate political support for Governor Hunt.

Finally, regarding the legislative arena, North Carolina has had an improving but still moderately staffed state legislature. There has been some development of legislative specialization in recent years, with a few legislators becoming identified as champions—notably, Representative Ernest Messer. However, the top leadership has not made aging a particular objective, and Lieutenant Governor Jimmy Green has even been viewed as openly hostile. No strong coalitions have emerged surrounding overall policy changes within the legislative arena.

Overall, North Carolina illustrates the extent to which virtually all states were taking a more active interest in aging issues by the late 1970s. In earlier periods, aging was simply not a major concern, and most of the activities that did occur were produced by a small group of professionals. It remained to be seen, as of the early 1980s, whether those recent efforts would ultimately lead to more substantial advocacy activities and a stronger overall program commitment.

Florida

Florida stands as a unique case in terms of state policy development for the aging. The state's growing percentage of persons over age 65 has, of course, produced a dramatic rise in its position among the states, from eleventh in 1955 to a strong first in 1975, with over 16 percent in the 65 and over category. This has taken place thorugh a uniquely high level of migration into the state, although interestingly enough, Florida also has a high level of out-migration of the aging, especially among the very old. Florida's aging, overall, are more culturally diverse and therefore less politically cohesive than is usually recognized, with substantial cleavages along regional and social class lines.

The rapid growth in the percentage of the state's older population has occurred in the context of very rapid overall population growth. In 1950, Florida was in many ways a fairly typical, relatively small (2.5 million persons), substantially rural southern state. By 1980, however, Florida had a population of almost 10 million persons and several major urban concentrations. With that growth has come new industries, new residents, and many new challenges to the state's traditional social and political values.

Politically, Florida in the 1960s constituted one of the classic cases of rural domination in state politics, largely through the activities of a large number of rural legislators who were able to maintain their positions because of a substantial lack of equality in the apportionment of legislative districts. The Democratic party dominated the state politically, particularly in the state legislature. Thus, in terms of party competition, Florida was thirty-ninth in the nation as of 1955 and moved only to thirty-third by 1975.

Major changes have occurred in some aspects of the state's politics, however, as is manifested even physically with the construction of an impressive new capitol building of modern design. Along with those actions in the 1970s has come the development of a more full-time legislature and a legislative staff system that is often ranked among the best in the country.

The extent to which Florida's political culture has moved away from an orientation of limited government and low tax effort is nonetheless substantially more questionable. On our general policy liberalism factor, Florida ranked only thirty-first. Perhaps even more significant, however, has been the drop in Florida's ranking on tax effort as the state's economic resources have increased. Thus, while Florida ranked thirty-seventh in 1960, its position had fallen to forty-fifth by 1975. The issue that Florida raises very pointedly, then, is the nature of the policy responses for the aging when large numbers and percentages arise but in a political culture that has not traditionally been very supportive of state government programs.

With some exceptions, the basic policy record suggests that Florida has not been particularly responsive to the needs of the aging. On our health and welfare factor, for example, Florida ranked thirty-seventh, last among our eight case study states. Similarly, on the income maintenance factor, Florida ranked thirty-fifth, and the level of commitment for OAA/SSI has been quite limited. Where substantial sums of money have been potentially involved, and in program areas in which need has been a requisite, Florida has simply not had a strong record.

Two exceptions to this picture of limited response need to be considered, however. First, in the area of regulatory policy, Florida has been fairly active. This activity has involved in part a reorganizational effort in the mid-1970s and represents the responses in part to a growing amount of interest group activity. Thus, Florida has been a fairly early adopter, and has had fairly broadly designed programs, in areas like generic drugs and, more recently, the regulation of denturists. Second, there are some indications of emerging action in the area of social services. Florida's ranking of seventeenth on the social services factor was fairly high, considering the size of the state (which seems to have dampened efforts in some large states) and the economic resources available to the state. In addition, while advocates going to the legislature often felt frustrated, there were some responses in the late 1970s in the form of state funds for community program development. Insofar as the size and proportion of Florida's older population has made a difference, then, it would seem to be in the areas of regulatory policy and social services.

The development of political forces for the support of aging programs, while difficult in all of the states, seems to have come up against particular obstacles in Florida. For example, the governors typically have had neither the inclination nor the political resources to move very decisively on aging issues. Colburn and Scher (1980, pp. 289–290), in their assessment of Florida's governors, conclude, for example:

> Because of the potential voting importance of this group, Florida's governors invariably promised to increase benefits for retirees. But, as in the case of education, the governors have not come forth with

very much, except to increase the homestead exemption. Funds have not been made available for other than the most minimal benefits needed to keep the elderly quiescent. Moreover, in spite of the potentially important electoral position occupied by retirees in the state, it is safe to say that no governor has ever set forth a comprehensive policy concerning the elderly, especially those who are poor and ill.

This statement, it should be noted, perhaps implicitly overstates what governors have done in other states. Nonetheless, despite the hopes some had with the election of Governor Reubin Askew in 1970, our interview responses would tend to agree with this interpretation. The Askew years did contribute some overall momentum to change in Florida's state government but no particular focus coming from the governor's office itself on aging issues. The election of Governor Robert Graham in 1978 brought to office an individual whose legislative expriences involved some promotion of health policies for the aging and whose campaigning clearly recognized the importance of the elderly vote. As of 1980, however, it remained to be seen whether the governor's office would emerge as a major force for aging-related policy development.

The Florida legislature has, in turn, shown a substantial increase in its involvement with aging issues and has displayed some ability to take a major role in program development. In the reorganization efforts that emerged in the early 1970s, for example, both legislative staff and key legislators played significant roles. More recently, a staff has been working actively on aging issues, along with several young legislators who have been clearly identified as spokesmen for the aging— most notably, Representative Richard Batchelor. At the same time, the continued important role for a number of senior legislators who are not particularly supportive, along with the difficulties in developing coalitions in what is essentially a no-party legislature, has hampered the overall potential for policy development.

The evolution of the SUA in Florida included, in the 1950s and 1960s, a group of professionals with backgrounds in areas such as social work and health care who provided the major voice for aging programs at a time in which there was very little organized activity. With nurturing at points from individuals and organizations at the University of Florida, the activities of those associated with the SUA in its early days provided an important initial voice, but it certainly was not a group that was able to mobilize significant involvement among the aging themselves. The 1970s, in turn, produced a series of organizational changes that ultimately found the SUA located deep within an integrated Health and Rehabilitative Services (HRS) Department, whose regional offices frequently thwart the development of local aging programs through their exercise of budgetary control. With a professional orientation in that department, the agency began to expand its programmatic activities. At the same time, the involvement with promotive activities was quite limited, ultimately producing a situation in which, as in a number of our other states, several other structures emerged in the effort to pursue lobbying more directly.

The growth of interest group activity in Florida has involved, in part, a fairly active role for the AARP. There has been a growth in the ability to mobilize a telephone and mail network on major pieces of legislation and a monitoring of lobbying activity in the state legislature with increasing skill. Within the Miami area, a number of local organizations have also emerged with some significance in statewide politics because of the concentration of seniors—and voters—in areas within that portion of the state.

As of 1980, the advocacy process in Florida was also seeking to adjust to the emergence of a fairly strong Silver-Haired Legislature. That activity was begun in 1978, with support from the state legislature and the SUA. Members of the Silver-Haired Legislature are elected among residents age 60 and over in each legislative district in the state. Each prospective candidate is required to obtain at least 100 signatures from residents age 60 and over in order to have his or her name on the ballot. In 1979, over 95,000 votes were cast to select the delegates. The delegates then meet for five days in Tallahassee while the legislature is not in session.

Research by Matura (1981) suggests that the Silver-Haired Legislature has been fairly effective in pursuing legislation for the aging. This conclusion is supported by both a survey of state legislators that Matura conducted and an effort to tabulate the number of recommendations that were ultimately passed into law by the state legislature. At the same time, in our interviews as well, there were some private references to legislative resentment in the wake of these activities and some uncertainty as to whether this structure would be the most conducive to effective advocacy over a longer period of time.

Advocacy in Florida, then, has shown some of the same tendencies we have noted in other states, with definite growth in the 1970s and a tendency for the aging to become more active themselves in that advocacy process. At the same time, the SUA, while it nurtured some of the early supportive efforts in the state, did not have a particularly strong role as a focal point for advocacy activities by the end of the decade. As in other states, much of the reputed clout of the aging operates through the perceptions of elected officials—notably, their fear of the potential (if not actual) senior vote, which is obviously larger in Florida than in any other state.

Florida stands, in sum, as a state in which the political processes through which the aging have sought expression have been undergoing substantial change. With the development of some mass-based advocacy, a number of legislative specialists, and an SUA that is carrying out a variety of solid programs, Florida is in a very different position than in the quiet days of the 1960s. However, the policy record also suggests that it can be very difficult to alter long-established patterns in a state's politics like the tendency to commit limited resources to the public sector. The Florida response, along with those from the other seven case study states, thus offers a number of insights into the forces that may produce policy responses for the aging.

Conclusion

The case studies forcefully underscore the importance of systematically assessing the differing patterns of state policy responses. Because the eight states have differed so widely, it is particularly important to consider the responses on a fifty-state basis and in relationshp to the basic forces that are included in our overall analytical framework. After considering the responses in specific areas on a fifty-state basis, we can then turn to a reconsideration of both the case-study findings and the quantitative comparisons of the sources of state policy.

4

Health and
Long-Term Care

Health and long-term care policies are becoming increasingly central in overall state efforts for the aging. Programs for the aging within Medicaid constitute a fundamental, and expensive, state policy. Issues of eligibility, scope, and reimbursement have made Medicaid decision making central to any assessment of state policies for the aging. Given the program's rapidly rising costs in recent years, it is not surprising to find Medicaid policies constituting an area of considerable controversy and action. The range of options being developed by the states has particular importance because the models and precedents being created are likely also to influence federal action in future years.

Specific issues in the recent debate over Medicaid, as well as aspects of our overall project model, pose key questions for consideration. First, in what ways have various socioeconomic and political factors been shaping Medicaid responses in the states? Second, in what manner and in response to what influences have the states sought to undertake cost containment strategies? Third, to what extent have objectives such as equitable distribution and effective regulation been achieved in the operation of Medicaid programs? To begin, it is useful to consider briefly the manner in which state health care programs have evolved.

Program Development

State roles in the development of health policies for the elderly have evolved gradually from modest beginnings to today's substantial financial and regulatory commitments. Initially, health assistance was provided primarily at the county level and was usually given on the basis of need (Stevens and Stevens 1974). With the development of nursing homes in the 1930s and 1940s, the states also began to establish at least a fledgling regulatory effort (Dunlop 1979, p. 63). State involvement with the establishment of nursing homes was also expanded by two developments in the mid-1950s. The amendments to the Hill-Burton Act in 1954, which provided modest financial assistance for nursing home construction, helped to generate some interest in the creation of new facilities. At the same time, state interest in nursing homes was also increased by the gradual expansion in federal assistance for OAA recipients who required nursing home care. The expansion of those opportunities that occurred under the Kerr-Mills program of Medical Assistance for the Aged (MAA) provided an additional nudge toward action in many states. Thus, by 1965, the combined federal and state spending on medical vendor payments under MAA had reached $1.4 billion (Stevens and Stevens 1974, p. 34).

The passage of Medicare and Medicaid in 1965 marked a major turning point in the development of state health policy roles. Because the primary debate focused on Medicare, however, the potential issues and problems involved with an expansion in Medicaid received very little attention (Marmor 1970). At least in part because of that limited initial debate, the full implications of Medicaid costs (for both the states and the federal government) became apparent only with the movement toward fairly substantial implementation in key states such as California and New York (Stevens and Stevens 1974).

Responses to the Medicaid program have included both repeated efforts by the federal government to contain costs and to develop a stronger role in the regulation of facilities. These responses came as early as 1967 in connection with mounting costs and involved a major expansion in the federal government's regulatory role for nursing homes as of 1972. With the changes provided in the extensive 1972 reforms, the states were given full federal funding of nursing home regulatory actions under Medicaid, and they were required, as of 1976, to design their cost reimbursement methods on a reasonable-cost-related basis. The complexity of the new requirements ultimately gave the states considerable latitude in developing their programs, but they clearly provided a major impetus for changes in both regulatory procedures and reimbursement practices among the states (Vladeck 1980, pp. 67–68). In the context of the continuing federal involvement, and pressures within the states for expansion throughout the 1970s, there was a tendency for the program efforts to grow for all aspects of Medicaid as it affected the elderly, especially in the states that initially had the weaker programs (Bovbjerg and Holahan 1982, p. 29).

Policy initiatives in the early 1980s illustrate the continuing controversy over appropriate state and federal roles. The Reagan administration, in an attempt to contain total program costs, sought a cap on Medicaid in 1982. In the wake of strong resistance in Congress, a compromise emerged in which the states were given incentives to reduce their program costs, and the federal share was to be reduced on a sliding scale ranging from 3 percent in 1982 to 4.5 percent in 1984. The states were also given more discretion in the handling of hospital and nursing home reimbursement. The more sweeping proposal involved the Reagan administration's New Federalism initiative in 1982 with its proposed program swap between the federal government and the states. As part of a general swap, the federal government would assume full responsibility for Medicaid, while the states would take over responsibility for AFDC and food stamp programs. Because of initial suspicions regarding the financial desirability of the proposed swap, negotiations between the Reagan administration and the governors broke down by summer 1982 (Schechter 1983).

State responses in the 1980s have often emphasized program curtailment and a reduction in total costs through changes in payment provisions. On the basis of an extensive monitoring of Medicaid changes conducted by Richard Merritt (1982), it was concluded that the first two years under the Reagan administration had produced quite varied responses. In 1981, the emphasis was on cutting costs through reductions in eligibility and, to some extent, reductions in the scope of services. In 1982, there was considerably greater focus on program cost containment through longer-term strategies like the use of rate-setting commissions. In some instances, there was also a shift toward less stringent income elibigility requirements.

The evolution of Medicaid has produced a widely diverse set of evaluations. Frequent criticisms, as reviewed in Spiegel (1979), have included lack of equity in the provision of services, poor quality of some services, confusion in some administrative procedures, inadequate procedures for cost control, and the inability to control fraud in some aspects of the program's operation. Several of these issues, including the question of fraud, became a major part of the national debate as a result of revelations by the Moreland Commission in New York State and the conviction of a major nursing home operator in New York City, Bernard Bergman, of defrauding the government of $1.2 million (Smith 1981; Underwood and Daniels 1982). Other critics of the program have argued that the provision of funds for nursing homes under Medicaid contributed in an unfortunate manner to the overuse of nursing homes in recent years. By tracking nursing home growth before and after 1965, however, Dunlop (1979) concluded that the growth had begun prior to the establishment of Medicaid as a new basis of financing. Finally, taking a more general perspective, Holahan (1975) reviewed the first years of the program and concluded that despite the expansion in health care services, Medicaid suffered from a lack of equity in the extent to which care was being made available to individuals in different circumstances throughout the country. The lack of uniformity in the development of Medicaid programs also emerged as a major point of emphasis in the extensive comparative state assessment by Davidson (1980). Given the severity of recent criticisms, it is not surprising that Medicaid stands as a continuing focus for reform proposals.

Medicaid: Sources and Characteristics

The debates over state health policy roles for the aging underscore the importance of considering both the characteristics and sources of those policies. In this section we consider the evolution of health policy efforts in terms of our analytical framework. In the search for a comprehensive assessment of state health policy efforts, we have employed both general measures and several specific dimensions, including the range of services, eligibility requirements, and the level of spending on specific types of programs. (For a review of specific variables, see chapter 1 and the appendix.) In the following discussion, we first present basic findings and then relate those findings to our analytical framework.

Early Health Policies

The consideration of health policy efforts begins with two measures focusing on the level of activity as Medicaid was replacing the existing MAA programs in 1966. As is evident in table 4–1, both the early health factor and the level of total Medicaid spending per capita show quite striking relationships. (See table 4–1 for the correlations and table

Table 4–1
Patterns of Relationship for Early Health Policies in the States:
Simple Correlations

	Early health	T19 Total Exp., 1966
Early Health	—	.72[d]
Diversity	.64[d]	.55[c]
Indust.-Urban.	.45[b]	.40[b]
Need	− .72[d]	− .56[c]
Gov. Power	.33[a]	.44[b]
Party Compet.	.59[d]	.57[d]
Voter Turnout	.70[d]	.49[c]
Tax Effort	.33[a]	.53[c]
General Lib.	.75[d]	.69[c]

[a]Significant at .05.
[b]Significant at .01.
[c]Significant at .001.
[d]Significant at .0001.

4–6 for the regression equations. Throughout our analysis, results will be presented only for those independent variables having a significant correlation with at least one of the dependent variables for at least one time period.) As might be expected, the two policy measures themselves are strongly and positively correlated. Among the socioeconomic variables, the industrialization-urbanization factor and the diversity index have moderately strong, positive correlations with both policy measures, and the magnitude of needy groups in the population has not unexpectedly but quite impressively negative correlations with the two indicators of early health policy. Both dependent variables also correlate strongly and positively with three of the political variables: party competition, voter turnout, and general policy liberalism. Both tax effort and governor's power correlate less substantially (but still significantly) with the early health factor than with expenditures.

In the regression equations, reported in table 4–6, fairly strong results are obtained for both policy measures. For the early health factor, the measures of diversity and turnout produce an R^2 of .63. For total spending, an R^2 of .52 is obtained with party competition and tax effort as the explanatory variables. Thus, our measures of state policy during the shift from MAA to Medicaid produced some strong explanatory results from a limited number of independent variables. As Medicaid began, efforts were stronger in states that had relatively few needy groups in their population, along with relatively high levels of party competition, voter turnout, and tax effort. Perhaps it is not surprising, given the limited state advocacy by the elderly themselves that existed during this period, that measures of advocacy and of higher concentrations of older persons in a state's population did not have a measurable impact.

Medicaid: 1970

In evaluating the development of Medicaid after its initial years of operation, it is helpful to start by considering the relationships among major program components as of 1970. Among the dependent variables, as reported in table 4–2, there is a very strong correlation between total per capita spending for all Medicaid programs and Medicaid spending for the aging per aging persons. Similarly, expenditures per aging persons for skilled nursing care correlate strongly with both total Medicaid expenditures per capita and expenditures per aging persons. Similarly, the correlations between inclusion of the medically needy and the expenditure measures are all significant. There are no significant correlations, however, between optional services and the other

Table 4–2
Simple Correlations among Dependent Variables: Medicaid, 1970

	T19 Total Exp.	T19 Aged Exp.	T19 SNF Exp.	T19 Needy Elig.
T19 Aged Exp.	.90[c]			
T19 SNF Exp.	.71[c]	.87[c]		
T19 Needy Elig.	.47[b]	.41[b]	.36[a]	
T19 Opt. Serv.	.11	.05	.11	.22

[a]Significant at .05.
[b]Significant at .001.
[c]Significant at .0001.

four measures. States that spent more on a per capita basis thus were somewhat more likely to include the medically needy in their programs, but they had virtually no tendency to provide a larger number of optional services.

The correlations between these dependent variables and our various independent variables for 1970 are given in table 4–3. Turning to the socioeconomic variables, a number of strong relationships emerge. Industrialization-urbanization continues to have a strong correlation with the expenditure-based measures but not quite a significant relationship with inclusion of the medically needy and optional services. The need variable, as expected, again correlates negatively with all of the policy measures, but the correlation with total per capita spending is substantially lower than in 1965.

Among the political measures, both general policy liberalism and tax effort show strong correlations with Medicaid effort in 1970. In both instances, however, the correlations are stronger for the expenditure-based measures. It is important to note that the tax effort measure is more strongly correlated with our policy measures for 1970 than for 1965. Regarding the political capacity measures, scope of state and local government correlates significantly with two of the three expenditure measures. Centralization, in contrast, correlates significantly only with optional services, and that correlation is inverse rather than direct. This in part reflects the tendency for southern states to be fairly centralized and to offer fewer optional Medicaid services; it also suggests that the development of a larger overall public sector, and not centralization in state government, is the most important influence of political capacity on aging health policy in the states.

Turning to the roles of specific political participants, fairly strong

Table 4–3
Simple Correlations between Independent and Dependent Variables: Medicaid, 1970

	Dependent Variables				
Independent Variable	T19 Total Exp.	T19 Aged Exp.	T19 SNF Exp.	T19 Needy Elig.	T19 Opt. Serv.
Indust.-Urban.	.63[d]	.58[d]	.41[d]	.22	.22
Need	-.32[b]	-.32[a]	-.26	-.34[a]	-.33[a]
Diversity	.67[d]	.64[d]	.49[c]	.25	.24
Scope of Govt.	.37[a]	.27	.32[a]	.05	-.12
Centralization	-.26	-.13	-.09	-.05	-.30[a]
Gov. Ambition	.30[a]	.39[b]	.29[a]	.17	.09
Gov. Power	.49[c]	.46[c]	.53[c]	.37[b]	-.02
Party Compet.	.34[a]	.20	.21	.30[a]	.35[a]
Voter Turnout	.16	.17	.14	.19	.21
Senior Orgs.	.44[b]	.41[b]	.40[b]	.10	.21
Tax Effort	.62[d]	.24	.40[b]	.20	.54[d]
General Lib.	.65[d]	.24	.41[b]	.21	.55[d]

[a]Significant at .05.
[b]Significant at .01.
[c]Significant at .001.
[d]Significant at .0001.

correlations emerge for both governors and senior organizations. Governor's power has the strongest correlations, followed by the governor's ambition and success score. The measure of the governor's reputation showed no significant correlations, and is therefore not included in the results. The number of senior organizations, finally, has significant correlations with the three expenditure-based measures.

The regression equations in table 4–6, as well as the correlations, show more explicable relationships for the expenditure-based measures than for the scope measures. The equations for total per capita Medicaid spending ($R^2 = .75$) and for Medicaid aging expenditures per aging persons ($R^2 = .63$) have similar results. In each instance, tax effort, industrialization-urbanization, and state and local scope enter the equation, with the governor's political ambition and success score also entering for aging expenditures. Expenditures for skilled nursing care are more difficult to explain because that measure produces an equation with an R^2 of only .40. Interestingly, the two variables that enter that equation are governor's power and senior organizations. The optional services measure produces a five-variable model that includes percentage change in income and four political capacity measures, again with a fairly low R^2 of .43. Surprisingly, all of the predictors in that model have an inverse impact on the dependent variable. Finally, inclusion of the medically needy fails to produce an acceptable model, except for its simple correlation with general policy liberalism. In terms of our project model, there are important roles, then, for some socioeconomic variables, some political capacity measures, tax effort, general policy liberalism, and some aspects of the advocacy process. Once again, the condition of the older population does not have a direct impact on state health policy efforts for the aging.

Medicaid: 1975

As in 1970, the dependent variables for 1975 show (with exceptons) stronger relationships among the expenditure-based measures than among the scope measures. Table 4–4 shows that the health and welfare factor, for example, correlates strongly with total per capita Medicaid expenditures and with both Medicaid expenditures for the aging and skilled nursing expenditures. Its correlation with intermediate care expenditures, however, drops to .16. Once again, the scope measures show limited relationships both with each other and with the expenditure-based measures.

Several changes begin to emerge in examining the correlations of these dependent variables with the 1975 independent variables, as shown

Health and Long-Term Care

Table 4–4
Simple Correlations among Dependent Variables: Medicaid, 1975

	T19 Aged Exp.	T19 SNF Exp.	T19 ICF Exp.	T19 Needy Elig.	T19 Opt. Serv.	Health/Welfare
T19 SNF Exp.	.73[c]					
T19 ICF Exp.	.58[c]	.02				
T19 Needy Elig.	.04	.11	.08			
T19 Opt. Serv.	.23	.24[a]	.01	.44[b]		
Health/ Welfare	.73[c]	.73[c]	.16	.23	.43[b]	
T19 Total Exp.	.21	.30[a]	.00	-.11	.21	.63[c]

[a]Significant at .05.
[b]Significant at .001.
[c]Significant at .0001.

Table 4-5
Simple Correlations between Independent and Dependent Variables: Medicaid, 1975

			Dependent Variables			
Independent Variable	T19 Total Exp.	Health/ Welfare	T19 SNF Exp.	T19 ICF Exp.	T19 Needy Elig.	T19 Opt. Serv.
Indust.-Urban.	.24	.49c	.35a	.06	.04	.21
Need	−.26	−.34a	−.16	−.34a	−.30a	−.28a
Unemployment	.12	.30a	.30a	−.03	−.17	−.05
Development	.34a	.51d	.41b	.31a	.16	.38b
Pop. Change	.25	−.16	−.03	−.02	−.41b	−.44b
Aged Migration	.44b	−.08	−.08	−.10	−.33a	−.35a
Aged Pct. Change	.42b	.04	.18	−.31a	−.14	−.01
N.H. Beds	−.06	.25	.20	.52c	.30a	.28a
Hospital Beds	−.10	−.05	−.17	−.11	.28a	.26
Diversity	.29a	.57d	.34a	.38a	.12	.28a
Pol. Culture	.10	.34a	.14	.20	.31a	.42b
Gov. Reputation	.21	.17	.48c	.00	.18	.11
Legis. Profess.	−.08	.54c	.47c	.07	.15	.29a
Party Compet.	.19	.26	.16	.25	.23	.35a
Voter Turnout	−.08	.15	.03	.16	.26	.33a
Tax Effort	−.05	.63d	.47c	.15	.31a	.31a
Senior Orgs.	−.04	.48c	.05	.10	.04	.20
NCSC Effort	.00	.39a	.28	.12	.13	.25
General Lib.	.02	.61d	.44b	.41b	.29a	.44b

[a]Significant at .05.
[b]Significant at .01.
[c]Significant at .001.
[d]Significant at .0001.

in table 4–5. (It should be noted that expenditures on aging recipients is not presented here because it is a component of the health and welfare factor.) The diversity index has a strong positive correlation with the health and welfare factor but a less extensive correlation with some of the other expenditure-based measures. Similarly, industrialization-urbanization has significant correlations with two of the expenditure-based measures but at markedly less substantial levels than in 1965 or 1970. A somewhat similar shift occurs with the need factor. That factor is still negatively correlated with all of the policy measures, as expected, but those correlations are even weaker than in 1970.

The impact of changes in the aging population is particularly intriguing. Increases in the older population are positively correlated with total spending on Medicaid, but they show no significant correlation with aging-related aspects of Medicaid except for an inverse correlation with intermediate care expenditures. Similarly, migration of the aging to a state is positively associated with total per capita spending on Medicaid but is slightly negatively correlated with skilled and intermediate care spending for the aging. Thus, increases in the older population through either migration or a combination of other forces are correlated with total Medicaid spending, but on nursing home expenditures, the impact of migration by the aging is negative. Thus, the aging clearly are not moving to states that spend extensively on Medicaid programs for their older citizens.

Regarding political variables, there are also several changes by 1975. Party competition and turnout, in contrast to 1965, do not produce any particularly strong correlations with either the expenditure-based measures or the scope measures—even less so than in 1970. General policy liberalism shows a strong relationship with the health and welfare factor and with both skilled and intermediate care nursing expenditures but not with total Medicaid expenditures. Tax effort shows correlations of .63 with the health and welfare factor and .47 with skilled nursing expenditures but no relationship with intermediate care expenditures or with total Medicaid spending.

Turning to the roles of political actors, measures for both governors and senior organizations again correlate significantly with the health policy measures at some points. Regarding governors, the correlations are not very strong, with the highest correlation being between gubernatorial reputation and skilled nursing expenditures. The senior organizations variable, at the same time, produces an equally strong correlation with the health and welfare factor but does not quite produce statistically significant correlations in the other Medicaid policy areas.

The regression equations for 1975, presented in table 4–6, once

Table 4–6
Best Regression Models for Explaining Selected Indicators of State Medicaid Policies for the Aging: 1965, 1970, and 1975

Dependent Variable	Independent Variables	Probability > F	R²	Probability > F	N
1965					
Early Health	Diversity	.0004	.63	.0001	39
	Voter Turnout	.0022			
T19 Total Exp.	Party Compet.	.0002	.52	.0001	44
	Tax Effort	.0002			
1970					
T19 Total Exp.	Indust.-Urban.	.0001	.75	.0001	42
	Tax Effort	.0001			
	Scope of Govt.	.0096			
T19 Aged Exp.	Indust.-Urban.	.0001	.63	.0001	44
	Tax Effort	.0066			
	Gov. Ambition	.0406			
	Scope of Govt.	.0434			
T19 SNF Exp.	Gov. Power	.0002	.40	.0001	44
	Senior Orgs.	.0110			
T19 Needy Elig.	General Lib.	.0033	.19	.0033	44
T19 Opt. Serv.	Centralization (−)	.0002	.43	.0004	44
	Income Change (−)	.0029			
	Scope of Govt. (−)	.0061			
	Legis. Apport. (−)	.0131			
	Gov. Power (−)	.0313			
1975					
Health/Welfare	Tax Effort	.0001	.52	.0001	39
	Indust.-Urban.	.0010			
T19 Total Exp.	Migration	.0001	.50	.0001	39

	p-value	R^2	Signif.	N
T19 Aged Exp.		.66	.0001	41
Development	.0001			
Party Compet. (−)	.0001			
Unemployment	.0001			
N.H. Beds	.0006			
Hospital Beds	.0196			
T19 SNF Exp.		.54	.0001	41
Gov. Reputation	.0004			
Legis. Profess.	.0005			
Tax Effort	.0140			
Senior Orgs.	.0210			
T19 ICF Exp.		.16	.0102	40
Diversity	.0102			
T19 Needy Elig.		.18	.0032	45
Pop. Change (−)	.0032			
T19 Opt. Serv.		.49	.0001	45
Pol. Culture	.0001			
Aged Pct. Change	.0008			
Aged Migration (−)	.0009			
NCSC Effort	.0066			

again show the greater explicability of the expenditure-based policies and the particular difficulty in explaining inclusion of the medically needy. The health and welfare factor attains an R^2 of .52 with an equation including tax effort and industrialization-urbanization. Total Medicaid expenditures per capita can best be explained by an equation containing only the net migration into the state. For Medicaid expenditures for the aging, a model with an R^2 of .66 emerges with an interesting set of five variables: party competition (inverse), unemployment, the development index, nursing home beds per aging person, and total hospital beds per capita. Skilled nursing expenditures produces a model with an R^2 of .54 and a predominance of political variables: senior organizations, governor's reputation, legislative professionalism, and tax effort. Intermediate care expenditures, finally, proved quite inexplicable, failing to yield a model containing anything beyond its simple correlation with the diversity index.

For the scope measures, optional services produces an equation with an R^2 of .49 generated by political culture, percentage change in the older population, migration of older persons (inverse) and lobby effort by NCSC. Inclusion of the medically needy fails to produce an acceptable model.

Summary

The results of the correlation and regression analyses for Medicaid and its precursor programs in the 1960–1975 period show several relationships that are central to our overall project model. In general, the expenditure-based aspects of the program have been substantially easier to explain than regulatory dimensions such as inclusion of the medically needy and the availability of optional services. Turning first to socioeconomic factors, there are fairly strong indications that the industrialization-urbanization dimension continues to be important, particularly for the expenditure-based aspects of Medicaid. The one other variable that does show a significant impact is net migration rate, which is positively associated with higher total expenditures per capita. For the regulatory component, in contrast, population change is inversely related to inclusion of the medically needy as of 1975, while aging migration contributes negatively to optional services, and growth of the aging population has a positive impact. Overall, then, the states with growing populations are apparently spending somewhat more but are apt to be more grudging in terms of their handling of the regulatory component of health care policy.

Regarding political factors, there has been a distinct change over the three time periods. The two political openness variables, party competition and turnout, have very clearly declined in importance. As of 1965, both of those variables produced strong correlations and had important roles in the regression equations. By 1975, however, the correlations were substantially more modest, and party competition on some occasions began to enter some of the regression equations as a negative factor. This would suggest a bureaucratization of Medicaid and its involvement with subgovernment politics (Redford 1969), along with a possible shift of other factors (such as a falling tax base), which have made efforts more difficult for the competitive and high-turnout states.

Indicators of political capacity, however, appear to have grown in importance. The impact of governors appears to increase between 1965 and 1970, and various measures of gubernatorial strength enter the regression equations for those two years, particularly the equations for nonfiscal-based aspects of the programs. For 1975, however, the results suggest that the overall importance of political capacity is fairly modest, particularly for expenditure-based aspects of Medicaid. A modest but occasionally significant impact emerges for aging-based lobbying. Specifically, the measure of senior organizations enters several of the regression equations in ways that suggest that states in which aging issues have a relatively high salience and aging-based interest groups are more active are somewhat more apt to expand their Medicaid efforts.

Tax effort relative to capacity and general policy liberalism also exhibit considerable importance, with tax effort having a particularly striking role. In reviewing the regression equations in table 4–6, for example, tax effort appears in five of the nine equations. A willingness to use available economic resources stands, in short, as an extremely important factor in shaping the nature of a state's Medicaid program. Finally, general policy liberalism, while not appearing extensively in the regression equations, did show a persistent positive correlation with several of the policy measures. Several of these findings, as we shall see shortly, have major implications for the present debate over the nature of Medicaid policies. Before turning to those issues, however, it is necessary to examine an additional key component of both Medicaid and state health policies for the aging more generally—namely, nursing home regulation.

Nursing Home Policies*

State policies for nursing home regulation and reimbursement policies within Medicaid have been areas of controversy in recent years. Within Medicaid, nursing homes have consumed an increasingly substantial

---

*This section was coauthored with Robert C. Myrtle.

portion of total program costs. As of 1979, for example, nursing home costs (for all age groups) made up just over 40 percent of all Medicaid costs. At the same time, Medicaid has come to assume over 50 percent of all public and private nursing home costs (see Bovbjerg and Holahan 1982). In addition, the use of regulation to increase the quality of care has been a major reform issue in many states (see Vladeck 1980). To adequately assess state nursing home policy responses, it is necessary to consider existing ideas about the forces that may shape those responses. We thus begin with a consideration of other recent studies and then review the components of state policy being examined in this book.

Major Policies and Potential Influences

Interpretations of state regulatory policies have moved toward an expanded range of considerations in recent years (Myrtle, Lammers, and Klingman 1982). Initially, regulatory policy discussions often emphasized costs and consequences (Salkever and Bice 1979; Drake 1980). More recent discussions, however, have begun to consider socioeconomic and political explanations (Wing and Craige 1979), along with analyses of the values of particular key participants (Koff 1981) and the importance of interest group activity (Feldstein 1980). As an additional major issue, attention has been directed increasingly toward the possibility that regulatory policies will be used as a basis for reducing pressures on state spending (see Abernethy and Pearson 1979; Feder and Scanlon 1980). Finally, some interpretations have suggested that the availability of nursing home beds constitutes an important dimension in the regulatory dynamic, both in terms of the underlying concerns of the regulators and the pressures that will lead to additional costs.

Several specific research issues that go beyond the key questions being raised in our analytical model thus emerge in looking at nursing home regulatory policies. First, what is the relationship between cost changes and reimbursement policies? Are states that are experiencing higher costs the ones that are responding with tighter regulatory policies? Second, are there indications that a potential demand for services, as reflected in demographic characteristics of the older population, is influencing regulatory responses? Third, are there indications that total supply, as measured by the number of beds available in a state, is influencing the nature of regulatory policy responses?

To examine basic questions about nursing home regulation, it is necessary to consider several different policies. The components being examined here are reimbursement rates, Certificate of Need (CON) programs, fire regulations, and patient care regulations. Turning first to reimbursement rates, considerable variation exists in areas such as payment mechanisms, costs deemed reimbursable under applicable standards, controls on depreciation and profit mechanisms, limits on administrative and other indirect expenses, and performance and occupancy standards. To examine these developments, variations in reimbursement approaches were factor analyzed to derive a measure of a state's control over cost reimbursement. Components of this reimbursement control factor included the characteristics of the reimbursement system: single fee (flat rate), retrospective cost-based reimbursement, and prospective cost-based reimbursement; basis for reimbursement: individual facility's costs, cost limit based on cost experience of similar facilities, or patient or service-specific cost limits; and use of occupancy requirements. In coding these provisions, maximum points were awarded to the establishment of regulatory provisions that were judged to be most likely to combine cost control with at least a substantial amount of concern for the quality of care. The more highly scored systems, then, would include provisions such as prospective reimbursement and cost limits based upon the experiences of similar facilities.

The second policy tool to be examined is the use of CON legislation. These programs have constituted a major component of state efforts to limit the supply of nursing home beds. Beginning with New York in 1964, states began to require institutional providers to demonstrate that a need existed for the additional beds or services they sought to provide. Later, the federal government sought to expand this concept to all states with the 1972 amendments to the Social Security Act, followed two years later by the Health Resources Development Act. The federal requirements were reduced, however, by the Reagan administration in 1981, thus reintroducing greater potential for future differences in state efforts. Two measures were employed to assess a state's performance in this regulatory area. The first was the length of time that the CON legislation had been in existence, and the second measure was the extension of CON requirements to home health agencies.

The use of fire and patient care standards has also been an important component of state nursing home policies. Although these standards emerged out of requirements established by various federal programs, the exact standards and enforcement policies were left to individual states. Considerable variation thus exists in the policies and procedures designed to comply with federal requirements and in the emphasis that states place on using these policies as part of their regulatory effort (Ruchlin 1977). In our assessment of these two policy efforts, we coded state legislation on the basis of the extensiveness of patient-oriented regulations (such as the existence of opportunities for raising criminal charges against nursing home operators and of provisions against misuse of a patient's personal financial resources). The fire code provisions, in turn, were evaluated on the basis of their conformity with the life safety code. State policies for nursing home reimbursement and regulation can thus be examined from a variety of perspectives.

Relationships among Policies

The relationships among our five policies (see table 4–7) show both expected and unexpected results. The strong positive and statistically significant relationship between the earliness of CON enactment and the extent of reimbursement controls shows an underlying commonality in moves toward some form of cost control, either by constraining supply or by modifying reimbursement policies. The negative correlation between fire safety standards and earliness of CON adoption is, on the surface, somewhat curious. Examination of the data reveal that smaller, less urbanized states tend to have more fire safety regulations than their urbanized counterparts. Many of these same states also were late adopters of CON legislation; hence, the relationship that emerges reflects these patterns.

While the lack of a significant relationship between fire safety and patient care regulations is not surprising, the absence of a relationship between patient care standards and reimbursement controls is more curious. As a general rule, patient care standards serve to increase the quality of care that is provided and, ultimately, its costs (Feldstein 1977). However, at least as of 1975, there was no consistent indication

Table 4–7
Simple Correlations among Dependent Variables: Nursing Home Regulation, 1975

	Fire Regs.	Patient Care	N.H. Reimburs.	CON Age
Patient Care	.23			
N.H. Reimburs.	− .23	− .11		
CON Age	− .29	− .11	.55[a]	
CON Home Health	− .19	− .03	− .05	.16

[a]Significant at .001.

that the states with higher patient care regulation efforts were trying
to avoid possible cost impacts with tighter cost controls.

Correlations between Independent
and Dependent Variables

The correlations between conditions believed to contribute to the
emergence of regulatory policies and the actual state responses are
surprisingly low. To convey a sense of that lack of strong relationships,
it is a simple task to summarize the very few strong relationships and
requires no separate presentation. Among the 31 independent variables initially used in this analysis, some 13 showed no significant relationship with any of the five policy measures. Among the
socioeconomic influences, the strongest correlation was for the industrialization-urbanization factor: this was a positive .43 for the age of
CON programs and a negative .41 for fire regulations. Among the
other factors, general policy liberalism was positively correlated with
both reimbursement and CON age and negatively correlated with fire
regulations. Similarly, tax effort was positively correlated with all but
patient care regulations and fire standards (which again showed a negative correlation). In terms of potential indicators of demand for regulation, the percentage of the population age 65 and over was positively
correlated with patient care regulations, while the number of nursing
home beds per thousand elderly persons was negatively correlated with
fire regulations and with the existence of CON coverage for home
health agencies but showed almost no correlation with the other three
policy variables.

   As a very striking finding, there was no indication that any of the
policy efforts was closely associated with changes in state Medicaid
expenditures. The changes in the percentage of state Medicaid spending for the elderly between 1970 and 1975 were examined separately
for total per capita costs and costs for acute care and for skilled nursing
facilities. In examining correlations with CON age, home health, and
patient care regulations, four of the correlations were slightly negative
and none was statistically significant. From the correlations, then, there
is simply no indication that expenditure increases are tied closely to
regulatory efforts.

Regression Analysis

On the basis of the weak correlations, plus the weak regression models
that emerged, it is appropriate to focus our discussion on the regression

analyses undertaken for two major aspects of state regulatory policy—
namely, reimbursement control and earliness of CON legislation.

The regression equations for earliness of CON provisions and the
cost control factor, as reported in table 4–8, produce R^2 of .58 and .44
respectively. It is useful in discussing those results to consider collectively the predictors that entered the two equations. For cost influences
in these equations, just as with the correlations, there is little relationship between either total cost or the rate of increase in costs and the
level of regulatory effort. The only hint of a cost impact comes with
the entrance of the tax effort measure, but this is probably better
interpreted as an indication of an active policy orientation in state
government. It is significant that the number of nursing home beds
does not enter either of the equations. Equally important, however, is
the entrance of the increase in the number of hospital beds betwen
1970 and 1975. Since the nature of the acute care industry in a state
often seems to be the primary regulatory focus, with nursing home
regulation following, this result gives a hint that growth in hospital bed
supply ultimately fosters nursing home regulatory efforts.

The characteristics of the older population did, however, have a
fairly strong impact, at least on the CON measure. Thus, life expectancy and the income of those 65 and over each make major contributions in that equation. This suggests that states having larger numbers
of persons with longer life expectancies and relatively larger incomes
may be nudged toward stronger regulatory action regarding their long-
term care facilities.

The political relationships that emerge from the two equations produce both surprising and important results. It perhaps comes as no

Table 4–8
Best Regression Models for Explaining the Sources of Nursing Home Regulatory Policies, 1975

Variable	Probability > F	R^2	Probability > F	N
Age of Certificate of Need Program (CON Age)				
Aged Income	.0001	.58	.0001	45
Life Expectancy	.0003			
Voter Turnout (−)	.0005			
AARP Members (−)	.0041			
Tax Effort	.0280			
Scope of Reimbursement Controls (N.H. Reimburs.)				
General Lib.	.0001	.44	.0001	45
NCSC Effort (−)	.0007			
Hospital Bed Change	.0085			
Legis. Apport. (−)	.0299			

surprise that regulatory policies would not be responsive to a number of our general political indicators such as turnout and legislative apportionment since they have not been significant positive influences in most sections of the results. While the actual contributions are somewhat minor (particularly for legislative apportionment), it is nonetheless surprising to find both of these variables entering with a negative impact. This suggests quite dramatically that simply having larger levels of participation through voting and a state legislature with equally apportioned districts will not help in the movement toward more extensive regulatory efforts and may actually contribute to a lower effort. A second political relationship also emerges in a surprising manner. Our measures of lobby activity for NCSC and for AARP size of membership both enter one of the two equations, but negatively. While it seems doubtful that there was a kiss-of-death phenomenon, with legislators consciously doing the opposite of what the aging-based groups were advocating, the strong negative influence indicates that these groups, as of the early 1970s, could not be seen as having a positive impact, at least on the basis of our measures.

The last of the political explanations is, however, both statistically stronger and intuitively satisfying. Each of the equations does contain one strong impact from a general political indicator. For CON adoption, this impact comes from tax effort and, for reimbursement controls, through the general policy liberalism factor. Thus, for nursing home regulation, along with a number of our other policy areas, we find an important impact stemming from the more general aspects of a state's political features, especially its general willingness to use the public sector.

Policy Issues

The pattern of state policy responses on Medicaid and nursing home policies that has evolved over the past two decades has major implications for the policy issues being debated in the 1980s. In considering those policy implications, it is important to address issues such as the sources of regulation, changes in the degree of equity in Medicaid, and the willingness to modify the scope of overall programs.

Regulation of Nursing Homes

The regulation of long-term care has produced a number of actions that are of interest in the overall debate over potential state responses.

Obviously, the increases in costs in the last several years, along with the fiscal constraints the states have been facing, may be producing changes in the forces prompting state regulatory responses. Nonetheless, the findings from this analysis have important implications for differing interpretations of responsiveness to cost changes and the nature of state political processes in this policy area. The analyses in this chapter have demonstrated a striking absence of a program cost impact on regulatory activity. The states simply have not displayed anything resembling an automatic tendency to increase regulations in the face of increasing costs. Apparently many other factors in a state's political system are apt to intervene. Similarly, a larger number of nursing homes does not seem to produce a more rapid response. Somewhat indirectly, however, an increase in the number of hospital beds appears to act as a stimulus toward regulatory reform in general, incuding the regulation of long-term care facilities. Somewhat more encouraging for those hoping for stronger state responses is the impact that stems from two variables that are likely to increase: per capita income and life expectancy. Overall, lack of cost-related responses provides an obvious potential for state action. Indeed, the efforts at cost control in the early 1980s in a number of relatively high spending states such as California, Illinois, and Washington may well constitute the beginnings of a shift in which cost factors will more substantially influence nursing home policy development.

In looking at the potential for state action on nursing homes more generally, the importance of a willingness to pursue public sector initiatives in a state emerges, very fundamentally, as an important and basic influence that is likely to continue. This includes both the importance of overall tax effort relative to capacity and the general policy liberalism factor. States that are using their public sector more aggressively, in short, seem more likely to move toward more extensive controls.

The regulatory policy area, while underscoring the importance of general political forces in a state, ultimately raises a major question about the extent to which specific lobbying efforts can alter those general tendencies. If other factors are working against more extensive regulation, then lobbying efforts would seem likely to be insufficient. It remains to be seen whether subsequent analysis—and action in the state capitols—will show a more direct impact of lobbying efforts in the quest for changes in the regulation of long-term care facilities.

Equity Questions

The state experiences with Medicaid raise basic questions of equity in the handling of similar cases in different parts of the country. The extent to which policies ought to include uniform expenditure and eligibility requirements throughout the country is obviously a point of legitimate public debate. It should be noted, however, that a concern with the level of variation in the handling of similar cases in different parts of the country has been a point of major concern among Medicaid's critics (see Holahan 1975).

On the basis of findings in our study, two different conclusions can be drawn regarding state responses on equity issues. First, if one looks at the sources of Medicaid spending, it is rather sobering to find that a strong predictor of a more generous program has been the relative absence of needy groups in a state's population. This correlation drops throughout the 1965–1975 period but is still significant for 1975. Similarly, if one looks more generally at the sources of the quite strong state efforts, they show very clearly that individuals in poorer states are being presented with less generous programs.

Second, if one looks at the direction of change, then a different view can be taken. Since its inception, Medicaid has moved on a number of measures toward greater uniformity. From our data, the calculation of coefficients of variation (standard deviations divided by the mean) offer important support for this view. Regarding Medicaid expenditures for aged recipients, most notably, the coefficient of variation drops from 1.02 in 1970 to .55 for 1975. Similarly, for skilled nursing expenditures under Medicaid, the coefficient of variation drops from 1.29 in 1970 to 1.03 in 1975. Since the programs, as received by individuals, pool federal and state dollars, and with formulas that aid the poorer states, this means that individuals are being helped by both an increased uniformity in state effort and the redistributive impact of federal funds.

On the basis of some evidence, this pattern does not hold for expenditures in the entire Medicaid program. In our study, the coefficient of variation for total Medicaid expenditures per capita over the entire period increases from .74 in 1965 to .85 in 1970 to 1.15 in 1975. On the basis of the extent of total coverage, however, there are also indications of greater uniformity in Medicaid programs among the states. According to Bovbjerg and Holahan (1982, p. 29), the disparity among the states has lessened between 1970 and 1979 when examined in terms of the ratio of persons in a state who are below the poverty line to those who are eligible for Medicaid. Of those states with below-average coverage of their poverty-level populations in the 1970s, 21 percent increased their position, 11 percent decreased, and 2 percent stayed the same. In sum, state Medicaid programs continue to show major differences among the more and less prosperous states, but some trends have been moving toward greater uniformity. The possibility of a change in these trends in the face of greater fiscal austerity caused by federal retrenchment and weak economies in some states nonetheless remains a key policy issue.

Summary

The states have shown, in balance, a fairly strong commitment to Medicaid. There has been a major expansion, including substantial state willingness to develop and maintain optional services. It is surprising that the states do not try to control costs by restrictions on optional services. Several of the poorer states, in fact, actually had rather strong records regarding optional services. Similarly, there were no noticeable indications in our data that states were acting decisively to reduce program costs through changes in cost containment strategies even when expenditures were increasing quite substantially.

Other assessments of Medicaid responses have also tended to emphasize the extent to which states have maintained major aspects of their programs even in the face of the degree of adversity being experienced in the 1981–1983 period. Thus, as Bovbjerg and Holahan (1982) conclude, "While states are constraining the scope of their programs, there are clear limits on their willingness to do so. The major problem is that the poor and chronically ill are in need of some level of medical care and are unable to pay for it" (p. 67). The role of the states in health care, in short, shows a substantial expansion in the first decade under Medicaid and some movement toward equalization. Issues of equity remain, however, and the willingness of the states to sustain programs, while surprisingly substantial in some instances, is clearly under greater question in the face of mounting budgetary pressures.

5 Social Services

The importance of social services as a central component in public efforts to assist the aging is reflected by the recent growth in such programs at all levels of government. The major emphasis on social services dates from the 1962 amendments to the Social Security Act, which established a separate category of grants to the states for the provision of social services to recipients of various federal welfare programs, including OAA and MAA. The intent was to slow the rapid growth in the welfare rolls and in federal welfare spending by shifting the emphasis from support to rehabilitation and prevention, thereby breaking the cycle of welfare dependency. Although the term *social services* was never defined precisely, "fundamentally and at a minimum, it meant casework by a trained social worker" (Derthick 1975, p. 9). It was thus hoped that professional counseling would help welfare recipients as well as people "who might reasonably be expected to need financial aid within one year of their request for services" (Gilbert 1981, p. 103) to get off and/or stay off welfare. In this chapter, we first review the manner in which the states have related to those efforts and then turn to sources of differing state efforts.

Program Development

Considerable uncertainty surrounded the early state social services commitments. At the outset, the definition of what constituted "social services" was left to the states. Coupled with open-ended reimbursement of 75 percent of the cost of social services programs by the federal government, this flexibility gave the states considerable incentive to expand those services. Consequently, federal expenditures for social services grants grew from $194 million in 1963 to $741 million in 1971, then exploded to $1.688 billion in 1972 (Derthick 1975, p. 8). In that year, Congress placed a ceiling of $2.5 billion on such grants and began allocating the funds according to each state's share of the national population. That same legislation included a requirement that 90 percent of social services expenditures go to welfare recipients, in view of the burgeoning numbers of nonrecipients availing themselves of social services. This trend was exacerbated by provisions in the 1967 amendments to the Social Security Act that liberalized the concept of "potential welfare recipient" to include those who might need income support within five years and introduced "the concept of group eligibility, whereby residents of low-income neighborhoods and other groups such as those in institutional settings became eligible for service" (Gilbert 1981, p. 103). The 1967 amendments also shifted the emphasis of social services from soft services like counseling to hard services such as day care, drug treatment, and work training, a diversification which tended to fuel cost increases (pp. 106–108).

In a further attempt to gain control of social services spending, Congress enacted Title XX of the Social Security Act in 1974, consolidating virtually all previous sections of the act relating to social services. The new program retained the 75 percent federal match, the broad definition of social services (leaving specifics to the states), the $2.5 billion ceiling on federal expenditures, and allocation of funds by population. However, it also wrought some important changes in program administration. First, it attempted to reverse the trend toward liberalized eligibility by requiring that at least 50 percent of federal funds be spent on welfare recipients. At the same time, it established income-related eligibility for services; that is, for people whose income fell between 80 percent and 115 percent of the state's median income, an income-related fee could be charged for services. Some types of services were even made available to everyone regardless of income (Gilbert 1981, p. 104). Second, Title XX opened the door to provision of services by private, nonprofit agencies by allowing the states to use donations, or contributed funds, from such agencies as part of the state's 25 percent matching funds, even if those donated funds were in turn used to purchase services from the donating agencies (p. 109). Finally, Title XX instituted requirements for annual planning and public participation therein, although it continued the tradition of considerable state discretion in the use of federal funds (pp. 111–114).

Social services provided through Title XX and its predecessor programs became an important source of funds for assisting the nation's aging population. Because the states were not required to allocate funds to specific target groups (except for income-related requirements, as specified earlier) or to report to the federal government on the target groups to which the funds were allocated, ascertaining such allocation patterns has required special survey studies. In perhaps the most extensive such study, Gilbert and Specht (1982, p. 73) estimate that of the roughly $2.5 billion expended for Title XX in 1980, approximately $580 million was spent on social services for the aging. Their study demonstrated that the aging receive at least their fair share of the Title XX program, comparing their proportion of the overall population or of the population in poverty with the proportion of Title XX funds going to all aging or the aging poor, or with the proportion of Title XX recipients who are aging or aging poor. Thus, between 1975 and 1980, the aging received an average of 13.8 percent of Title XX allocations and constituted 15.4 percent of the Title XX service population, compared with their 10.9 percent share of the total population (p. 74). Similarly, in almost 75 percent of the cases (the fifty states at every year from 1976 to 1980), the percentage of Title XX funds going to the aging poor was at least twice the percentage of aging in the poverty population, while in over 15 percent of the cases it was at least three times as large (p. 82).

Other analysts have asserted, in contrast, that the aging are not receiving their fair share of social services funds because the aging have greater need and are at greater risk than the nonaging (Lindeman and Pardini 1983, p. 152). Moreover, the trend toward more generous allocation to the aging poor may be reversing, in part due to the recent movement toward group eligibility for all aging persons regardless of income, a feature found in 23 states by 1979 that "could serve as a mechanism for the redistribution of resources from the poor to the nonpoor elderly" (Gilbert and Specht 1982, p. 85). Similar concerns about group eligibility are expressed by Alfaro and Holmes (1981) in their comparative survey of state officials and service providers in a sample of both group-eligibility and non-group-eligibility states. They found that the latter "are serving a higher proportion of older persons who are disabled, living alone, and living below the poverty level" and that "the availability of free services on a group basis seems to encourage the more able elderly with greater resources to apply for services, while it does not reach as readily the elderly most in need" (Alfaro and Holmes 1981, p. 380). Despite hopes that it might induce increased state appropriations for aging services or improvement in the quality of those services, group eligibility "has been adopted with greater emphasis on helping to relieve bureaucratic pressures than on helping elderly clients" (p. 381).

Group eligibility is only part of a larger trend toward the universalization of social services, a movement advocated in part by social service professionals that no doubt is attractive to politicians who seek support from the working and middle classes, more regular voters than the poor (Schram 1981, p. 87). Thus, "the politics of social services in a time of scarcity appears to be very much one of entrenched providers seeking to get political influentials to perpetuate their established position in the social service network" (p. 89). This pattern also reflects a related trend toward decentralization of decision making for social programs that promotes "goals which are inconsistent with national standards without attracting national attention" (p. 90). These trends, along with those (mentioned earlier) toward a broader range of services, broader distribution of funds according to state population, and expansion of service delivery by private, nonprofit agencies (Gilbert 1981), have been fostered in part by the shift in federal program design from categorical grants to block grants. Strictly speaking, Title XX was not a block grant because it did not allocate specific amounts of federal funds to the states for broadly defined purposes yet with considerable state discretion in use of the funds; rather, Title XX reimbursed the states for 75 percent of the cost of providing social services and involved several restrictions and requirements, as discussed earlier. Nevertheless, the states did enjoy considerable discretion in allocating the funds for various services within the broadly defined goals of achieving self-support and preventing abuse and institutionalization but assisting those already in institutions.

In 1981, federal funding of social services took on more of the features of a block grant when Title XX was replaced by the Social Service Block Grant (SSBG) as part of the consolidation of some 57 categorical grant programs into 9 block grants in the Omnibus Budget Reconciliation Act. SSBG merged the Title XX social services program with two smaller Title XX programs: training of state and local social workers and child day care. The original goals of Title XX were retained, but several restrictions and requirements were dropped, including the requirement for state matching funds, targeting of welfare recipients, and income limitations. Other requirements, like the reporting requirement, were further eased. Thus, SSBG is essentially a continuation of Title XX with broadened eligibility and even greater administrative discretion for the states (Ellwood 1982, pp. 219–222).

The principal feature of the shift from Title XX to SSBG, however, was a 20 percent reduction in federal funds for the program. Far more than the administrative changes, this reduction severely affected state and local social services effort. In a survey of eight states, Lindeman and Pardini (1983) found that most of them had made extensive cuts in their programs since 1981, primarily by reducing state funding, decreasing personnel and otherwise lowering administrative overhead costs, eliminating some services, creating waiting lists for some other services (mostly optional services aimed at enhancing quality of life or preventing difficulties), and even lowering the income eligibility standard. Only one state, Massachusetts, actually increased its program, by increasing state funding. In other states where social services programs were maintained or larger cuts were avoided, many used recipient fees and copayments or shifted costs to other federal programs (for example, Medicaid waivers for in-home care) or to local governments. Despite the elimination of the federal requirements for 25 percent state matching funds and income-related eligibility, most states maintained both, although a few adopted group eligibility for the aging. Most states also continued monitoring service delivery, but most also reduced their planning efforts.

Overall, the states used the federal cutbacks in funding and requirements to consolidate their control over social services programs. The results of these changes are not likely to improve program operations or to benefit program recipients. Personnel reductions, plus curtailed planning and evaluation activities and staff training, will only result in increased case loads and lower program efficiency. But more important, although the aging have fared rather well in comparison with other clientele in an era of increased competition among such groups, "the elderly may receive fewer, more crisis-related services at a greater out-of-pocket cost" (Lindeman and Pardini 1983, p. 149), hurting the frail, low-income aging the most.

Equally as important as Title XX/SSBG in the provision of social services to the aging have been the various programs developed under the Older Americans Act of 1965, for which approximately $650 million was allocated in 1980 (Gilbert and Specht 1982, p. 72). Enacted during the flood of legislation known as President Lyndon Johnson's Great Society, the Older Americans Act defined all citizens over the age of 60, regardless of income, as constituting a group in need of social services. This universal approach resulted in part from a feeling that the poor of all ages were already being served by various programs in the War on Poverty, including the predecessors to Title XX (Estes 1979, p. 36). The act established a small Administration on Aging (AoA), buried deep within the bureaucracy of the federal Department of Health, Education, and Welfare, for distributing funds to social services to a designated SUA in each of the states and territories. The SUA then disbursed funds to local service providers for delivery of various social services to the aging. A significant addition to those programs, nutrition services, came in the 1972 amendments to the act.

Reflecting the Nixon administration's decentralizing New Federalism, the 1973 amendments required the SUAs to establish Planning and Service Areas (PSAs) within their jurisdictions and to designate at least one Area Agency on Aging (AAA) within each PSA for coordinating the delivery of services. Funds are disbursed automatically to the states and territories according to their share of the nation's population aged 60 and over and with no matching requirements, while distribution patterns to AAAs within states vary widely. Although the SUAs are required to submit to AoA plans for coordinating their service programs, they and their AAAs still have considerable flexibility in the use of federal funds (Lowy 1980, pp. 36–41). Although the AoA budget declined for the first time in fiscal year 1982 ($720 million, down from $748 million in the previous year), the cut was modest compared to programs serving other clientele. Moreover, the 1982 extension of the Older Americans Act gives the states even greater discretion in the use of program funds (Gutowski and Koshel 1982, p. 320). As with most Great Society programs, however, the amount of federal funds appropriated has never been adequate to achieve the broad and ambitious goals stated in the act, even though the elderly are widely perceived as the recipient group most deserving of help. It has instead fostered the development of an extensive aging network comprised primarily of social service professionals, researchers, and leaders of aging interest groups.

One clear mandate the 1973 amendments to the Older Americans Act directed toward the SUAs and the AAAs was to serve as advocates for the aging in seeking a greater share of state and local resources for such programs, reflecting in part the efforts of the Nixon administration to devolve more federal responsibilities to the subnational level. Perhaps the major tool available to the agencies for this purpose is pooling of Older Americans Act funds with state and local funds—and with funds from other federal programs—in designing programs for the aging. It is significant that the most obvious target for pooling has been Title XX social services funds, and the federal requirement for public participation in Title XX planning provides SUAs and AAAs an opportunity to influence the distribution of Title XX funds in favor of the aging. In a survey of AAA efforts in this type of advocacy, Gilbert and Specht (1979) found that direct contact with Title XX officials by AAA staff personnel was more effective than efforts to mobilize aging constituents and interest groups or allies in non-aging-based agencies and interest groups. Thus, pooling of funds appears to be pursued more effectively by larger, better funded, and more established AAAs with stabler leadership. According to another report from the same survey, AAAs that secure more Title XX funding for the aging are more likely to emphasize life-sustaining services for the at-risk aging rather than life-enhancing services for those aging who are better off. However, the trend toward group eligibility for Title XX programs, discussed previously, could undermine this emphasis on the aging poor (Nelson 1980). Furthermore, the Reagan administration's recent reductions in funding for all social programs, including those for the aging, will make it even more difficult for the aging network to design and implement effective programs for the aging (Brown 1983). The states, especially those hardest hit by the recent economic recession and those that have traditionally been less generous in their social programs, may be unable and/or unwilling to replace those lost federal funds.

While federal funding of social services for the aging has remained rather modest, especially in comparison with Western European countries such as the United Kingdom and Sweden, the trend toward decentralization in the administration of such programs has fostered increasing variation among the states and localities in their policy efforts in this and other areas. This chapter seeks to account for that variation by examining the patterns of interrelationship among various measures of state policy effort in the area of social services, and between those measures and relevant socioeconomic and political characteristics of the states.

Sources of Policy Effort

Three major questions require examination as we turn to an assessment of social services policies. First, how extensively, and in what socioeconomic and political contexts, have different states responded in developing more extensive aging networks, as initially envisioned in the Older Americans Act, in terms of expanded staff and institutional development? Second, to what extent, and in what contexts, have the states been willing to allocate state funds for social services programs? Third, in the area of social services funding under Title XX of the Social Security Act, how have the states differed in their levels of commitment to the aging and in their approach to targeting for low income groups? Answers to these questions provide important insights into both the sources of state policy and the nature of state responses to federal strategies over the past two decades. This section thus first reviews the social services policy measures and then reports our findings, including both correlations and stepwise regression.

The Policy Measures

Our consideration of social services policy efforts is based upon measures that include both the results of factor analysis and a focusing on selected individual policy components. The composite social services factor was created through factor analysis, as described in chapter 1 and the appendix. As a related variable, the SUA budget per 1,000 older persons did not help constitute the social services factor and was thus employed as a separate indicator. The second composite factor to be used here was labeled the SUA size factor, and the third was the SUA status factor (for details, see chapter 1 and the appendix).

Several dependent variables that focus on specific aspects of state responses to federal programs have also been included. For responses pertaining directly to the aging, we have examined percentage of Comprehensive Annual Service Program (CASP) social services allocated for elderly persons (labeled CASP percent aging) and percentage of Title XX social services expenditures for the aging going to aging persons receiving SSI payments (labeled Title XX percent SSI). In addition, for comparative purposes in our discussion of regression results and policy implications, we have included, as a more general social services response measure, Title XX utilization, which is based upon the speed with which the states moved to match their full allotment of Title XX funds (for all eligible groups in the population) after the ceiling was placed on those funds in 1972. As in other chapters, the full battery of socioeconomic and political variables for 1975 has been employed as potential predictors of these dependent variables.

Correlations among Dependent Variables

To a surprising extent, the states show a quite varied rather than uniform pattern of effort. Table 5–1 presents the simple correlations among the dependent variables, or indicators of state social services policy for the aging. The most prominent feature of these correlations is their low magnitude. Only one correlation, between the social services factor and SUA budget, is significant beyond .001 and greater in magnitude than .5, which still represents only 25 percent of the variance shared between the two variables. Furthermore, a relatively strong and positive correlation might be expected between these two expenditure-based measures. Interestingly, the correlations between those two measures and all the others except Title XX percent SSI are inverse, and the majority of them is significant at least beyond the .05 level. Most of the other correlations in the table approach statistical significance, except those involving Title XX percent SSI, which has no significant correlations. All the statistically significant correlations involve either the social services factor or SUA budget.

It is important to emphasize that the largest (though still not significant) correlation for Title XX percent SSI is its only inverse correlation—namely, with the non-SUA indicator, CASP percent aging. This helps explain why Title XX percent SSI shows nonsignificant but

Table 5-1
Simple Correlations among Dependent Variables: Social Services, 1975

	SUA Budget	SUA Size	SUA Status	CASP Aged Pct.	T20 Pct. SSI
SUA Size	−.187				
SUA Status	−.304[a]	.243			
CASP Aged. Pct.	−.307[a]	.207	.154		
T20 Pct. SSI	.148	.156	.069	−.193	
Social Services	.575[c]	−.289[a]	−.225	−.366[b]	.036

[a]Significant at .05.
[b]Significant at .01.
[c]Significant at .001.

positive correlations with the social services factor and SUA budget, whereas CASP percent aging has significant but inverse correlations with those two SUA-oriented measures. This pattern among the significant correlations suggests that states with higher levels of overall social services policy effort for the aging actually tend to have smaller SUAs that are lower in administrative status and to devote fewer of their CASP funds to aging persons. This intriguing and somewhat unexpected pattern heightens one's interest in the correlations between each of these dependent variables and the various socioeconomic and political variables.

Correlations between Dependent
and Independent Variables

Table 5–2 presents the simple correlations between each of the 6 indicators of state social services policy for the aging and each of the independent variables that had at least one significant relationship with those dependent variables. Again, as in the correlations among the dependent variables, the overall magnitude of the correlations is rather low, although a few attain rather substantial levels. It is interesting that CASP percent aging, which in table 5–1 had two significant although inverse correlations with the social services factor and SUA budget, here shows only one significant correlation, with percentage of the population aged 65 and over. This is quite surprising, given the large number of independent variables with which that dependent variable could form a significant correlation based solely on chance.

At the other extreme, the SUA size factor successfully formed significant correlations with almost half of the independent variables, including one above the .9 level. That one independent variable was total population size, reflecting the fact that the various indicators comprising the SUA size factor were not standardized with any size-related denominator such as total population or size of the elderly population. It is interesting to note, nonetheless, not only that larger states have larger SUAs but also that the size factor overwhelms any other relationship. This finding in turn implies that the SUA size factor should be expected to correlate substantially with all indicators strongly related to state size. Most notable among those indicators are the legislative professionalism factor and the industrialization-urbanization factor. Like total population size, these two indicators (and the others with which the SUA size factor correlates) reflect the overall level of complexity of the state's society.

The dependent variable with the second largest number of signif-

Table 5-2
Simple Correlations between Dependent and Independent Variables: Social Services, 1975

	Dependent Variables					
Independent Variable	Social Services	SUA Budget	SUA Size	SUA Status	CASP Aged Pct.	T20 Pct. SSI
Total Pop.	-.457[c]	-.247	.917[d]	.303[a]	.242	.193
Indust.-Urban.	-.057	-.167	.685[d]	.385[b]	.099	.061
Need	-.277	.194	.110	.075	-.100	.410[b]
Status	.363[b]	.456[c]	.107	-.005	-.225	-.098
Development	.285[a]	.106	.300[a]	.066	-.126	-.082
Unemployment	.095	.039	.415[b]	.081	-.215	.263
Union Members	.122	.043	.491[c]	.081	-.236	.081
Income Change	.231	.452[b]	-.301[a]	-.183	-.233	.237
Pop. Change	.288[a]	.428[b]	-.343[a]	-.198	.216	-.014
Diversity	.224	.098	.371[b]	-.394[b]	.072	-.082
Pol. Culture	.173	.057	-.053	.076	.094	-.316[a]
Aged Pct. Pop.	-.322[a]	.428[b]	-.343[a]	-.127	-.216	-.014
Aged Pov. Pct.	-.238	-.128	-.267	-.394[b]	-.028	.359[a]
Aged Poor	-.334[a]	-.387[b]	-.156	-.043	.132	-.031
Aged Income	.539[c]	.530[c]	.091	.030	-.216	-.070
Aged Pct. Change	.112	-.563[d]	.170	.081	.352[a]	-.398[b]
Aged Migration	.259	.201	-.163	.081	.217	.162
Scope of Govt.	.351[a]	.741[d]	-.062	-.305[a]	-.266	.388[b]
Centralization	.508[c]	.385[b]	-.515[c]	-.276	-.185	.192
Gov. Power	-.039	.087	.283[a]	-.134	-.120	-.095
Gov. Reputation	.309[a]	.246	.104	.028	-.131	-.048
Legis. Profess.	-.320[a]	-.137	.848[d]	-.215	.194	.254
Legis. Apport.	-.406[b]	-.558[d]	.328[a]	.378[b]	.011	-.076
Voter Turnout	.106	-.177	.152	.067	.026	-.470[b]
Tax Effort	-.039	-.162	.376[b]	-.127	.174	.209
Tax Pct.	-.269	-.560[d]	.525[c]	.423[b]	.282	.245

Table 5–2 continued

Independent Variable	Dependent Variables					
	Social Services	SUA Budget	SUA Size	SUA Status	CASP Aged Pct.	T20 Pct. SSI
Tax Regress.	.168	.315[a]	-.132	-.066	.008	-.359[a]
AARP Members	.311[b]	.357[a]	.018	-.184	.024	-.233
NCSC Effort	-.093	-.176	.658[d]	.194	.192	-.075
Senior Orgs.	-.144	-.134	.441[b]	.361[b]	.171	.091
General Lib.	-.017	-.036	.464[c]	.122	.176	-.140

[a]Significant at .05.
[b]Significant at .01.
[c]Significant at .001.
[d]Significant at .0001.

icant correlations was our broader measure, the social services factor, which correlated with about a third of the independent variables. Its highest correlation was with aging family income, but it also had fairly strong correlations with degree of government centralization and, inversely, total population size. Centralization is strongly but inversely related to population size, meaning that the smaller states tend to have more centralized governments, probably because smaller states tend to have fewer large urban areas whose governments often dominate state politics. Furthermore, states with higher levels of aging social services policy effort also tend to have less-well-apportioned legislatures, which fits with their smaller size and greater degree of centralization, since apportionment is positively correlated with centralization. But the status factor and aging family income, which are both not significantly related to population, centralization, or apportionment, are both positively and substantially correlated with the social services factor. Thus, based solely on these simple correlations, states with high levels of aging social services policy effort appear primarily to be wealthier, smaller, more centralized, and less well apportioned.

Given the fairly strong correlation between the social services factor and SUA budget (.575; see table 5-1), one would expect their patterns of correlation with the independent variables to be rather similar. And indeed they are, except that the order of magnitude of the correlations is somewhat different. Specifically, with SUA budget, the scope of government factor, aging population, and to a lesser extent, legislative apportionment, the status factor, and aged poor as a percentage of the total population increased in strength and importance, whereas aging family income and centralization decreased in strength and importance. Tax percentage of revenue, income change, and population change emerged as major inverse correlates of SUA budget but not of the social services factor, whereas total population size correlated substantially and inversely with the social services factor but not with SUA budget. The substantial inverse correlations between SUA budget and both aging population and tax percent are most interesting and may be quite significant substantively.

It might initially seem quite surprising that states with fewer elderly persons would direct more funds into their SUAs and that states with more elderly persons would direct fewer funds into their SUAs. However, given that the dependent variable measures expenditures per elderly person, the correlation could simply reflect the spreading of a fairly constant amount of available dollars over larger numbers of elderly persons in some states and over smaller numbers of such persons in other states. In addition, the positive correlation between SUA budget and scope of government, along with the inverse correlation between scope of government and tax percent, suggests that states with higher levels of policy effort in the areas of aging social services do indeed have larger public sectors but that those public sectors are financed by sources of revenue that are easier to extract than taxes; that is, apparently the states that devote more public funds to their SUAs tend to be wealthy states that finance their larger public sectors with windfall revenue from sources like royalties on natural resources rather than from taxes that, in at least some instances, are apt to cause greater voter resistance. Those states in these instances are not necessarily smaller than others in total population size; the correlation between SUA budget and population is still inverse, but it is not significant, as it was between the social services factor and population. With these two exceptions, the correlates of both the social services factor and SUA budget are quite similar.

Finally, both the SUA status factor and Title XX percent SSI show far less numerous and fewer substantial correlations than do the other dependent variables. (Again, CASP percent aging had only one significant correlation, with aging population.) Tax percentage of revenue again proves to be a significant correlate of state policy effort in the area of aging social services, showing the highest correlation with the SUA status factor. But this time, the correlation is positive rather than negative, which fits with the inverse correlations between the SUA status factor and SUA budget. The SUA status factor is also inversely correlated with population change, which might be expected on the basis of a significant and inverse correlation between tax percent and population change. Furthermore, the SUA status factor is also significantly correlated with the industrialization-urbanization factor, which could be expected on the basis of a strong positive correlation between tax percent and industrialization-urbanization. Similarly, an even stronger positive correlation between legislative professionalism and tax percent helps explain the significant correlation between legislative professionalism and the SUA status factor. Interestingly, the latter also correlates significantly with the senior organizations measure, although again this could be explained by the latter's fairly substantial correlation with the other three independent variables. Nonetheless, in addition to having higher levels of industrialization and urbanization, stagnating population growth, more professional legislatures, and a higher tax percentage of revenue, states with higher status SUAs also tend to have a greater level of aging-based interest group activity than other states.

As for Title XX percent SSI, only four correlations are significant beyond the .01 level. The strongest is with voter turnout, and the second strongest is with the socioeconomic need factor. As with many of the other correlations in this policy area, however, the signs of the correlations for these two independent variables are the opposite of their usual pattern; that is, here the correlation for voter turnout is inverse, whereas that for the need factor is positive. Given the strong inverse correlation between turnout and need, this pattern suggests that states that devoted a greater percentage of Title XX social services funds to recipients of SSI-Aged tended to have greater numbers of needy persons in their populations, and such persons tended to vote less often. Similar to total SUA budget, Title XX percent SSI is inversely correlated with aging population, indicating that states with higher levels of Title XX funds devoted to the aging actually tended to have smaller aging populations. Finally, like SUA budget, Title XX percent SSI is positively correlated with the scope of government factor, indicating that states with higher levels of social services effort for the aging tended to have larger public sectors.

In summary, the patterns of correlation between the dependent variables for the social services policy area and the various independent variables differ from one dependent variable to the next. The composite social services factor and total SUA budget tend to attain higher levels in states that are wealthier, more centralized, less well apportioned, and more public sector oriented. States that score higher on the social services factor also tend to be smaller in population size, and states with larger SUA budgets also tend to have higher rates of income and population growth, to derive more public revenue from nontax sources, and to have smaller aging populations. States with larger and higher status SUAs tend to be more industrialized and urbanized and to have more professional legislatures and a higher level of aging-based interest group activity. Larger SUAs also tend substantially to be located in states that are larger in population, and higher status SUAs also tend to be supported in states with greater proportions of nontax revenue and stagnating population growth. States that devote a higher percentage of their Title XX social services funds to recipients of SSI-Aged tend to have greater numbers of needy persons who vote less often and also tend to have larger public sectors. Finally, the percentage of CASP social services devoted to aging clientele shows only one significant correlation, with aging population.

These correlation results lend only modest support to the conceptual model presented in chapter 1, at least for the area of social services. Taking into consideration the differing number of indicators belonging to each concept in that model, several key predictors nonetheless did not have the largest number of significant correlations. However, fiscal capacity, along with political capacity, did have the second highest number. General socioeconomic development and aging advocacy were not far behind, although their correlations tended to be much weaker. The socioeconomic status of the aging population, while barely having the largest number of significant correlations, likewise tended to have weaker ones. Fiscal capacity and political capacity had the strongest correlations, even considering their sparse number of indicators. Considering both number and strength of correlations, social services policy effort would appear to be associated most closely with fiscal capacity and political capacity and to a lesser extent with socioeconomic status, particularly that of the elderly population. Interestingly, the association with status is direct rather than inverse, suggesting that states with stronger social services programs tend to be those with populations lowest in need. That is, they are the states with the capability to provide more generous programs, regardless of the extent of need or demand for them and regardless of general liberalism in other policy areas or political openness.

Stepwise Regression Analysis

Once the overlap among the independent variables that correlate with a particular dependent variable is removed, the picture on some of the measures ironically becomes cloudier. Recall that in using stepwise regression analysis to identify the best combination of predictors for each policy measure, models were rejected not only if they had any insignificant regression coefficients or an insignificant overall R^2 but also if they showed signs of multicollinearity, or sufficient intercorrelation among the predictors to cause increasing standard errors of the regression coefficients. This had the consequence of eliminating some of the more easily interpretable patterns of relationship involving mutually reinforcing predictors—that is, independent variables that indicated a single general syndrome such as wealth or development. Instead, the procedure forces each predictor in a model to represent a separate dimension of state characteristics, and the very fact that they therefore do not go together makes their co-occurrence in a given model more difficult to interpret. A model may even include predictors that did not have significant simple correlations with the dependent variable.

Table 5–3 presents the best regression models for explaining each of the measures of social services policy for the aging in the states. Despite the uncertainty of some theoretical relationships noted at the outset, the overall level of variance explained for this policy area is quite high, with four of the coefficients of determination higher than .5. The social services factor did retain in its model the two independent variables with which it correlated most highly—aging family in-

Table 5–3
Best Regression Models for Explaining Selected Indicators of State Social Services for the Aging, 1975

Dependent Variable	Independent Variables	Probability > F	R²	Probability > F	N
Social Services	Centralization	.0001	.608	.0001	45
	Aged Income	.0004			
	Gov. Reputation	.0005			
	Migration	.0036			
SUA Budget	Legis. Apport. (−)	.0001	.661	.0001	45
	Gov. Reputation	.0075			
	Scope of Govt.	.0500			
SUA Size	Total Pop.	.0001	.855	.0001	45
	General Lib.	.0244			
SUA Status	Tax Pct.	.0002	.431	.0001	45
	Party Compet. (−)	.0010			
	Pop. Change (−)	.0324			
CASP Aged Pct.	Union Members (−)	.0007	.285	.0030	45
	Total Pop.	.0020			
	Need (−)	.0289			
T20 Pct. SSI	Tax Effort	.0001	.543	.0001	44
	Aged Pct. Pop. (−)	.0001			
	Aged Income (−)	.0027			
	Pol. Culture (−)	.0165			
T20 Utilization	Centralization	.0003	.461	.0001	45
	Status	.0016			
	Legis. Profess.	.0062			
	Gov. Ambition	.0074			
	Income Change	.0353			

come and degree of government centralization—plus another variable with which it had a far weaker but still significant correlation: the governors' reputation index. However, the model also included a variable with which the social services factor did not significantly correlate—namely, the net migration rate for the entire population. Thus, the regression results partially confirm the correlation results in that states with higher levels than others in overall social services policy effort for the aging tend to be more centralized (and hence to be smaller and less urbanized) and to have wealthier aging populations. In addition, they also tend to have more reputable governors and show a slight tendency to be gaining in total population through in-migration.

The measure of total SUA budget per 1,000 elderly persons also retained in its regression model two of the four independent variables with which it correlated most highly: the legislative apportionment factor (still with an inverse relationship with the dependent variable) and the scope of government factor. However, the third predictor included in the model, the governors' reputation index, did not correlate significantly with the dependent variable but was included in the model for the social services factor. This one common predictor provides a slender thread of continuity from one model to the next, although the similarity in the models is far less than the similarity between the patterns of correlation for the two dependent variables. At any rate, the regression results again partially confirm the correlation results in that states with larger SUA budgets tend to have less-well-apportioned legislatures but more reputable governors and to show a very slight tendency to have larger public sectors.

As might be expected from the discussion of the correlation results, the SUA size factor is explained quite substantially by total population size, largely due to the fact that the measures of expenditures, personnel, and number of AAAs are not standardized to control for the effects of state magnitude. The general policy liberalism factor also contributes significantly to the model, although it only boosts the R^2 for population alone from .841 to .855. Thus, states with larger SUAs than in other states are definitely larger in total population size and have a slight tendency to be more generally liberal in their nonaging policies.

The SUA status factor retained in its best regression model the two independent variables with which it correlated most highly—namely, tax percentage of revenue and the rate of total population change (inverse)—and added one variable with which it did not significantly correlate: the index of interparty competition, which is also inversely related to the dependent variable. Thus, states with SUAs that are higher in organizational status still tend to be more willing to raise revenue through taxation and to have stagnating population growth. (Recall that the correlation analysis showed that states with higher budget SUAs tend to raise less revenue through taxation and thus apparently rely more on windfall revenue to finance extras like aging-related programs.) But in addition to willingness to tax and stagnating population growth, states with higher status SUAs also tend to have less competitive political parties. It should be noted, however, that this is one of the social services models that accounts for less than 50 percent of the variance in the dependent variable.

Interestingly, the model with the lowest coefficient of determination is that for percent of CASP devoted to aging social services, the variable that had only one significant simple correlation. The regression model for this variable is nevertheless statistically significant and contains not the one with which it correlated (aging population) but rather three predictors: union membership, total population size, and the socioeconomic need factor, with unionization and need having inverse relationships with the dependent variable. Thus, states that devote more CASP funds to aging programs tend to have smaller labor unions but larger populations and relatively smaller groups of needy persons.

The measure of the percentage of Title XX funds devoted to recipients of SSI-Aged, in turn, retained in its best regression model only aging population and the Elazar (1972) culture index. The model pulled in two primary predictors that did not correlate significantly with the dependent variable and still produced a coefficient of determination greater than .5. The four variables thus comprising the model are tax effort in relation to tax capacity, population aged 65 and over, aging family income, and the Elazar culture index, with all except tax effort having inverse relationships with the dependent variable. Thus, states that devote more of their Title XX funds to the aged poor tend to have higher levels of tax effort but smaller and poorer aging populations. However, they also tend to have more Traditionalistic political cultures.

Finally, the regression analyses of Title XX utilization deserve brief discussion. Centralization, legislative professionalism, and governors' political ambition and success entered the equation as an indication of the impact of political measures, while status and income change also contributed to that equation with its modest ($R^2 = .464$) ability to explain state eagerness to match Title XX funds at a full level. This finding will be important in our consideration of policy implications.

In summary, the regression results only partially confirm the correlation results, yielding patterns of relationship that are considerably more difficult to interpret substantively, even though they account for quite substantial proportions of variance. States that score higher on the composite social services factor tend to be more centralized (and hence to be smaller and less urban) and to have wealthier aging populations, more reputable governors, and higher rates of in-migration. States with higher budget SUAs tend to have less-well-apportioned legislatures but more reputable governors and show a very slight tendency toward larger public sectors. States with larger SUAs have larger total populations and a slight tendency to be more generally liberal in their nonaging policies. States with higher status SUAs tend to be more willing to raise revenue through taxation but tend to have less competitive political parties and stagnating population growth. The proportion of variance explained in this latter model, however, is substantially lower than it is for the earlier models. The coefficient of determination is far lower still for CASP percent aged, whose model suggests that states that devote more of CASP to aging programs tend to have larger populations, smaller labor unions, and larger groups of needy persons in their populations. Finally, states that devote more of their Title XX funds to the aged poor tend to have higher levels of tax effort but smaller and poorer aging populations. However, they also tend to have more Traditionalistic political cultures.

As with the correlation results, these regression results furnish little support for the conceptual model presented in figure 1–1, at least for the area of social services. No indicators of aging advocacy appeared as predictors in the best models for the six dependent variable measures of aging social services, and general policy liberalism appeared only once. Thus, two of the concepts hypothesized to influence policy effort most directly did not contribute substantially to the explanation of social services effort. Again, taking into consideration the differing number of indicators belonging to each concept in the conceptual model, however, measures of fiscal capacity, along with several for political capacity, did appear in the regression equations more often in proportion to their numbers than did measures of the other concepts. Similarly, those two concepts furnished the lead predictor in four of the six models. General socioeconomic development also contributed substantially in terms of both the number of occurrences and the number of lead predictors. Thus, in assessing our conceptual model, the regression results appear to agree with the correlation results in suggesting that the states that exert stronger social services effort tend to be those with the capability to do so rather than those with the greatest need or demand for such programs. They also are not necessarily those states with generally liberal policies in other areas or states with open political systems.

By way of comparison, the regression results for the non-aging-based measure of social services effort, Title XX utilization, affirm the

importance of political capacity and general socioeconomic development in the explanation of this policy area. Interestingly, indicators of
fiscal capacity are conspicuously absent from the model for Title XX
utilization, perhaps suggesting a stronger overall commitment to general social services, independent of financial resources, than for aging-
oriented services specifically, on the part of high capacity states. Such
an interpretation runs counter to the results of previous studies, most
of which support the view that the aging tend to be favored over nonaging clientele. Caution must be exercised in deciphering such a con-
trary finding, however, because stepwise regression is an exploratory
procedure for identifying patterns of relationship rather than an exact
and infallible test of the truth or falsity of specific propositions. Furthermore, Title XX utilization is only one indicator for aging-oriented
social services. At any rate, our regression results suggest that fiscal
capacity is an important predictor of aging-oriented social services effort but not of general social services effort. Both types of efforts, in
contrast, tend to reflect the political capacity and general socioeconomic development of the states.

It is useful to emphasize, in conclusion, that the development of
social services commitments has been influenced by the level of political capacity in a state and the willingness to use that capacity on the
part of a state's governor. The absence of a stronger relationship with
factors that have been instrumental in moving states to larger financial
commitments in other policy areas, however, has held social services
to a secondary position in the evolution of state policy.

Policy Implications

The efforts to build a state-supported network of social services have
produced mixed results. It is important to recognize once again that
we were unable to measure systematically some aspects of state social
services commitments and have thus not included them in this analysis.
Similarly, at points, local financial assistance may also emerge to provide some social services support. Nonetheless, one clear conclusion
to be drawn from our analysis is that social services efforts, as measured in particular by the social services factor, have not expanded in
relationship to the size of the older population in the larger states. This
is in contrast, one should note, to the relationship that has emerged
for our expenditure measures for Medicaid (see chapter 4).

However, some useful indications of the factors in a state did appear to contribute to stronger social services efforts. Several of these
point to the significance of political capacity, along with a desire to use

that capacity. Thus, centralization emerges in our regression model for the social services factor and in the model for the comparative dimension of Title XX utilization. As an indication of the importance of a willingness to use state capacities for program development, it is also interesting to find that the governors may have a significant role. Thus, the measure of governor's reputation appears in the regression models for both the social services factor and the SUA budget measure, and the governors' political activity score emerges in the model for Title XX utilization.

The regression results for social services effort suggest, finally, a possible reason for the lack of a more extensive social services response in the states. There is a tendency for these policies to emerge without an impact from some of the measures we have identified in other chapters as important factors in areas such as overall Medicaid spending for the aging and income maintenance policies. In this regard, while the general policy liberalism factor does emerge in the regression model for the size of the SUA, neither general policy liberalism nor tax effort even has a positive correlation with the two financial measures—the social services factor and SUA budget.

In conclusion, if it is true that, as our analysis suggests, state effort in social services for the aging depends heavily on state fiscal capacity as well as general socioeconomic development and political capacity, then those services could well be in jeopardy, considering the recent decline in the economic and fiscal health of precisely the states with the highest levels of capacity—namely, the industrial states of the Northeast and Midwest. It is uncertain whether liberalism in non-aging policy areas and strong advocacy on behalf of the aging in an open political system will be sufficient to maintain high levels of effort in those states. Coupled with the findings of previous studies concerning the universalization and decentralization of social services, it is not entirely clear whether cutbacks in the area of social services will affect the aging disproportionately more than other clientele. Unfortunately, our interpretation of the sources of state social services policy effort for the aging could mean that the only way an adequate level of effort will be restored (in states that have recently imposed extensive cutbacks) or attained (in states that have lagged behind) is through continued development of economic, political, and fiscal capacity. The aging may not be able to rely upon strong advocacy efforts or the general liberalism of their states in other policy areas to boost their levels of social services policy effort. Despite its apparent ineffectiveness, however, stronger advocacy may be the only recourse because the need for social services among the aging cannot wait for lengthy processes of development to yield their anticipated benefits.

6 Income Maintenance

The increasingly diverse set of state income maintenance policies constitutes an important aspect of state efforts for the aging. Analytically, besides the basic questions surrounding sources of overall policy effort, income maintenance policies also raise the question of possible differences in the nature of support for different types of assistance. Are there differences, for example, between efforts in the area of property tax relief and those that occur with cash payments such as OAA and SSI? Because of the importance of the comparison of policy approaches, it is useful to examine that issue directly before turning to the results of the fifty-state analysis.

Policy Issues

Present income maintenance policies can be distinguished broadly along two fundamental dimensions. The first involves universal eligibility for benefits versus targeted benefits that are means tested on the basis of criteria such as need or, conversely, assets and present income. The second dimension involves direct (cash) versus indirect (in-kind) forms of assistance. To illustrate this basic typology, certain specific national-level policies for the aging may be categorized as follows. In the category of universal-direct policy are Social Security retirement benefits. In the category of universal-indirect policy, Medicare stands as the most prominent example. The category of means-tested direct policy is best illustrated by SSI. Finally, in the category of means-tested indirect policy, the food stamp program constitutes a major example. Classification schemes utilizing these dimensions are widely used in the literature (see, for example, Garfinkel and Skidmore 1978). In the debates over these respective approaches, efforts at quantifying as well as evaluating them have been undertaken by Moon (1977) and Viscusi (1979). General comparative interpretations have been presented by Garfinkel and Skidmore (1978), Herzog (1978), and Schulz (1980). Tax policies that provide support for the aging have been evaluated by Fairholm (1978) and Gold (1979) and direct income support policies by Plotnick and Skidmore (1975) and Grimaldi (1980). A related study by Kasschau (1978) examined differing views of key elite groups. The desirability of using means testing in various types of direct and indirect income maintenance programs is thoroughly examined by several analysts in Garfinkel (1982).

Each of the alternative policy strategies has had proponents and critics. Advocates of universal-direct approaches have stressed that these programs are most likely to be supported politically and that they give individuals an opportunity to spend their incomes at their discretion. Critics, in turn, argue that universal-direct programs are expensive in relation to the benefits actually reaching persons most in need of help and that they have little redistributive impact.

Universal-indirect programs are seen as an effective way to cover a major segment of the population with a given, and presumably needed, type of assistance. This has been the defense, for example, for the Medicare program since its inception in the mid-1960s. Critics of this approach have stressed its cost and the lack of discretion for the individual in the allocation of personal income.

The third category, means-tested direct programs, is seen by its supporters as providing assistance to the neediest segments of the population at the least cost and at the same time giving those individuals maximum discretion over their personal income allocations. The critics of this approach, in turn, have argued that these programs are vulnerable politically since programs for poor people too often turn out to be poorly funded. The fourth and final category, means-tested indirect programs, is supported as a vehicle for addressing a particular need such as excess amounts of personal income being devoted to housing costs or energy costs on the part of lower-income segments of society like the aging poor. Critics of these programs, as with universal-indirect approaches, question the lack of discretion given to the individual and the frequent absence of assistance to the near-poor.

The income maintenance policies being implemented by the states for the aging provide an opportunity for assessing the magnitudes and forms of income assistance that are produced in different socioeconomic and political contexts. The two income policies for the aging that were most extensively pursued by the states by the mid-1970s were supplements to SSI and various forms of tax relief. In terms of the basic typology, these two policies involve aspects, respectively, of direct and indirect forms of income assistance; that is, supplements to SSI represent direct cash payments to eligible recipients, whereas tax relief involves a reduction in payments owed by eligible individuals. At the same time, supplementation of SSI represents a clear example of a means-tested program, while tax relief, by the mid-1970s, involved substantial but not exclusive targeting for the low-income elderly. A brief description of these policy areas provides a basis for their categorization and the information needed for our analysis of their respective sources of variation among the states.

Supplements to SSI stand, since the mid-1970s, as a clear case of state efforts to extend the initial federal levels of guaranteed income for the impoverished elderly (Grimaldi 1980). SSI went into effect in 1974, replacing OAA, one of the major original components of the Social Security Act of 1935. Along with Aid to the Blind (AB) and Aid to the Permanently and Totally Disabled (APTD), OAA operated in a similar manner to AFDC and Medicaid, as an open-ended, formula-based entitlement program, with the federal government reimbursing the state for at least 50 percent (for the wealthier states) and up to about 85 percent (for the poorer states) of program costs. Due to vastly different payment levels and eligibility criteria, those costs varied considerably from state to state, with the largest and most generally liberal states spending the lion's share of the funds. SSI "federalized" OAA, AB, and APTD by establishing a nationwide income floor (essentially a guaranteed income for the aging, the blind, and the disabled). However, the states were allowed to supplement the standard federal payment according to their own eligibility criteria and payment levels.

Technically, states that had levels of assistance under OAA that were higher than the new federal SSI standards in 1974 were required to supplement the federal payment enough to bring the total payment up to the previous OAA level. Thus, the efforts were not at that point in time a voluntary action on the part of those states. However, since those higher levels were the result of past decisions, they reflect a combination of socioeconomic and political forces that had been at work in the state policy process. The SSI supplements also are based upon a stringent form of means testing since individuals whose incomes exceed the SSI level are immediately terminated from all assistance through that program.

Tax relief for the aging has emerged since 1964 as a major alternative form of assistance. Its growth has progressed to a point at which each of the 50 states now has some kind of property tax relief for the elderly, and 37 states provide tax and/or sales tax exemptions (Viscusi 1979, pp. 90–92). The most common type of property tax relief is a circuit-breaker program, which pegs the amount of relief to the taxpayer's income level in relation to his or her property tax liability. The amount of relief tapers off, as taxpayer income increases, via a formula that avoids abruptly cutting off the amount of relief at some arbitrary level of income. For example, the Vermont circuit-breaker program takes effect when the property tax exceeds 7 percent of household income; for Minnesota that figure is 6 percent; and for many other states it is 3 to 5 percent (Schulz 1980, p. 27). The number of states having circuit-breaker tax relief programs reached 25 by 1974 and 28 plus the District of Columbia by 1978. Of these programs as of 1979, 5 pertained only to aging homeowners, another 15 pertained to elderly homeowners and renters, 1 (Maryland) applied to homeowners of all ages plus elderly renters, and 7 states applied their programs to both homeowners and renters of all ages (Gold 1979).

In terms of other forms of tax assistance, all states that do not have a circuit-breaker program have either a homestead exemption or a tax credit provision. Fifteen of the states that have circuit-breaker programs also have some other forms of tax relief. In 8 states plus the District of Columbia, there are no age restrictions. In 15 states there is a higher exemption or credit for the aging than for other groups. In 14 states the assistance is only for older persons. Some 18 of the 37 states with homestead exemption or tax credit programs do provide, at the same time, either a partial or a clear income ceiling for the relief being provided (Gold 1979).

Property tax relief and SSI supplements also differ in terms of magnitude and redistributive impact. One of the few efforts to systematically assess income support policies for the aging was undertaken by Moon (1977, p. 101). As an estimate of the relative incidence of tax assistance, the author concluded that public assistance (exclusive of Social Security) was providing $1.09 billion of assistance to 10.3 percent of aged families. Among all aging families, regardless of income, public assistance was providing an average $80.64 annually. Of those families receiving public assistance, the average was $782.91 per recipient family. The distribution of property tax assistance was somewhat larger, at $1.83 billion. A much larger percentage of aging families, some 70.85 percent, were receiving such assistance, with the average assistance for all aged families coming to $134.89. The average payment per recipient family, however, was much smaller for property tax relief, at $172.71. Tax relief thus involves a larger total outlay due to a substantially larger number of recipients, even though the average assistance per recipient is substantially smaller than for SSI.

The research by Moon (1977) also provides an important indication of the incidence of assistance through SSI-Aged among the lowest income aging. Among the lowest 15, 30, and 40 percent of aged families, public assistance ranks first in "target efficiency," defined as the extent to which the programs provide aid for the intended group of beneficiaries. Unfortunately, there is no assessment of the incidence of property tax relief for the elderly. However, all the tax measures that are assessed (double exemptions, exclusion of transfers, and retirement credit) have the lowest target efficiency. This finding compares with the assessment of Surrey (1973) that nearly half of the federal tax assistance for the aging went to the few aging individuals with annual incomes over $10,000.

The study by Gold (1979) constitutes the most recent effort to assess the degree of targeting for lower income groups that occurs through property tax relief. Overall, Gold (p. 62) is quite critical of property tax relief for the aging, arguing that claims like potential loss of home are overstated and that singling out the aging is inappropriate when other groups may be in equal, or even worse, need of assistance. At the same time, he is less critical of the increasingly common form of relief, the circuit-breaker program, arguing in contrast to Aaron (1975) that, at least at the state level, such programs can be fairly sensitive to the income needs of the poorer segments of the aging population. Gold specifically states:

> The results of the survey allay fears that a large proportion of circuit breaker benefits goes to the rich. While average benefits to recipients do increase as income rises in several states, there are many programs with the opposite pattern. Overall, the results of the survey demonstrate that the benefits of all existing circuit breakers go mostly to households with below-average income. [p. 68]

Finally, in terms of alternative state income maintenance policy efforts for the aging, as noted earlier, as of 1973 some 37 states gave some form of income tax concession to the aging. These provisions, and a review of their impacts, are presented in Viscusi (1979). In many instances, however, the dollar amounts of these tax credits are very small. Nonetheless, those amounts are included along with the amount of property tax relief in our overall measure of the amount of state tax relief for the aging, as compiled by the U.S. Department of Housing and Urban Development (1975).

The two policy areas for our study may thus be summarized as follows. State supplementation of SSI-Aged, as of 1975, paid more in average dollar terms to the low-income elderly than did the various forms of tax relief. The benefits for tax relief were less on a per person basis but involved larger overall expenditures because of the larger number of beneficiaries. Both programs provided assistance disproportionately to the lower-income elderly, and tax relief, by the mid-1970s, was increasingly focused in that direction. However, since a large proportion of SSI recipients are both poorer than homeowners and less apt to own their own homes (although home ownership is exempted in the SSI assets test), SSI is clearly focused more directly on the aging with the lowest incomes. Finally, the two policies offer a classic case of opportunity for choice between direct and indirect policy strategies. How, then, have the states chosen between these two policy alternatives?

Policy Sources

The research findings presented in this section focus initially on state income maintenance policies as of the mid-1970s, including the level and scope of state supplements to SSI for the aging (SSI-Aged), tax relief for the aging (including both income tax and property tax provisions), and our broader measure that incorporates elements of both of the first two areas, the income maintenance factor. As in previous chapters, the analysis begins with the correlations among the various dependent variable indicators of state policy effort and between those indicators and various socioeconomic and political characteristics of the states, conceptualized as independent variables. Also presented are results of stepwise regression analysis, designed to explore combinations of the best predictors of the dependent variable policy measures. This section also includes the results of a type of analysis not possible with the other substantive areas of state policy efforts for the aging due to lack of availability of data for more than two or three time points: an examination of the trends over all five time points in the patterns of relationship for one key indicator of state income maintenance policy effort for the aging—namely, state payment level under OAA and its successor in 1975, SSI. The concluding section for this chapter offers interpretations of these changing patterns of influence on state policy efforts in the area of income maintenance for the aging and discusses some implications of these trends for the development of such policies.

Relationships among Dependent Variables

Table 6–1 presents the simple correlations among the original set of dependent variable indicators of state income maintenance policy for the aging. The table shows quite substantial correlations among all of those indicators except the level of state supplemental payment for SSI-Aged and earliness of adoption of a circuit-breaker property tax relief program. Because those two variables are not related to each other either, they apparently constitute two entirely separate dimensions from the remainder of the indicators of state income maintenance policy for the aging. The SSI state supplement level does correlate significantly, but at very weak levels, with all those remaining indica-

Table 6–1
Simple Correlations among Dependent Variables: Income Maintenance, 1975

	SSI Aged Pay.	SSI Pct. Aged	SSI Pct. Poor	SSI Ratio	SSI Limits-I	SSI Limits-C	Tax Relief
SSI Pct. Aged	.171						
SSI Pct. Poor	.307[a]	.882[d]					
SSI Ratio	.187	.850[d]	.913[d]				
SSI Limits-I	.384[b]	.587[d]	.703[d]	.681[c]			
SSI Limits-C	.385[b]	.668[d]	.870[d]	.780[d]	.842[d]		
Tax Relief	.389[b]	.492[c]	.606[d]	.559[d]	.754[d]	.656[d]	
Circuit-Breaker	.175	.215	.258	.289[a]	.127	.250	.375[b]

[a]Significant at .05.
[b]Significant at .01.
[c]Significant at .001.
[d]Significant at .0001.

tors except SSI-Aged state supplement recipients as a percentage of all elderly and the ratio of SSI-Aged state supplement recipients to federal SSI-Aged recipients. Because it will be included in our analysis of the changing sources of state income maintenance policy for the aging in a later section, the SSI state supplement level is not treated further in the mid-1970s analyses. Earliness of adoption of a circuit-breaker program, however, is included here as a separate dimension. It correlates significantly only with the average dollar amount of tax relief for the aging and, to an even less extent, with the ratio of SSI-Aged state supplement recipients to federal SSI-Aged recipients.

Table 6–1 does, nonetheless, contain an extremely important finding that addresses the distinction between direct and indirect forms of assistance discussed in the introduction to this chapter. That finding is the substantial correlation between the average dollar amount of tax relief for the aging and each of the indicators of the scope of a state's SSI-Aged program. This result suggests that no substantial trade-off exists between direct and indirect forms of assistance and that they are not treated by the states as competing alternatives. Instead, states that exert greater effort in providing direct cash support for the aging (in the form of supplementation of SSI-Aged) also tend to provide the aging with more generous levels of indirect assistance (in the form of tax relief). The pattern of interrelationship among these indicators was in fact strong enough to produce a composite factor-score measure of state income maintenance policies (for a more complete discussion of that factor and the procedures that created it, see chapter 1 and the appendix). That factor is used in the mid-1970s analyses to follow in place of its several component indicators. The amount of tax relief for the aging, however, because of its conceptual separateness from the indicators of scope of SSI-Aged and the fact that it is indeed the weakest component of the income maintenance factor, is also presented as a separate indicator of state income maintenance effort for the aging. Despite this separation, the substantial relationship between amount of tax relief and the various indicators of scope of SSI-Aged undermines the notion that direct and indirect forms of assistance constitute separate, competing dimensions of income maintenance policy effort, at least for the states and the aging.

Correlations between Independent and
Dependent Variables

The high degree of internal cohesion among the dependent variable indicators in the area of income maintenance makes the patterns of relationship among the three separate dimensions of that policy area and the various socioeconomic and political measures conceptualized as independent variables particularly interesting. Table 6–2 presents the simple correlations for those independent variables that correlated at the .05 level of significance or better with at least two of the three indicators of income maintenance policy: earliness of adoption of a circuit-breaker tax relief program, average amount of tax relief for the aging (both income and property tax provisions), and the composite income maintenance policy factor. Perhaps the most striking feature of table 6–2 is the difference among the three dependent variables in their numbers of significant correlations and the strength of those correlations. The circuit-breaker measure shows the fewest and weakest correlations, and the income maintenance factor shows the most and strongest, with amount of tax relief for the aging in between. The circuit-breaker measure correlates significantly with only 7 of the 21 independent variables and only very weakly at that. Only two of those

Table 6–2
Simple Correlations between Dependent and Independent Variables:
Income Maintenance, 1975

	Dependent Variables		
Independent Variable	*Circuit-Breaker*	*Tax Relief*	*Income Maint.*
Indust.-Urban.	.120	.295[a]	.508[b]
Union Members	.378[b]	.298[a]	.433[b]
Status	.111	.435[b]	.526[d]
Need	−.331[a]	−.313[a]	−.367[a]
Aged Income	.052	.388[b]	.442[b]
Aged Pov. Pct.	−.223	−.441[b]	−.531[d]
Income Change	−.363[b]	−.066	−.366[b]
Diversity	.125	.415[b]	.584[d]
Pol. Culture	.353[a]	.369[b]	.351[a]
Tax Pct.	.243	.283[a]	.570[d]
Property Tax	.223	.394[b]	.469[c]
Tax Effort	.212	.423[b]	.605[c]
Legis. Profess.	.161	.430[b]	.527[d]
Party Compet.	.354[a]	.389[b]	.327[a]
AARP Members	.120	.397[b]	.430[b]
NCSC Effort	.279[a]	.328[a]	.377[b]
Senior Orgs.	.080	.486[c]	.532[d]
AFDC Payment	.195	.575[d]	.624[d]
SSI-Blind Pay	.119	.418[b]	.556[d]
SSI-Disab. Pay	.066	.436[d]	.445[b]
General Lib.	.308[a]	.522[d]	.647[d]

[a]Significant at .05.
[b]Significant at .01.
[c]Significant at .001.
[d]Significant at .0001.

correlations are significant at a level higher than the .05 level, and those are only barely so. In contrast, the correlations are distributed fairly evenly among the various components of our conceptual model (figure 1–1). States that were early adopters of a circuit-breaker type of property tax relief thus tended to have slightly higher levels of union membership, interparty competition, lobbying effort by the NCSC, and general policy liberalism. They also tended to have lower levels of socioeconomic need and economic growth and to have more Moralistic political cultures. As tenuous as this pattern is, it still projects a faint image of states in the snowbelt region of the country.

The other two dependent variables in table 6–2, in contrast, correlate significantly with almost all the independent variables. The income maintenance factor indeed does correlate significantly with all of them, and amount of tax relief for the aging correlates significantly with all but percentage change in per capita income. Moreover, both of these two dependent variables show several rather substantial correlations, although the income maintenance factor produces by far the strongest and most numerous significant correlations, reflecting the tenuous status of tax relief as a component of that factor. The strongest correlations for amount of tax relief are with measures of state policy effort in non-aging-policy areas: AFDC payment level and the general policy liberalism factor. It is interesting to note that its third largest correlation is with senior organizations. The same two measures of non-aging-policy effort also yield the strongest correlations with the income maintenance factor, but at even higher levels of strength, and several other independent variables correlate more strongly with that factor than do any of the measures of aging advocacy—most notably, tax effort relative to capacity, the Sullivan diversity index, and tax percent of revenue. As with the circuit-breaker measure, but not amount of tax relief, the income maintenance factor correlates significantly and inversely with percentage change in per capita income. Of similar interest is the fact that all three dependent variables correlate negatively with not only the socioeconomic need factor but also with the percentage of the aging who are living in poverty; that is, the states exerting greater policy efforts in the area of income maintenance are not those with the largest numbers of needy older Americans. Indeed, amount of tax relief and the income maintenance factor are both positively correlated with the median income of families whose head is over 65 years of age. At the same time, states making greater income maintenance efforts do seem to have more active aging-based interest groups. The higher levels of both advocacy and policy effort in these states apparently do not stem from having more substantial numbers of needy aging, however. Instead, they appear to flow from higher levels of socioeconomic development, fiscal capacity, political capacity and openness, and general policy liberalism.

Stepwise Regression Analysis

The patterns evident in the results of the simple correlation analysis are, rather surprisingly, only partially reflected by the results of the stepwise regression analysis. Table 6–3 presents the best regression models for explaining each of the three dependent variables that were treated in the correlation analysis. It is interesting that the lead predictor in the model for amount of tax relief and the model for the income maintenance factor is not the independent variable with the highest correlation for that dependent variable in table 6–2. This is because the stepwise regression analysis procedure can substitute one predictor for another in its search for the best combination of predictors for a given dependent variable. The best model for the circuit-breaker measure, however, is indeed anchored by the independent variable that showed the strongest correlation with that dependent variable in table 6–2—namely, union membership. Joining that socioeconomic measure in the model was the index of Elazar's (1972) political cultures. It should be noted that we decided to accept that model despite the fact that the regression coefficient for political culture did not quite achieve statistical significance beyond the .05 level. Rejecting it would have left no acceptable model for the circuit-breaker measure other than the one-variable model containing unionization only. At any rate, the proportion of variance in the circuit-breaker measure accounted for by that model was quite meager ($R^2 = .229$).

It is interesting that the political culture measure not only appeared in the best regression model for amount of tax relief for the aging but also served as the lead predictor, even though its simple correlation with the dependent variable was only moderate. Another notable feature of this model is the appearance of two separate indicators of aging-based interest group activity: the number of senior organizations supplying witnesses before the Senate Special Committee on Aging and the rating of lobbying effort by the state's chapter of the NCSC. These two measures not only appeared in the model but also made fairly substantial contributions to the explained variance in amount of tax relief. Finally, the measure of gubernatorial activity makes a barely significant and curiously inverse showing in the model. The overall proportion of variance in amount of tax relief accounted for by this model is a fairly substantial 54.6 percent. Thus, states with more generous provisions for tax relief for the aging tend to be those with more

Table 6–3
Best Regression Models for Explaining Indicators of State Income Maintenance Policies for the Aging, 1975

Dependent Variable	Independent Variables	Probability > F	R^2	Probability > F	N
Circuit-Breaker	Union Members Pol. Culture	.0217 .0527	.229	.0042	45
Tax Relief	Pol. Culture Senior Orgs. NCSC Effort Gov. Ambition (−)	.0011 .0017 .0059 .0466	.546	.0001	45
Income Maint.	Tax Effort Senior Orgs. Migration	.0001 .0017 .0017	.611	.0001	43

Moralistic political culture, higher levels of aging interest group activity, and slightly less active governors. It should be noted that this model is somewhat similar to that for the circuit-breaker measure in that both contain the political culture variable and an indicator of labor-union-related activity, for the NCSC is affiliated with local chapters of the AFL-CIO.

Finally, the best regression model for the income maintenance factor is anchored by tax effort relative to capacity and contains the senior organizations measure and the net migration rate, both of which make similar levels of contribution (substantially lower than the tax effort measure) to the explanation of the variance in the dependent variable. Again, tax effort was not the independent variable having the highest correlation with the income maintenance factor. Nonetheless, its emergence as the prime predictor of that factor serves to underscore the importance of fiscal capacity in enabling states to provide direct income support. The absence of an indicator of fiscal capacity from the two tax relief models, along with their similarity in terms of combinations of predictors, highlights the separateness of tax relief as an indirect form of support. At the same time, however, the appearance of the senior organizations measure in both the model for the income maintenance factor and that for amount of tax relief for the aging reminds us that the two dimensions are indeed related, as is most apparent in the inclusion of the tax relief measure in the income maintenance factor. The emergence of the net migration rate indicates that states with higher levels of income maintenance effort not only have higher levels of fiscal capacity and aging interest group activity but also are states that are gaining in population. This is an intriguing indication of higher levels of effort in the sunbelt region of the country rather than the snowbelt, as hinted in the correlation analysis. This combination of predictors achieves a rather substantial proportion of variance accounted for in the income maintenance factor ($R^2 = .611$).

Summary

The results of the correlation and regression analyses for the indicators of state income maintenance policy efforts for the aging as of the mid-1970s leave a somewhat confused picture of the sources of those efforts. Some similarities emerge between the patterns of relationship for the three dependent variables (earliness of adoption of a circuit-breaker tax relief program, amount of tax relief for the aging, and the composite income maintenance factor) and between the correlation and regression analyses. However, quite a few discrepancies exist among these sets of results as well. The patterns of correlation for the circuit-breaker measure suggest a slight tendency for snowbelt states to be early adopters of such provisions, while its best regression model emphasizes unionization and political culture. Amount of tax relief shows patterns of correlation similar to those for the income maintenance factor, although at weaker levels, while its regression model is in some ways similar to that for the circuit-breaker measure, emphasizing political culture and labor-union-related interest group activity among the aging (NCSC lobbying effort, along with the senior organizations measure). This regression model for the income maintenance factor also includes a measure of aging interest group activity (the senior organizations measure) but is dominated by an indicator of fiscal capacity (tax effort relative to capacity) and includes net migration rate, more characteristic of sunbelt than snowbelt states. Many of the variables included in these models, even the lead predictors, were not those having the strongest simple correlations with the dependent variables.

Despite this somewhat confusing pattern of results from the correlation and regression results, one very important finding did emerge from the examination of the patterns of interrelationships among the various indicators of state income maintenance policy for the aging as of the mid-1970s. That finding is the substantial relationship between amount of tax relief for the aging and each of the indicators of the scope of a state's SSI-Aged program. This result suggests that direct and indirect forms of assistance do not constitute separate, competing dimensions of state income maintenance policy, at least for the aging. Instead, states that exert greater effort in providing direct cash support for the aging also tend to provide the aging with more generous levels of indirect assistance.

Income Maintenance Policy over Time

As an additional dimension of explanation, results for policy indicators available for more than one time period can be compared. In the study of state policy efforts for the aging, only one indicator is available for all five time points used in the present study: average monthly state-local payment for OAA for 1955, 1960, 1965, and 1970 and for SSI for 1975. Table 6–4 presents the simple correlations between OAA-SSI and selected independent variables that were also available for most of the five time points used in this study, plus those considered to be enduring traits of the states and therefore applicable to several time points. Only variables having correlations statistically significant at the .05 level in at least one time period are shown. Average state-local

Table 6–4
Simple Correlations between Average State-Local Payment for OAA or SSI and Selected Independent Variables, 1955–1975

Independent Variable	Dependent Variables				
	OAA, 1955	OAA, 1960	OAA, 1965	OAA, 1970	SSI, 1975
Total Pop.	.200	.283[a]	.319[a]	.301[a]	.225
Indust.-Urban.	.500[c]	.468[c]	.426[c]	.286[a]	.170
Union Members	—	—	.457[c]	.304[a]	.039
Diversity	.651[d]	.679[d]	.659[d]	.590[d]	.193
Pol. Culture[e]	.554[d]	.633[d]	.637[d]	.513[d]	.024
Status	.669[d]	.632[d]	.637[d]	.649[d]	.182
Need	-.644[d]	-.703[d]	-.683[d]	-.534[d]	-.093
Scope of Govt.	.372[b]	.334[a]	.274	.344	.094
Centralization	-.458[b]	-.430[b]	-.408[b]	-.098	-.213
Gov. Power[f]	—	.380[b]	.413[b]	.372[b]	.135
Gov. Ambition	—	.146	.224	.294[a]	-.268
Legis. Profess.	.332[a]	.395[b]	.460[c]	.401[b]	.355[a]
Party Compet.[g]	.592[d]	.610[d]	.551[d]	.378[b]	.146
Voter Turnout	.567[d]	.576[d]	.509[c]	.323[a]	-.193
Senior Orgs.	—	—	.287[a]	.384[b]	.278
Tax Effort	—	.250	.325[a]	.398[b]	.293[a]
Tax Pct.	.384[b]	.365[b]	.300[a]	.240	.301[a]
AFDC Payment	.849[d]	.844[d]	.728[d]	.706[d]	.253
Innovation/General Lib[h]	.698[d]	.737[d]	.728[d]	.670[d]	.189

[a]Significant at .05.
[b]Significant at .01.
[c]Significant at .001.
[d]Significant at .0001.
[e]Measured at one time point, but considered applicable to all.
[f]The 1967 time point is used for both 1965 and 1970.
[g]The 1946–1963 measure is used for 1955, 1960, and 1965, and the 1962–1973 measure is used for 1970 and 1975.
[h]Innovation is used for 1955 and 1960, and general policy liberalism is used for 1965, 1970, and 1975.

payment for AFDC, though not conceptualized as an independent variable, is included for purposes of policy area comparisons. It should be noted that many other independent variables not included in table 6–4 because they were available for only one or two time points did have significant correlations with OAA-SSI payment. The focus here is on patterns of change over time in the significant correlations with this key indicator of state income maintenance policy.

Table 6–4 reveals that OAA-SSI payment correlates most strongly and consistently not only with most socioeconomic indicators but also with several political variables—most notably, innovativeness/general policy liberalism, party competition, and voter turnout. Several indicators of the structure and development of state government—most notably, legislative professionalism—also show fairly consistent, although somewhat weaker, correlations with OAA-SSI. Some of the political indicators that were not available for the earliest time points might also have shown rather consistent levels of relationship, although again the strength of their correlations is lower than for the socioeconomic variables. Perhaps the most notable feature of table 6–4 is the drastic drop-off in the correlations with the advent of SSI in 1975. In general, the strongest correlations appear to peak around the early 1960s and then decline into the 1970s; but still the drop-off from 1970 to 1975 is extremely abrupt. This suggests that the patterns of explanation that might have characterized OAA certainly did not continue for SSI. The only three variables to maintain significant, but very weak, correlations with SSI were legislative professionalism, tax effort relative to capacity, and tax percent of revenue. This sparse pattern suggests the importance of institutional and fiscal capacity in launching what was then a new program and shows that the changeover washed out all other previous patterns of socioeconomic and political influence over policy in that program area; that is, the states that began exerting the highest level of effort in supplementing SSI were no longer necessarily the same ones that had been paying generous levels of OAA benefits. Indeed, the familiar patterns of relationship found in most comparative state policy research, emphasizing socioeconmic development and political openness, had evaporated, leaving only institutional (specifically legislative) and fiscal capacity to associate with SSI supplement, and only at very weak levels at that.

Examination of stepwise regression analyses of OAA-SSI payment over time tends to support the patterns noted here in the correlation analysis. Table 6–5 presents the best models produced by stepwise regression analysis for explaining OAA payment in 1955, 1960, 1965, and 1970 and SSI supplement in 1975. As with the correlation analysis for these indicators, the most notable feature of table 6–5 is that the

Table 6–5
Best Regression Models for Explaining Average State-Local Payment for OAA and SSI, 1955–1975

Dependent Variable	Independent Variables	Probability > F	R²	Probability > F	N
OAA, 1955	Innovation	.0001	.747	.0001	46
	Scope of Govt.	.0001			
	Party Compet.	.0005			
	Unemployment (−)	.0071			
OAA, 1960	Innovation	.0001	.835	.0001	45
	Scope of Govt.	.0001			
	Party Compet.	.0018			
	Unemployment (−)	.0067			
	Aged Pct. Pop.	.0207			
OAA, 1965	Need (−)	.0001	.724	.0001	45
	Legis. Profess.	.0018			
	Aged Migration (−)	.0109			
	Scope of Govt.	.0155			
	Legis. Apport.	.0246			
OAA, 1970	Status	.0001	.561	.0001	45
	Aged Migration (−)	.0068			
	Senior Orgs.	.0492			
SSI, 1975	Tax Pct.	.0006	.302	.0023	44
	Union Members (−)	.0428			
	Tax Regress. (−)	.0431			

proportion of variance (R^2) in OAA-SSI payment explained by the various models is very high in the early periods, peaking in 1960 at .835, but declines steadily into the 1970s. The drop-off from 1970 to 1975 does not appear to be as drastic as in the correlation results; instead, the decline is steep but rather steady from 1960 all the way to 1975.

The models are rather complex and difficult to interpret in substantive terms. For 1955, the lead predictor is the Walker index of policy innovativeness, with two other political variables, the scope of government factor and the index of interparty competition, showing a somewhat less substantial effect, and one socioeconomic variable, the unemployment rate, having a rather weak and inverse impact. Thus, three of the four best predictors of OAA payment in 1955, and the most powerful predictors at that, are political rather than socioeconomic indicators. These predictors suggest that the states with higher levels of OAA payments in 1955 primarily had more innovative state governments but also had larger public sectors, more competitive party systems, and to a lesser extent, lower rates of unemployment. The model achieves a quite substantial proportion of variance explained (R^2) in the dependent variable, .747.

The model for OAA payment in 1960 is very similar to that for 1955, except that a fifth predictor, relative size of the elderly population, enters the model, although its influence is quite weak (but still statistically significant). Furthermore, the overall proportion of variance explained is even higher $(R^2 = .835)$. Thus, the states with higher OAA payments in 1960 apparently had more innovative state governments, larger public sectors, more competitive party systems, slightly lower rates of unemployment, and slightly larger aging populations. Political indicators continued to dominate the explanation of state income maintenance policy in 1960.

The socioeconomic need factor dominates the model for OAA payment in 1965, showing a strong inverse impact on the dependent variable. Among the other four predictors, legislative professionalism shows somewhat more of an impact than the scope of government factor, the legislative apportionment factor, or aging migrants as a percentage of the aging population. Both the latter variable and the socioeconomic need factor should be expected to have inverse effects on the dependent variable because, once again, the southern states tend to have larger groups of both needy persons and elderly migrants; yet those states also tend to have lower OAA payments. It is also not surprising that charactersitics of the state legislatures would emerge as significant explanatory factors in the mid-1960s because that is the period during which the more progressive legislatures were beginning to professionalize and reapportion themselves. Thus, states with higher OAA payment levels in 1965 tended primarily to have fewer disadvantaged groups and, to a far less extent, fewer elderly migrants in their populations, and to have more professional and well-apportioned legislatures and larger public sectors. The overall proportion of variance explained for this model ($R^2 = .724$) is somewhat lower than for the 1960 model and is even slightly lower than for the 1955 model.

In the 1970 model for OAA payment, the socioeconomic status factor replaces the socioeconomic need factor as the principal predictor, again showing by far the greatest impact on the dependent variable. Since these two factors are fairly strongly but inversely correlated at any given time point (that is, states with fewer needy groups tend to have higher levels of socioeconomic status), the influence of the status factor on OAA payment for 1970 is positive, whereas the influence of the need factor in 1965 was negative. Moreover, the effect of the status factor is slightly higher than the effect of the need factor. The number of senior organizations represented before hearings of the Senate Special Committee on Aging replaces the two legislative indicators found in the model for 1965. (Those two measures happen to be the best predictors of the senior organizations measure for 1970.) However, the contribution of that measure to the explanation of OAA payment for 1970 borders on being statistically nonsignificant. Finally, the number of aging migrants as a percentage of the aging population continues to have a weak and inverse influence on the dependent variable. Thus, states with higher levels of OAA payment in 1970 tend to be substantially higher in socioeconomic status and to have slightly fewer aging migrants but slightly more active senior organizations. The proportion of variance explained for this model, however, is considerably lower than for previous models.

Finally, the model that best explains state supplemental payment levels in 1975 under SSI for the aging, the program that succeeded OAA, reflects to a considerable extent the patterns observed in the correlation results. Once again, the radically different nature of SSI yields a vastly different set of relationships than those evolving under OAA. The change from a formula matching grant program (OAA) to one with a uniform federal floor and optional state supplements apparently invited a substantial change in the forces shaping state effort in the area of income maintenance policy. In addition, by 1975 there were decreasing numbers of potentially eligible individuals in some states because of the expansion in Social Security coverage in previous years. Thus, rather than socioeconomic status or need or overall policy innovativeness, SSI-Aged state supplemental payment in 1975 is best explained primarily by fiscal capacity measures—most notably, tax percent of revenue. Much weaker impacts on the dependent variable are registered by the index of tax regressivity (inverse) and the extent of unionization (also inverse). States with higher state supplements to SSI-Aged in 1975 therefore tended to be primarily those more willing to extract revenue in the form of taxes and, to a far less extent, those with more progressive tax structures and those with weaker labor unions. This set of predictors differs somewhat from the independent variables showing the strongest correlations with SSI-Aged state supplement in that legislative professionalism and tax effort relative to capacity, two of three variables having significant correlations with SSI-Aged (the third being tax percent of revenue), are not included in the regression model. The best explanation of SSI-Aged state supplement thus emphasizes fiscal capacity rather than institutional capacity in the launching of the new program. But the regression results confirm the correlation results in depicting the drastic shift in the patterns of relationship with state income maintenance policy wrought by the changeover from OAA to SSI. The regression results also reflect the precipitous drop in the explainability of state policy efforts in this area because the 1975 model for SSI-Aged state supplement manages a proportion of variance explained (R^2) of only .302. State income maintenance efforts for the aging appear to be increasingly difficult to explain, at least at the macro level of analysis. To the extent of explainability attained, the shift from OAA to SSI somehow apparently induced fiscal capacity to supplant the more familiar socioeconomic and political concepts as the major source of those policy efforts.

In summary, the temporal pattern of explanation for the single but important indicator of state policy effort in the area of income maintenance—namely, OAA-SSI payment—reveals a shift over time in the nature of the primary predictors of that indicator. The best regression models for both 1955 and 1960 highlight the central role of overall policy innovativeness, a political variable. In 1965 and 1970 the models are dominated by the socioeconomic need factor (inverse) and the socioeconomic status factor respectively. The models for 1955, 1960, and 1965 all contain a political capacity measure—namely, the scope of government factor—and the models for 1955 and 1960 both contain another political variable—namely, interparty competition. (These two earliest models also both contain the unemployment rate, a socioeconomic variable, as a weak and inverse predictor.) Two political measures of legislative capacity—namely, professionalism and apportionment—also make a brief appearance in the model for 1965. But the last indicator conceptualized as being political in nature that emerges in this sequence of models is the senior organizations measure in 1970, and its contribution is barely significant. Another aging-related indicator, the net migration rate for aging persons (inverse), does appear in the models for both 1965 and 1970, but it is a socioeconomic rather than a political measure.

In 1975, however, apparently induced by the shift from OAA to SSI, the contribution of both socioeconomic and political variables is virtually eliminated from the explanatory models, supplanted by two measures of state fiscal capacity—most notably, tax percent of revenue but also the index of tax regressivity (inverse). (Union membership, conceptualized as a socioeconomic variable, does make a weak but inverse contribution to the model.) Thus, one major trend in the regression results over time is a decline in the explanatory power of political variables and a rise in that of socioeconomic variables until 1975, when both types of variables are abruptly replaced by state fiscal capacity as the best explanation of state income maintenance efforts for the aging. However, the proportion of variance in those efforts that can be accounted for by the various independent variables peaks around 1960 and then declines precipitously until less than a third of the variance is explained in 1975. Of utmost importance is the apparent fact that the decline in the explanatory power of political variables and the rise in socioeconomic and then fiscal capacity measures has been accompanied by a decline in the explainability of state income maintenance policies for the aging.

Changing Patterns and Prospects

The results of our correlation and regression analysis of state income maintenance efforts for the aging, for a variety of policy indicators as of the mid-1970s and for the single but important measure of state payment levels under OAA and SSI from 1955 to 1975, suggest that the usual forces that have been shown to shape state policy in the past may be changing. Although the bulk of past research in the area of comparative state politics and public policy has rather consistently demonstrated the dominance of socioeconomic variables over political ones in explaining the cross-state variation in public policy at any given point in time, our longitudinal results indicate that political variables actually may have been more important in the past but that in more recent years they have been declining in influence. At least in the area of income maintenance policy for the aging, overall policy innovativeness was the dominant influence in 1955 and 1960. Thus, states with higher levels of OAA payments were primarily those that were quicker to adopt new policy initiatives in a wide variety of policy areas (Walker 1969) In 1965, legislative characteristics (notably, professionalism but also apportionment) briefly emerged as significant contributors to the explanation of OAA payment, replacing innovativeness. Two additional political variables—namely, the scope of government factor and interparty competition—also made substantial contributions to those early models. By 1965, however, the socioeconomic variables were already dominating the explanation of state income maintenance efforts for the aging, with the need factor (inverse) in 1965 and the status factor in 1970 making the largest contributions; that is, the states with relatively few disadvantaged groups and relatively more advantaged groups tended to make greater efforts in this policy area.

By 1975, with the shift from OAA to SSI, fiscal capacity measures clearly emerged as the most important forces shaping state policy effort in the area of state income maintenance policies for the aging. Not only the best regression model for state SSI-Aged payment in 1975, in which tax percent of revenue was the dominant predictor and the tax regressivity index was also included, but also the model for the broader income maintenance factor, in which tax effort relative to capacity was most important, displayed this important emphasis. This shift in the patterns of relationship with OAA-SSI is supported by the simple correlation analysis over time, which revealed that the only three indicators to maintain significant (though rather weak) correlations with SSI in 1975 as well as with OAA in the earlier periods were measures of fiscal and institutional capacity: tax effort relative to capacity, tax percent of revenue, and legislative professionalism.

An equally important feature of these results over time is the precipitous decline in the strength of the relationships with the various indicators of state income maintenance effort for the aging. Both the correlations between those indicators and the various socioeconomic and political measures conceptualized as independent variables, and the proportion of variance in each of the dependent variable policy measures accounted for by its best stepwise regression model, tend to peak around 1960 and then decline steadily but precipitously until 1975, with the drop-off being particularly pronounced for the last time period. The correspondence between this decline in the explainability of state income maintenance efforts for the aging and the decline in the explanatory power of political variables, coupled with the rise in the explanatory power of socioeconomic indicators and then measures of fiscal capacity, could signal an extremely important shift in the determinants of public policy in the states. This temporal pattern could be interpreted as representing the decay of traditional political institutions and processes as important influences on the making of public policy.

In their place may be developing the processes of subgovernment politics and policymaking so characteristic of nonfiscal policy areas, primarily regulatory policies, as discussed in previous chapters. On the one hand, such processes involve less visible and hence less measurable patterns of influence, primarily because they involve lower stakes for major interests (although very high stakes for the regulated interests). Policies involving large amounts of expenditure, on the other hand, have typically been characterized by wider conflict over limited revenues among numerous powerful interests with high stakes in the outcome of the conflict. It could be that expenditure-based policy is becoming more like regulatory policy in the patterns of influence that shape it. This would certainly not be due to any lowering of the stakes involved, and the scope and intensity of conflict over limited resources is assuredly increasing rather than decreasing as budget surpluses disappear in this era of austerity.

The key to this change may be the emergence in recent years of advocacy as a significant determinant of expenditure-based state policy effort, at least in the area of aging. As our case studies in chapter 3 suggested, lobbying by aging-based interest groups at the state level did not really get started in earnest until the 1970s. Furthermore, while such lobbying has typically focused on social services, it may have begun to have spillover effects in the area of income maintenance. Although our aggregate measures of such advocacy activity are certainly limited, the appearance of the senior organizations measure in the best regression models for both OAA for 1970 and the income maintenance factor for 1975 (although not for SSI-Aged in 1975) may be a hint that advocacy is emerging as an important force in state policymaking, at least in the area of aging. Advocacy may indeed be serving to undermine the stabler patterns of socioeconomic and political influence by cross cutting the processes by which traditional political institutions shape public policy. Thus, as aging-related interest groups develop their capacity to engage in effective advocacy, they may increasingly be able to circumvent the institutional constraints and forces that have traditionally dictated the form and content of state policy efforts for the aging.

The results of our analysis also reveal an increasingly important constraint that may be more difficult to overcome—namely, state fiscal capacity. Within the bounds of this powerful force, however, advocacy just might come to have an increasing impact in the future, not through traditional political institutions and processes but through the backdoor avenues of subgovernment politics and policymaking. This strategy could wield considerable leverage on behalf of the aging in the area of state income maintenance policy in light of our finding that direct and indirect forms of assistance are not separate, competing dimensions of that policy area, at least for the aging. Instead, states that exert greater effort in providing direct cash support for the aging (OAA-SSI) also tend to provide the aging with more generous levels of indirect assistance (tax relief). Thus, advocacy efforts on behalf of the aging might succeed in boosting the levels of state effort in both types of support rather than merely causing a trade-off between them. Of course, such optimism must be tempered by recognition of the severe constraints on state fiscal capacity likely to be imposed by continued economic stagnation, particularly in those states that traditionally have been most generous in providing assistance to the aging.

7

Regulatory Protection

State regulatory policies have an impact on the lives of the aging in increasingly diverse ways. Although the aging are often not the only segment of the population with interests in a given issue, they have a major stake in policy areas such as employment opportunities, drug costs, utility rates, and housing industry regulation. The uncertainties being expressed in Washington, D.C., in the 1980s over the use of federal regulatory provisions also increase the significance of possible state action. In an era of likely budgetary constraints, regulatory policies seem particularly destined to attract attention because of their potential for allowing public officials to show some responsiveness to key clientele groups—and without increasing direct financial outlays.

In this chapter, we examine both past patterns and future prospects for state regulatory action. The record on past regulatory efforts such as generic drug substitution laws, consumer-oriented provisions for improved operations of the funeral and hearing aid industries, job discrimination, and public guardianship protection provides a basis for identifying several patterns of regulatory policy activity and evaluating future prospects.

Dimensions of Regulatory Policy

Regulatory policies affecting the aging in recent years have varied on several dimensions. These include the nature of the policy design, the scope of conflict, and the magnitude of the likely impact. A brief review of major characteristics provides a basis for subsequent empirical analysis of the resulting patterns of policy development.

Age Discrimination

State interest in age discrimination legislation substantially predates the initial federal involvement in 1967. Legislative action to protect older workers (initially defined as persons between age 40 or 45 and age 65) emerged in the late 1950s along with other aspects of the nation's slowly developing interest in problems of the aging. Passage

of age discrimination legislation occurred primarily in the late 1950s
and early 1960s, and by 1967 (when federal protection for those between the ages of 40 and 65 was established) some 23 states had enacted provisions against age discrimination. Few of these enactments
appear to have been surrounded by substantial controversy, perhaps
in part because they were not often followed by aggressive enforcement
efforts. In addition, although the potential impact was broad, no one
industry was intensely motivated to oppose initial passage.

Another wave of interest in job discrimination issues took place in
the mid-1970s with a push for the elimination of nonmandatory retirement prior to age 70. California was the first state in the nation to pass
nonmandatory retirement legislation for private sector as well as public
sector employees, with legislation predating the 1978 amendments to
the 1967 federal law. Several other states, including Maine and Florida,
were leaders in eliminating mandatory retirement for public employees. Congress then moved rather quickly to establish a federal minimum age of 70 as the age to which most public and private sector
employees could work without termination on the basis of age. Some
states have continued to experiment with provisions that are more
generous than the federal law, however, in either eliminating mandatory retirement for those of any age or by including some of the few
remaining groups that are excluded in the present federal legislation.
At points in the 1970s and, in particular, before the federal legislation
in 1978, state age discrimination policy controversies were fairly intense
(Walker and Lazer 1978, pp. 27–31). In Maine, for example, the elimination of age requirements for state employees became a hotly contested issue in the early 1970s.

Generic Drugs

Conflicts involving proposed changes in laws governing the use of generic drugs have been quite intense in a number of states during the
past decade. Technically, the movement for the use of generic drugs
involved an effort to repeal the legislation that had quickly passed the
states in the 1930s and 1940s to prevent substitution in the sale of
prescription drugs and thus the opportunity for unwarranted profits by
druggists who substituted a lower cost drug without either alerting the
customer or passing along the price advantage. In 1972, Kentucky
became the first state to repeal its antisubstitution law; it passed a bill
that allowed pharmacists to substitute generic drugs if they were included on a list of generics approved by a state drug formulary council.
New Hampshire followed in 1973, along with Florida and Minnesota

in 1974, and some 45 states had enacted some legislation allowing the use of generic drugs by 1979 (Silverman et al. 1981).

The generic drug controversy has clearly involved large stakes for various parties to the conflict. For all consumers, per capita expenditures on drugs had exceeded $60 annually by 1976, and the allocations for aging consumers were substantially higher. Overall, Americans, by the late 1970s, were allocating almost 1 percent of the gross national product (GNP) for drug expenditures. Savings to the consumer on generic drugs could in turn be quite substantial, with some wholesale prices for generic drugs running less than 10 percent of the price of comparable brand name drugs (see Silverman and Lee 1974, p. 334). Since about three-fourths of the drugs presently on the market are being sold under patent, however, major savings cannot be achieved in all prescription areas. Silverman and Lee (1974), taking an initially optimistic perspective, saw total consumer savings of a quarter of a billion dollars as of the early 1970s. (For a somewhat less optimistic view expressed more recently, see Silverman et al. 1981).

The economic stakes were also enormous from the perspective of the drug industry. Historically, U.S. drug firms have been among the most profitable enterprises in the country. They have also used major and expensive promotional campaigns in their efforts to sell new brand name drugs. The prospect of generic drug use and the resulting price competition would clearly stand to disrupt established practices. It is thus not surprising, as reported in Silverman and Lee (1974, p. 166), that as one Kentucky legislator viewed the fight over his state's proposed new approach to generic drugs, he concluded that a bomb in the state capitol would wipe out half the pharmaceutical vice-presidents in the country. High stakes were clearly producing substantial conflict.

Funeral Industry Practices

Interest in reform of the funeral industry emerged sporadically in many states in the 1960s and somewhat more substantially in the 1970s and 1980s. The staunch assault on industry practices by Mitford (1963) was followed by an increasing amount of concern and lobby activity. The sheer size of the funeral industry would seem to justify that concern. As of the late 1970s, $2.35 billion was spent directly on funerals, another $1.75 billion on cemetery charges, and at least $1.3 billion on related expenses, for a total of $6.4 billion being spent on funeral costs, according to estimates by the Federal Trade Commission's (FTC) Consumer Protection Bureau (1978a).

The evolution of funeral regulations prior to the 1970s had been a fairly typical example of a trade association using regulatory processes for the purposes of protecting public health, enhancing the prestige of practitioners, and reducing opportunities for competition. An industry with some 20,000 funeral homes and over 50,000 licensees was regulated by state boards that were almost invariably composed of individuals from within the industry, and both state regulations and common practices of the industry served to reduce effective price competition. Through the National Funeral Directors Association (NFDA), which led the fight for expanded regulation early in this century, the directors had a trade association whose members conducted between 70 and 75 percent of all funerals and memorial services in the nation. The separate organization of black morticians into the National Funeral Directors and Morticians Association (NFDMA), the growth of a small Federated Funeral Directors Association (FFDA) that desired price competition, and the emergence of various memorial societies seeking greater ease in organizing crematory programs did little to undermine the hegemony of the NFDA as a spokesman for the funeral industry.

Interest in funeral industry reform has focused in recent years on four basic issues. First, reformers have pursued requirements allowing customers to consider specific needs from a range of potential services. Second, considerable emphasis has been placed on the availability of price information through measures like required telephone disclosure of prices. Third, reformers have sought to remove restrictive provisions that work against nontraditional approaches to funerals and the handling of last remains. In some states, for example, embalming has been required even when a body was to be cremated, and many states have placed trust requirements on memorial societies at levels that make it difficult to generate funds to build a larger organization. (Not surprisingly, NFDA spokesmen have been frequent leaders on both of these provisions.) Fourth, there has been some interest in expanding nonindustry membership of funeral boards. This thrust has occurred in a context in which no state has placed a majority of nonindustry members on its board and in which the only states with more than 20 percent nonindustry representation were California (38 percent), Colorado (43 percent), Delaware (29 percent), Mississippi (29 percent), North Dakota (25 percent), South Dakota (38 percent), and Wisconsin (25 percent). Despite a decade of reform interest, assessments of state legislation as of 1978 found that in comparing present requirements with the initially proposed FTC rule, only about 5 percent of those proposed provisions had been enacted in the states (see FTC 1978a, p. 103).

Hearing Aid Industry Practices

Controversies over hearing aid industry regulation also occurred fairly often in the 1970s. A variety of consumer groups, as well as aging-related interest groups, began examining an industry that had grown rather quietly to significant proportions and that affected both the 650,000 individuals buying hearing aids annually by the mid-1970s and potentially the 14.5 million persons estimated to suffer from hearing problems. It is not surprising that the aging-based interest groups took some interest in the issue, since estimates show approximately 30 percent of the nation's 20 million older persons to have hearing impairments and since a substantial proportion could profit from the use of hearing aids (see FTC 1978b, pp. 19–20).

The practices uncovered in initial investigations were highly discomforting in terms of both the level of medical attention being provided at the time of sale and the opportunities for exploitation of potential customers. Hearing aid salespersons had minimal training, existing training emphasized primarily sales techniques, few opportunities for consumer complaints were available, and instances of inadequate diagnosis were widespread. The cases of abuse documented in one of Ralph Nader's Public Interest Group reports (Public Citizen's Retired Professional Action Group 1973) and the analysis by the FTC's Consumer Protection Bureau (1978b) were painfully numerous. The title of the Nader Report, *Paying Through the Ear,* seemed all too apt.

The reform agenda for hearing aid legislation has been articulated both by some interest groups and more recently by the FTC in its positions on trade regulation rules. One major issue has been the establishment of a trial period after which a hearing aid could be returned. This has been emphasized by reformers because of the too-frequent impact of high pressure sales techniques and/or improper diagnosis. A second key reform has involved provisions for examination prior to the sale of a hearing aid by either audiologists or doctors with expertise in ear problems. In addition, reform efforts among the states have included educational and continuing education requirements and provisions for more accurate advertising. The hearing aid industry, including related segments like manufacturers of batteries, has fought intensively against the new regulations. After Minnesota established a fairly broad requirement for audiologist exams, for example, the next issues of the *Hearing Aid Journal* urged strong action to prevent disruption of the industry and loss of dealer control over sales practices. The possibility that the dealers would, in their eyes, also lose in most states or through a tougher Federal Trade Commission rule remains in question.

Public Guardianship

Interest in the use of public guardianship for the aging has emerged in recent years due in part to the recognition that institutionalization of the aging has at points occurred when a combination of less intensive services, including guardianship, would constitute a more humane public policy. Because of past abuses, guardianship laws have provoked substantial criticism. Although the advocacy effort has not been as extensive as in many other aging-related policy areas, some interest has been expressed by the aging-based lobbies, spokesmen for legal aid programs, and agency personnel in social service organizations and state and local units on aging.

The major reform thrusts have been toward rationalizing procedures, protecting individual rights through due process and procedures for review, and intensifying provisions that reduce the possibility that individuals will personally profit from their role as guardian. Model statutes for the states have thus emerged as individual-rights-oriented standards against which recent reform efforts, or the lack of response, can be measured. Those issues are extensively reviewed by Schmidt et al. (1979). Guardianship, along with age discrimination, generic drugs, and funeral and hearing aid industry regulation, thus constitutes a substantial range of regulatory policies affecting the aging.

Underlying Issues

Studies of regulatory policies have only begun to explore the factors that lead to differences in state-level commitments. Nonetheless, interpretations in several recent works can provide a basis for explorations of major regulatory areas. In addition, the study of state regulatory policies is creating important opportunities for the development of expanded approaches to the measurement of those multifaceted endeavors.

The most general study of state regulatory policies in the area of consumer-oriented legislation was undertaken by Sigelman and Smith (1980). They examined a range of some 28 different consumer protection policies in existence as of 1974, including mobile home construction, eyeglasses advertising, and opportunities for the sale of generic drugs. From this broad range of policies, the authors found that larger,

more urbanized states, and states with better educated and more prosperous citizens, are more likely to enact consumer protection laws.
Their strongest socioeconomic predictor was median family income.
Two political factors also had a strong statistical impact. The impact
of differences in political cultures could be seen in the tendency for
the Traditionalistic states (as defined by Elazar 1972) to act less rapidly.
The measure of legislative professionalism showed a strong positive
influence on consumer protection. Thus, when a large number of regulatory measures covering a variety of clientele groups are examined
collectively, a pattern emerges that can be explained fairly well with a
combination of socioeconomic and political variables.

Another major contribution to the study of state regulatory policies
has emerged in the work of Gormley (1983). This research proposes a
theoretical orientation for the analysis of regulatory policies through
the development of several typologies of regulatory policy and policymaking patterns. Although not all of the types of regulatory policies
that Gormley identifies are present in the policies that have been examined in this study, the two dimensions Gormley uses for his typologies can be used to help interpret the differences among the states in
regulatory policy effort for the elderly. These two dimensions are the
degree of complexity that the policy issue presents and the salience of
the issue for major groups in a state.

Several of the issues being raised throughout this book are also
relevant for the assessment of regulatory policies. Among the respective components of our overall model, several questions stand out.
Regarding socioeconomic conditions, is there an indication that greater
complexity in society, as is generally assumed to occur with urbanization, leads to more extensive regulatory activity (see Ellul 1967)? As
for the characteristics of the older population, it is important to consider the extent to which larger numbers of older persons, and their
financial conditions, may be associated with more extensive regulatory
policy efforts. Finally, regulatory policies for the aging raise important
questions about the possible impact of political culture. Is there a tendency for regulatory policies for the aging to correlate with other efforts to use state government more extensively as part of a pattern of
general policy liberalism, or are these efforts fairly unique?

The study of regulatory policy is now increasingly being undertaken with an extensive set of measures. These include earliness of
adoption, provisions for nonindustry representation on regulatory
boards, and the scope of protection being granted. The importance of
date of adoption has been borne out by the usefulness of the Walker
(1969) innovation index. For our analysis, speed of adoption proved
to be a useful measure for age discrimination legislation, generic drug

substitution provisions, and the establishment of provisions regulating the hearing aid industry. Dates are available for initial regulation of the funeral industry, but they often reflect a public health rather than a consumer protection approach so that date of initial legislation does not necessarily show the beginning of consumer protection interests. Similarly, dates of adoption for guardianship laws do not necessarily reflect an interest in codifying the patient rights dimensions.

The importance of examining non-industry-related board memberships is also increasingly apparent. In an extensive study of the impact of drug price regulation, Cady (1975) found that the amount of consumer representation on state pharmaceutical boards had a significant impact in reducing drug costs. In addition, while some have argued (see FTC 1978b) that nonindustry representatives tend to be intimidated by technical experts and thus usually ineffective, the measure of nonindustry representation can also be viewed as an indication of the level of responsiveness to a practical step that has been frequently advocated by the aging-related consumer movement. We have thus included the composition of regulatory boards in the two cases in which they occur: the funeral industry and the hearing aid industry.

The basic strategy involved in assessing the scope of regulatory policy is to measure the range of provisions enacted but to discount provisions established for public health rather than consumer protection purposes. A second strategy is to examine independently the provisions that have had the greatest weight in the consumer protection controversies. We have been guided by the recent reform agenda, as discussed in the previous section, in the coding process. Thus, for funeral regulation, it is essential to discount the provisions that pertain primarily to industry-related interests in establishing, for example, provisions for particular sizes of facilities, which have the primary purpose of restricting competition. Measures of the scope of consumer-oriented legislation were thus created for each of our five policy areas. The study of regulatory policy for the aging, in sum, offers opportunities for the use of important new approaches to measurement as well as the examination of basic theoretical issues.

Findings

The analyses we have undertaken to examine regulatory policy efforts include both simple correlations and stepwise regressions. As in previous chapters, we begin by reporting the results and then relate those findings to major theoretical issues.

Simple Correlations

The simple correlations among the aging-related regulatory policies show a surprising absence of common underlying regulatory efforts among the states. As suggested by table 7-1, there is no general dimension of regulatory protection policy for the aging; the only significant correlations occurred within the subareas of aging-related consumer protection policies rather than among different subareas. None of the correlations between the subareas was significant; thus, states that have strong policies in a subarea like generic drugs do not necessarily have strong policies for age discrimination or funeral industry regulation. It is thus not surprising that factor analysis could not reduce these multiple indicators of consumer protection policy for the aging to a single dimension.

Table 7-2 presents the simple correlations between each of the characteristics of aging-related consumer protection policy and a variety of socioeconomic and political variables for the states. The patterns of correlation in the table indicate that the policy variables had differing levels of relationship to the independent variables. In general, measures of the scope of state regulatory legislation were more often and more substantially related to the macrolevel characteristics of states than were measures of earliness of adoption of legislation or measures of regulatory board composition. As for the policy subgroups, age discrimination had the most and largest significant correlations, with generic drug substitution and hearing aid regulation next. It is interesting that the latter subarea's significant correlations (and most of its nonsignificant correlations) were all negative, except with the socioeconomic need factor, which is a negative indicator. Funeral industry regulation had fewer significant correlations, and public guardianship had none at all.

Regarding the independent variables, AARP size, party competition, general policy liberalism, and socioeconomic status had the most frequent and the strongest correlations, largely with age discrimination, generic drug substitution, and hearing aid regulation policies. The indicators of socioeconomic need among the elderly (income and poverty) had the highest correlations (along with the general policy liberalism factor) with the scope of age discrimination legislation but had only one other significant correlation, a negative one between aging income and early adoption of hearing aid regulation. Percentage of the population age 65 and over had a significant correlation only with scope of funeral regulation, which also had the only significant correlations with total population size, scope of state government, and legislative professionalism. The industrialization-urbanization factor

Table 7-1
Simple Correlations among Dependent Variables: Regulatory Protection, 1975

	ADEA Scope	ADEA Age	Generic Scope	Generic Age	Hearing Scope	Hearing Age	Hearing Board	Funeral Scope	Funeral Board
ADEA Age	.428[a]								
Generic Scope	.110	.085							
Generic Age	.210	.087	.665[b]						
Hearing Scope	.008	-.115	.027	-.033					
Hearing Age	.016	-.181	.043	-.141	.690[b]				
Hearing Board	-.095	-.247	.010	-.040	.579[b]	.436[a]			
Funeral Scope	-.008	-.066	.111	.146	.066	.233	.063		
Funeral Board	.004	.261	.167	.129	-.024	-.096	.078	-.037	
Guardianship	-.014	-.025	-.095	.122	.051	.033	.067	-.079	.214

[a]Significant at .01.
[b]Significant at .0001.

Table 7-2
Simple Correlations between Dependent and Independent Variables: Regulatory Protection, 1975

Independent Variable	Dependent Variables									
	ADEA Scope	ADEA Age	Generic Scope	Generic Age	Hearing Scope	Hearing Age	Hearing Board	Funeral Scope	Funeral Board	Guardianship
Total Pop.	.158	.176	-.031	.105	-.139	-.044	-.132	.397b	.077	-.098
Indust.-Urban.	.328a	.366b	-.062	.141	-.090	-.161	-.029	.243	-.119	-.030
Status	.409b	.352a	.173	.122	-.361b	-.351a	-.157	.076	.180	-.010
Need	-.320a	-.176	-.290a	-.162	.348a	.220	.099	-.139	-.093	-.045
Aged Pct. Pop.	-.161	-.151	.149	.216	.213	.184	.103	.279a	-.013	-.173
Aged Income	.492c	.238	.023	.049	-.254	-.317a	-.069	-.009	.168	-.044
Aged Pov. Pct.	-.508c	-.257	-.218	-.222	.273	.230	.072	-.286a	-.148	.011
Scope of Govt.	.138	.044	-.108	-.095	-.054	-.200	.011	-.305a	.065	-.159
Gov. Power	.056	.151	.152	.072	-.160	-.191	-.145	.163	.066	-.046
Gov. Ambition	.222	.152	.190	.026	.047	.049	-.019	.183	.018	-.076
Gov. Reputation	.206	.164	.093	.040	-.076	-.021	-.148	.134	-.066	-.160
Legis. Profess.	.229	.263	.009	.131	-.090	-.062	-.110	.332a	.144	-.110
SUA Status	.047	-.028	-.168	-.094	.132	.087	.041	.081	-.177	.157
Voter Turnout	.203	.156	.340a	.233	-.139	-.181	-.022	.139	.193	-.039
Party Compet.	.426b	.110	.373b	.350a	-.279a	-.214	-.040	.264	.146	-.031
AARP Members	.346a	.184	.337a	.345a	-.296a	-.313a	-.162	.097	.175	.053
NCSC Effort	.255	.235	.067	.356a	.004	-.123	.021	.192	-.003	-.131
General Lib.	.500c	.522c	.397b	.400b	-.247	-.275	-.166	.180	.166	-.144

aSignificant at .05.
bSignificant at .01.
cSignificant at .001.

correlated only with the two indicators of age discrimination legislation; the socioeconomic need factor correlated only with scope of age discrimination legislation and hearing aid regulation (positively); and the rating of NCSC lobbying effort correlated only with earliness of adoption of generic drug substitution. Overall, the scarcity and weakness of significant correlations suggest that aging-related consumer protection policies in the states have limited relationships with macro level state characteristics.

Regression Analysis

The regression equations that emerge for our regulatory measures, while they do not typically produce very strong relationships, are revealing on several issues. As shown in table 7–3, there tends to be an R^2 of .3 to .4 for each of the regulatory policy measures.

Turning first to the scope of age discrimination legislation, one finds a regression model for 1965 that has an R^2 of .43. Although it would seem unfortunate that only one variable enters this equation, the emphasis that emerges on the importance of general policy liberalism in a state does represent a theoretically satisfactory result. General policy liberalism also emerges as the sole predictor in a one-variable model in 1975, but the ability to explain falls to only .26. For 1955, a one-variable model also emerges, with industrialization-urbanization as the best predictor but with an R^2 of merely .18. The best explanation of age discrimination in employment legislation thus comes in 1965, utilizing the general policy liberalism factor in state politics.

On generic drug legislation, a fairly substantial degree of overlap between the equations emerges for the scope and speed of adoption. Political culture enters the equation for scope, while general policy liberalism enters the equation for speed of adoption. Unemployment makes a contribution on both. It is interesting that for speed of adoption, aging poor enters, along with population change, while for scope, reliance on the property tax also enters, negatively.

Funeral industry regulation, rather interestingly, shows some relationship to the characteristics of the aging population. The size of the aging population contributes to the scope of funeral regulation, while aging migration contributes to board composition. However, aging population change (in percentage terms) has an inverse effect in the equation that explains board composition. In addition, the centralization measure works against scope, but legislative professionalism contributes to board composition, along with income change.

Hearing aid industry regulation produces regression equations that

Table 7-3
Best Regression Models for Explaining Selected Indicators of State Regulatory Policies for the Aging, 1975

Dependent Variable	Independent Variables	Probability > F	R²	Probability > F	N
ADEA Scope, 1955	Indust.-Urban.	.0030	.184	.0030	46
ADEA Scope, 1965	General Lib.	.0001	.431	.0001	45
ADEA Scope, 1975	General Lib.	.0003	.260	.0003	45
Generic Scope	Pol. Culture Unemployment Tax Percent (−)	.0002 .0080 .0406	.314	.0013	45
Generic Age	General Lib. Aged Poor Pop. Change Unemployment	.0002 .0035 .0384 .0542	.396	.0004	45
Funeral Scope	Centralization (−) Aged Pct. Pop.	.0002 .0259	.339	.0002	45
Funeral Board	Aged Pct. Change (−) Aged Migration Income Change Legis. Profess.	.0010 .0033 .0175 .0217	.334	.0027	45
Hearing Scope	Union Members (−) Unemployment Gov. Ambition Scope of Govt. (−)	.0016 .0033 .0147 .0224	.324	.0030	45
Hearing Age	Aged Pop. Change Unemployment Scope of Govt.	.0016 .0018 .0076	.380	.0002	45
Hearing Board	Aged Pop. Change Voter Turnout Aged Poor	.0003 .0063 .0293	.318	.0012	45
Guardianship	Scope of Govt. (−) Aged Pop. Change (−) Pop. Change Pol. Culture	.0008 .0044 .0149 .0455	.345	.0017	45

have modest R^2 values but a few interesting relationships. In particular, for both speed of adoption and board composition, there is an apparent impact from size of the aging population. In looking at the states in which that increase has occurred (see table 2–2), it is useful to recall that this includes a number of relatively small states in the plains and mountain sections of the nation and areas in which the range of hearing aid regulatory activity has been fairly strong. Aged poor, it should be noted, also enters the equation for board composition. Thus, these regression equations suggest that the proportion of older people in a state's population may make a difference in its level of hearing aid industry regulation. At the same time, however, the other measures that enter are somewhat puzzling. Unemployment level enters for two of the measures, unionization enters one measure inversely, and rather curiously, scope of government enters but with a positive coefficient in one instance and negative value in the other.

Finally, regarding guardianship, political culture again contributes, along with population growth, but rather curiously, size of older population has an inverse effect. This relationship occurs in part, one suspects, because of the negative correlation between culture and size of older population. In addition, scope of government enters, this time negatively. On the basis of the correlation and regression analyses, it is possible to consider more general patterns in the evolution of regulatory protection for the aging.

Patterns

State regulatory policymaking for the aging does not produce a high level of uniformity in levels of activity in a given state. Strong actions on job discrimination policies, for example, do not necessarily mean that a state will also have a strong record on generic drug substitution laws. It is rather striking that this lack of uniformity among different regulatory areas affecting the aging is much more pronounced than the pattern that occurs for regulatory policies across a broader range of clientele groups (see Sigelman and Smith 1980).

Turning first to socioeconomic factors, the more urban and industrial, or the wealthiest, states do not consistently emerge as consistent leaders. A number of the early adopters rather persistently have been fairly small and relatively less developed states. On generic drug laws, for example, Kentucky and New Hampshire were among the first states, and on hearing aid regulations the more rural states tended to predominate in the early and more substantial responses. There is little support, in sum, for the view (Ellul 1967) that increased complexity in society will directly produce increases in regulatory activity.

The characteristics of the older population produce impacts that, while not very extensive, are nonetheless suggestive of some political responsiveness to conditions of the aging. It should be emphasized here that our case study analysis of policy development in Florida showed a level of interest in regulatory policies that surpassed the attention being given to those issues in many other states. In the simple correlations, the only statistically significant correlation with the percentage of the population age 65 and over was for the scope of funeral industry regulation, and in several instances the simple correlations were negative. In the regression analyses, however, predictors of stronger effects included changes in the aged population in several instances. A more slowly growing older population was associated with public guardianship protection and public representatives on funeral boards. Conversely, a more rapidly growing older population was associated with the two measures of consumer protection in relationship to the hearing aid industry. Thus, the characteristics of the older population may make a difference, but not with a consistent nudge in particular directions of policy effort.

Regarding political influences, the respective policy areas show some different relationships. Either political culture or general policy liberalism enter for age discrimination, both generic drug measures, and guardianship. Conversely, in terms of the impact of more specific measures of capacity, openness, and lobbying activity, the relationships are very limited. Turnout does relate to hearing aid board composition, and legislative professionalism relates to funeral board composition. Overall, however, the predominant thrust of the regression equations for the funeral and hearing aid regulatory efforts shows an absence of a measurable impact from most political factors.

The frequently rather weak findings in the correlation and regression analyses, combined with recent theoretical writings, suggest that it may be useful to consider differences in state uses of regulatory policy in another way. To a surprising extent, some states not normally known for innovativeness will rank near the top of any given list of adopters of a particular innovation. It thus seems useful to view regulatory policy innovation on the basis of two types of adopters: traditional innovators and mavericks. Several factors that increase the likelihood that a given regulatory policy reform will include some of each among its stronger performers can be identified. (For a listing of state dates of adoption of major regulatory policies, see tables 2–3 and 2–4.)

The traditional innovators are states that over time have had strong records in their general tendency to innovate. This is reflected in high scores on the initial Walker innovation index and high scores on political culture measures focusing on a willingness to use the public sector more extensively. These states are also more likely to have substantial capacity in their public sectors, as indicated by the relationship to legislative professionalism. In addition, the traditional innovators are apt to have larger populations, to be more industrialized, and to have higher levels of personal income than less innovative states. Frequent representatives in this category include, for example, California, Massachusetts, Minnesota, New York, Oregon, and Wisconsin, followed by a second group of states possessing some, but not necessarily all, of these characteristics.

The potential maverick states lack aspects of both the political capacity and the tendency to use the public sector that are associated with the traditional innovators. These states are also more likely to be smaller and less prosperous than the traditionally innovative states. Regarding the lack of an active political tradition, Florida would be a good example, while the lack of capacity would be reflected by small states such as New Hampshire and Maine. However, each potential maverick state did emerge as a leading innovator on a specific issue. Florida and New Hampshire were among the leaders in the early establishment of generic drug substitution laws, and Maine was a leader in the movement toward nonmandatory retirement. The relatively low correlations with socioeconomic characteristics on a number of the regulatory measures provide one indication that there are, in fact, tendencies for regulatory issues to produce groupings that include states with fairly diverse characteristics among the leaders.

It is thus necessary to consider whether there may be differences in the likelihood that traditionally innovative states will predominate on a given issue. The traditionally innovative states do have substantial advantages on many proposed innovations in regulatory policy. This may account in part for the results reported by Sigelman and Smith (1980) in which a combination of some 28 different policy areas produced a pattern of correlations basically suggesting that the traditional innovators were predominating. In traditionally innovative states, the capacity for policy development is apt to be a major advantage, particularly on the complex policy issues. A dramatic example here is the role of public utility commissions in the traditionally innovative states. As reviewed by Anderson (1981) and Weiss (1981), the capacity for handling complex issues makes a handful of states such as California, New York, and Wisconsin the states to which others look for policy cues. Generic drug substitution would stand to some extent as a similar example among the issues we have considered. The traditionally innovative states are also apt to manifest significant interest group activities, and possibly an active level of party support, if there is a substantial amount of conflict. The attitudes in the electorate are also apt to be somewhat more supportive of new policy initiatives.

Despite their advantages, however, the traditionally innovative states may not be leaders on some issues. A key aspect involved in those periodic delays appears to be the high stakes involved for key interests. If California or New York takes a new policy step, for example, there is a realization that considerable interest will develop in other states as well. Thus, controversies over funeral industry regulation in California or generic drugs in New York are apt to produce extensive lobbying activity, including interest group actions from outside the state in some instances. The high stakes may thus lead to levels of controversy that will slow down the development of a new regulation in some of the traditionally innovative states. It should be emphasized that the correlations with the scope of protection, more than with the date of first enactment, tend to be significant for characteristics that are more extensive in the traditionally innovative states. Once they do act, the traditionally innovative states may also act more comprehensively. A good illustration of this phenomenon would be the development of the nation's toughest generic drug law in New York—but five years after the initial legislation had been passed in Kentucky and after New Hampshire and Arkansas had taken some action.

The potential mavericks possess characteristics that periodically elevate them to the ranks of an early regulatory innovator on specific issues. In part, the stakes may be substantially smaller and thus may not generate the level of opposition that occurs in the more populous states. Second, a number of the regulatory reforms that the states have been undertaking are relatively simple and do not require extensive analytic capacity prior to their enactment or extensive implementation roles once adopted. Placing an additional consumer representative on a board or stating that a certain type of exam must be given for hearing aids is a fairly simple task. Third, there may be opportunities for significant action by a few persons, or even an individual, to be effective in the often more informal policy processes of some of these states. In the development of legislation eliminating age requirements for the mandatory retirement of state employees in Maine, for example, the actions of a few leaders in the legislature were critical to that early adoption. Fourth, the tight budgets that less affluent states often confront may make it attractive for a political leader to instigate a regulatory step in the absence of initiatives that require substantial tax dollars. It is useful to recall here that on the adoption of regulations pertaining to nursing home reimbursement, there were some indications that poor states had a greater tendency than wealthier states to develop some type of rate reform.

The mix of traditional innovators and potential mavericks thus seems likely to vary from one policy area to another. Those that raise high levels of controversy and are quite complex are apt, over a several-year period, to find the traditionally innovative states having fairly strong responses. In the initial enactments involving most regulatory policy, however, some potential mavericks do emerge. From this perspective, one might expect to find that future regulatory protection controversies will involve somewhat different potential for different types of states. What, then, is that agenda, and how do past conflict patterns help one in developing an interpretation of potentials for action?

Prospects

Opportunities for expanded use of regulatory policies are emerging on both several of the policies that emerged in the 1970s and on major new issues. Among the issues we have examined for earlier years, funeral industry regulation and, to a less extent, generic drug substitution laws seem likely to produce additional interest. There are also likely new areas of regulatory interest, including the increasingly debated issue of utility rates. Some of the new issues fall quite nicely into our categorization of responses on the basis of traditionally innovative states and mavericks, and we consider these before reviewing responses in the areas of generic drugs and funeral industry regulation.

The impact of changes in utility costs on the elderly may well be the most important regulatory issue to emerge in the 1980s. Initially, this issue surrounded the rapid increases in the costs of gas and electricity that began in the mid-1970s. In the wake of the Supreme Court decision requiring the break-up of the nation's telephone system in 1982, the impact of increasing phone rates quickly got the attention of both consumer groups and interest groups representing the elderly in a variety of states. Several points can be made about the emerging policy conflicts on the basis of our interpretation of the factors contributing to past regulatory policy responses.

Utility policy is apt to involve both high levels of conflict and considerable complexity. As suggested by Gormley (1983), this type of situation may produce policymaking characterized by crisis management. One might expect considerable controversy in some of the large states that are traditional innovators. At the same time, it seems likely that the states that have the higher levels of capacity than others for handling complex policy issues will have a major advantage.

The responses of the states on lifeline rates and on peak-load pricing in the 1970s suggest the types of regulatory policy developments that may occur. As discussed by Anderson (1981), the lead in establishing lifeline rates came with actions in California and Wisconsin. In establishing peak-load rates, New York played a major role. The actions in these traditionally innovative states need to be watched carefully. Given past patterns, one can expect that those opposing rate relief from other states will join in the conflict, and advocates may well undertake a similar strategy. Victories on utility issues in these states may make it easier for other states to act, in part because of the staff work that is initially done in the traditionally innovative states.

Expanded interest in regulatory policy may also occur in other policy areas. Significantly, several of these issues are apt to involve less conflict and in some instances do not require involvement with particularly complex policy questions. These policy questions thus seem likely to receive some attention on the part of the maverick states that do not have a lengthy tradition of innovativeness.

The possibility of state laws allowing for the establishment of reverse annuity mortgages (RAMs) is illustrative of state potentials in less controversial areas. In these plans, as developed experimentally by a few states in the 1970s, individuals are able gradually to sell the equity in their home back to a savings institution in return for immediate monthly income. Theoretically, the development of RAMs makes considerable sense. Homes are now owned by approximately two-thirds of the aging, and they are owned free and clear by over 6 million elderly persons (Struyk and Soldo 1980, pp. 2–3). Conversely, there is a clear income need for segments of that older population. Resolution of questions of fairness in the administration of RAMs will result in definite opportunities for additional state initiatives.

The distribution of potential sources of conflict on RAMs is not likely to be intense since few groups are likely to offer strong opposition. Real estate groups may not like RAMs since they constitute another infusion of complexity into the real estate market. For the banking industry, there appears to have been a reluctance to act aggressively, in part out of a fear that if plans work badly and individuals lose their homes, then public responses may be intensely adverse. Given the absence of intense stakes, and the relatively simple legislation involved, RAMs constitute a regulatory policy area in which opportunities exist for a few individuals or an aging-based interest group to have a significant impact. From this perspective, one might also expect that some of the maverick innovators might be among the leaders in developing alternative approaches to the handling of mortgage equity for the elderly.

Among the issues we have previously examined, questions on those of generic drugs and funeral industry regulation seem likely to have an important place on the issue agenda of the states in the 1980s. For generic drugs, the period of extremely heated controversy may have passed, leaving the important task of clarifying the laws in some states and working toward more effective methods of implementation. This is the basic view taken by Silverman et al. (1981). The peak level of conflict on generic drug legislation may well have come in 1977 with the passage in New York of an unusually stringent law. In that law, pharmacists were required to substitute the cheapest of the generics unless the physician specifically wrote out *no substitution* on the prescription. In the wake of the passage of that law, the Food and Drug Administration became involved with the development of a model state law that called for some discretion on the part of the pharmacist and that also sought to clarify the question of the physician's role in deciding when generic drugs could not be used.

As of the early 1980s, it was also less clear just how much consumer savings might be anticipated. Clearly, drugs were an expensive part of the nation's total health care costs, with an outlay of at least $20 billion annually estimated for 1979 by Silverman et al. (1981). The potential savings were reduced, however, by the continued existence of patents on a wide range of drugs. As an additional factor contributing to a likely reduced level of conflict, it was also clear by the 1980s that the nation's major pharmaceutical companies were increasingly involved with the production of generic drugs. Thus, while resistance to the stronger laws continued, there was less at stake than when generic drug laws were first being proposed in the early 1970s. Generic drug laws thus stand as a policy area in which clarification and adjustment might be anticipated and, from many perspectives, recommended. One might anticipate movement toward the model code approach in an increasing number of states—but probably without the pitched battles that occurred in some states in the 1970s.

Despite the 1982 federal rule that was passed in Congress, conflict in the area of funeral industry regulation seems likely to continue. In the wake of the federally established rules in 1982, states were given the option of following those standards or using more stringent state rules. In the short run, those seeking more extensive consumer protection would have to return to the state capitals. Changes in the nation's preferences for various forms of services also portended greater conflict. Led by a strong surge in California, there has been a major shift away from traditional funeral services with burials and toward the use of cremation. In California, in 1982, some 31 percent of those who died were cremated (*Los Angeles Times,* 13 April 1983, pt. I, p. 24). Nationally, the figure climbed from 5 percent in 1972 to 12 percent in 1982. Some experts now see a shift toward cremation that will involve between 30 and 40 percent of those who die by the turn of the century. This shift in consumer preferences has major implications for an industry that historically has been characterized as having an oversupply of service providers. One might anticipate continued strong resistance in the state capitals—as well as in Washington, D.C.—to consumer-oriented measures that have the net impact of reducing the level of expenditures on funeral industry services.

The politics that began to emerge in the early 1980s also suggested the existence of a high conflict issue (Pertschuk 1982). In California, the funeral industry fought intensively over the proposed rules for crematory societies. In an interesting twist in politics, spokesmen for the funeral industry became keenly interested in establishing financial reserve requirements that would prevent individuals from losing their deposits if a memorial society became insolvent. Although the question of how to protect consumer deposits was very valid, the nature of the conflict also suggested that the funeral industry was involved in a major effort to retard the development of memorial societies in the state.

The development of regulatory policies for the nation's funeral industry in the 1980s thus seemed likely to show major aspects of high conflict regulatory politics. One could anticipate, as began to happen in California, a battle that achieved a fair degree of visibility in state politics. One could also anticipate very strong action on the part of the affected industries. In this situation, the results in a few of the key traditionally innovative states need to be watched carefully as potential models for actions in other states. Because the policy issue is not very complex, one might also anticipate action by some of the maverick innovators.

The area of regulatory protection for the aging, in short, offers substantial potential for new policy initiatives. This includes both new policy approaches and innovative action on the part of states that might not initially be perceived as places in which new policies might emerge. We have seen in this chapter that regulatory protection policies for the aging take on a variety of patterns in the states and do not consistently show a few states as the top innovators. The oft-quoted view of Justice Brandeis (*New State Ice Co.* v. *Liebmann* 285 U.S. 707 [1932]) regarding the potential for states in a federal system to operate as experimental laboratories for developing new policy approaches is aptly supported in the widely varied state responses involving regulatory policies for the aging.

8   Sources of State Policy

The sources of state policy effort for the aging are multiple. They include major political as well as socioeconomic factors, and they show some differences in their relative importance among policy areas and at different points in time. With few exceptions, they are not related to characteristics of the older population in the respective states.

This chapter explores sources of change from several perspectives. To begin, we examine the roles of major political actors and institutions, drawing upon the case study findings coupled with the statistical analysis of the major policy areas. These findings are then placed in the context of our basic analytical framework.

Political Capacity: Leaders and Institutions

The roles of key political participants and the underlying state institutional capacities constitute a major component of our conceptual model. Thus, in this section we examine the role of governors, legislators, and administrative agencies.

Governors

The role of the governors has undergone major changes since the 1950s. In the 1950s and 1960s, governors would occasionally become personally involved with aging policies, and there were a few instances in which the climate of expectations surrounding a state government would change with the emergence of a new governor in ways that would influence policy outcomes for the aging. In the 1970s, however, governors were much more likely to show interest in the aging, at least in terms of electoral politics, and at some points they became directly involved in policymaking. Nonetheless, the manner in which governors have been influencing policy outcomes has most often been indirect, and in a number of instances it is difficult to detect any significant policy impact. It is thus appropriate to review the reasons for gubernatorial involvement and the direct and indirect ways in which governors have influenced policy outcomes.

Only on rare occasions were there indications that interest in aging issues was kindled by personal experience. One interesting example of this phenomenon came in Minnesota, as Governor Wendell Anderson developed an intensified interest in property tax relief in the context of his strong identification with his boyhood neighborhood in St. Paul (only a short distance from the capitol) in which property taxes were a hotly debated issue among relatives and longtime neighborhood acquaintances. One staff aide suggested, for example, that Anderson's interest in property tax relief came in the wake of a family Thanksgiving dinner in which the property tax level was a major topic of debate. In some other instances—with Governor Harold Hughes in Iowa, for example—there was some suggestion that his mother's experiences in a nursing home had served to increase his interest in aging-related issues. As for personal experiences with aging, the oldest of the governors to serve in our case study states were James Rhodes in Ohio and Dixy Lee Ray in Washington. In both cases it has been suggested that the governor's age made him or her somewhat more sensitive than other governors to aging issues and more anxious to participate in functions in which older persons were included. Overall, however, there were limited indications that personal experiences played a major role in the development of interest in aging policy issues.

In a few instances, gubernatorial involvement came as the result of immediate controversies. Fortunately, there are fewer cases now in which governors have become involved in nursing home issues in the wake of major fires or other scandals. In an earlier day, nursing home fires would on occasion become a major factor in both gubernatorial involvement and regulatory reform. A charge of questionable practices within an SUA, if aired in the newspapers, in recent years could also produce gubernatorial involvement. Somewhat surprisingly, however, during the period of nursing home reform in the early 1970s, in which officials in several states were charged with serious conflicts of interest, the governors appear to have been quite reluctant to become personally involved. Major issues might produce direct involvement, but they were no guarantee that the governors would not defer to legislative or agency action.

Regarding reasons for interest, it is also clear that governors in the 1970s began to discover the aging in terms of electoral politics. As an indication of this motivation, the number of instances in which governors found time to visit retirement communities, senior centers, and nursing homes increased sharply. In at least one instance (Governor Robert Graham of Florida), a governor also encouraged his wife's involvement with senior activities. It should be noted, of course, that this type of interest was not an entirely new development. Governor Orville Freeman in Minnesota in the 1950s, for example, was interested in so-called senior day visits to nursing homes and in personally signing letters of congratulations to the state's centenarians on their one hundredth birthday. While it is clear that public actions that show an interest in the aging have increased, the more difficult question surrounds the extent to which this interest has been translated into specific actions to alter public policy rather than merely to reflect electoral considerations.

In terms of their contribution to policy development, the governors' actions have had some impact in increasing the recognition of aging as an important political issue. Besides their election campaign activities, governors have been involved with the promotion of various commissions and annual conventions for the study of specific aging-related issues; yet it is difficult in the area of issue raising to find instances in which the governors have engaged in sustained attempts to focus attention on aging-related policy questions.

Turning to the question of specific policy design, the impact of the governors has usually been indirect. This is the case, of course, in most policy areas. Only rarely will a particular policy design become the favorite of a governor in policy areas affecting the aging. The impact that governors have thus tends to come through their involvement with budgetary proposals in support of particular programs and in their selection of appointees who will shape specific pieces of legislation. In terms of budget calculations, it is clear that the governors have at points been involved in issues such as Medicaid and SSI supplement levels (for one example of this relationship, see the discussion of Governor Evan's role in Washington in Riley 1975). There is little indication, however, that governors have often had much direct involvement with changes in the budgets for the SUAs.

In their administrative relationships with the SUAs and their directors, the governors have had little substantive contact. One of the stronger relationships occurred in Ohio, in which the position of director of the Commission on Aging was that of a political appointee, Martin Janis, who had a long-standing association with Governor Rhodes. Cabinet status does appear to have some influence on the likelihood that the SUA directors will have at least some direct contact with the governor, at least in the context of group meetings. The lack of frequent contact is not surprising, given the fact that there were usually several layers of administrative hierarchy between the governors and the directors of the SUAs. Given the lack of substantial direct contact, the influence of the more aggressive governors on social services policy development is appropriately seen occurring through the appointment process and through the general climate of expectation they create within a state government.

The relationships of the governors to the larger administrative structures in which the state units are housed was often quite extensive. This tended to emerge in part through an interest in reorganization. Thus, among our case study states, Florida, Iowa, and Washington in recent years went through the process of establishing major integrated human services departments. In Washington, in particular, this led to substantial involvement by Governor Daniel Evans in that reorganization effort and in the subsequent selection of Charles Morris as the first head of the new department. In their selection of department heads, the governors were at points helping to shape the nature of the overall human services programs in their states and, thus, indirectly having some impact on the manner in which the opportunities for changes in policies affecting the aging might occur.

Governors were also involved on some occasions with their legislative programs in terms of key issues of budgets and taxes and clearly used various political resources on behalf of those programs. The list here includes considerations such as patronage, personal persuasion, and appeals to party loyalty in states in which party was a significant aspect of the voting process. The governors have increasingly been maintaining legislative liaison operations that in some instances have provided substantial channels of influence on some key votes in a given session.

It is important to emphasize that the instances in which the governors have had the strongest impact on policy development in terms of building support for new initiatives have come in elections representing the victory of a different coalition in a state and demonstrating that some different policy steps should be taken. At points, as with Governor Pat Brown in California, a governor may also be working very closely with a state legislature that is also manifesting significant change in its dominant coalitions and, as one consequence, contributing indirectly to the evolution of new policy initiatives for the aging. The selection of a governor seeking to make fundamental changes may run into roadblocks that substantially curtail ultimate accomplishment, as some would say occurred with Governors Gilligan in Ohio and Askew in Florida. Nonetheless, Governors Hughes in Iowa, Curtis in Maine, and Freeman in Minnesota, for example, exemplify political victories that did produce important reorientations on a number of state policies. This fundamental realigning potential in a state, and the support it tends to create for new policy directions, need to be recognized as infrequent but potentially significant phenomena in which the impact of governors goes well beyond bargaining roles on specific bills.

The findings from our fifty-state comparison, in turn, give only modest indications of gubernatorial influence on policy development. Perhaps it is not surprising, because of the financial issues involved, that the formal powers of the governor (which include the strength of this budgetary role) did emerge occasionally on aspects of Medicaid. There were also rather striking indications that the governors have been involved with aspects of social services program development. In this area, the reputational evaluation and the degree of ambition and success for the respective governors did emerge in our regression equations in the areas of Title XX utilization and the social services factor. (See also Lammers 1982.) The suggestion that relatively ambitious and highly regarded governors would work to maximize their state social services programs does correspond to other discussions of the roles of contemporary governors. Ransone (1982), for example, emphasizes the extent to which governors are apt to become involved with aspects of programs that involve federal support. Uslaner and Weber (1977, pp. 134–135) argue, on the basis of a survey of state legislators, that governors are apt to become involved in issues with limited potential for negative reactions. The provision of some expansion in social services for the aging, which often gives governors some political credit while not representing a large budget item (in the context of programs being adopted in recent years), would seem to constitute a good example of a likely area for potential involvement.

The relative absence of contributions from our governors measures in other policy areas also relates to aspects of the interpretation presented by Uslaner and Weber (1977). They argue that executives are most likely to take the lead where leadership is most likely to be productive, both electorally and in terms of specific policy successes. Thus, on some regulatory matters such as generic drug substitution laws and patient care provisions for nursing homes, governors may well conclude that the potential political hazards do not warrant extensive involvement. From this perspective, it is not surprising that a number of our statistical analyses as well as the case studies produced numerous instances in which the governors had quite peripheral roles.

Governors, in sum, have become more interested than before in aging-related issues in general but are not often directly involved with many specific aspects of political development. However, their appointment and budgetary roles may be important for aging-related policy, along with their ability to provide some additional attention to aging-related issues. These roles are often of very real significance, even if they fall short of the model sometimes envisioned by advocates for the aging, in which governors emerge with a strong personal commitment to aging-related issues and to the development of aging as their particular area of concern.

Legislators

The assessment of legislative involvement with policy development must include both the roles of the legislators and the actions of their increasingly substantial legislative staffs. Our considerations in this section include, as with the governors, an assessment of sources of interest, roles in policy initiation, and participation in the coalition-building activities needed to develop support for particular policies.

Reasons for Interest. A wide variety of responses emerged to case study questions involving reasons for legislative interest in aging issues. Since state legislatures do not usually have a large number of senior members, it is perhaps not surprising that we found few instances in which individuals might be characterized as having become interested in aging on the basis of experiences they or their peers were having. Furthermore, since those who were in the legislature at an advanced age were usually quite financially successful, they were by no means uniformly enthusiastic about policy initiatives in areas like social services. Phrases like "stingy *old* committee chairman" do indeed emerge in the halls of the state capitols. Since the senior members also tend to be on some of the key committees—appropriations and taxation, for example— they sometimes emerged as significant opponents of programs that would include some help for the aging.

There were, at the same time, a number of legislators who specialized in aging issues at a decidedly young age. In Iowa, Ohio, Maine, and Florida, for example, some individuals in their late twenties or early thirties were prominently identified with aging-related issues. The availability of prominent roles for young legislators in these states may reflect in part the less pro-welfare orientation in these states when compared with the other four states in our study and the greater opportunity for recognition on the basis of advocacy for the elderly.

In all the states there was some tendency for individuals who specialized in aging-related issues to be somewhat younger than average, to have a somewhat more liberal view than was average for that state, and to come (particularly in the 1970s) somewhat disproportionately from urban areas, often from districts with large numbers of elderly voters. In Minnesota, for example, the group of legislators that was most involved with aging-related issues was quite disproportionately from the Minneapolis–St. Paul metropolitan area. It is significant that the rural elderly, who constitute sizable proportions of the population in areas like rural Iowa, do not seem to have developed legislative champions in a manner that their number might suggest would be likely. Their involvement is handicapped in part by the often quite conservative nature of the representatives from these areas and the difficulty in developing visible programs in sparsely populated areas.

There was also specialization in aging-related issues on the basis of the professional training and career backgrounds of the legislators. This was particularly apt to occur in states in which aging issues were less salient as well as in earlier time periods. As was characteristic of state legislatures in general in the era prior to the development of a more substantial legislative staff in the 1970s in most states, there was a tendency for individuals to take committee assignments and to develop specializations on the basis of personal qualifications. Thus, we found a variety of health practitioners including doctors, chiropractors, dentists, and nurses serving on aging-related committee assignments. This practice, in some instances, has produced charges of conflict of interest and consequently appears to have declined somewhat in recent years. At its worst, this relationship produced instances in which legislators in positions to make decisions affecting a state's nursing homes were also partial owners of such homes. Fortunately, while our responses on this issue must be judged very tentatively, there were indications that the combination of a post-Watergate orientation against manipulative transactions and lower levels of profitability had reduced this form of conflict of interest. Besides the greater concern with conflict-of-interest issues, backgrounds have changed with the emergence of an increasing number of individuals who are anxious to develop a specialization in aging-related issues on the basis of ideology or constituent interests.

Patterns of Conflict. The dominant manner in which aging-related policies are handled in the state legislatures is in committee deliberations and with little open conflict on the floor producing hotly contested votes. The tendency for policies to be worked out among the proximate actors and then ratified by the legislative body is, of course, common to a variety of policy areas. There were, at the same time, indications of particular concern among some of the legislators that they not be forced to take positions for or against the aging on floor votes. Thus, in Iowa, for example, our case study analysis produced interpretations very similar to Bruner's (1978) assessment that conflicts were settled primarily in committee.

Significant legislative battles would nonetheless emerge on occasion, particularly over the more expensive policy commitments. Often, these controversies involved potentially significant alterations in the general configuration of human services policies in the state. In California in 1973–1974, for example, the question of the size of the SSI supplement became the focus for an extensive controversy between Governor Reagan and the legislature, which included a number of controversial votes. While we were not able to undertake roll-call-voting analyses in a systematic manner on instances like this, the persistent interpretation of our interviewees was that the conflicts tended to take on the characteristics associated with general welfare conflicts in state policies. Thus, if a two-party system was aligned according to differing views of the appropriate scope of state government, then the conflict tended to take on a substantial partisan division. In other instances, like in Florida in the late 1970s, the legislators tended to divide along lines resembling liberal and conservative positions on human services issues.

Legislative Capacity. Finally, in assessing the legislative impact, it is important to consider the increasing role played by legislative professionalism, meaning full-time legislatures with adequate staff support. The eight states we examined include a number that have relatively high rankings for legislative professionalism, both on our rankings and on those produced by the Citizens' Conference on State Legislatures (1971). California, as of the early 1960s, had what many observers consider to be the most highly developed of any state legislative staff at that time, and it has continued to occupy a strong position, with one of the most extensive staff systems in the nation. All of our case-study states, with the partial exception of North Carolina and Maine, have gone through a significant improvement in their levels of staff support in recent years.

The role of legislative staffs in developing new proposals, and in providing the information and general support that would make it easier for legislators to act on new legislation, has in some instances been quite pronounced. Legislatures have developed specialists among legislators, as well as staff personnel who have played important roles, in a number of areas including nursing home regulation, Medicaid rules and requirements, opportunities for funding through federal grants [for a good example of the importance of legislative staff in California in the expansion of Title XX programs, see Derthick (1975)], various consumer protection provisions, and various tax reform proposals. Our experiences in the field suggest overall that legislative staffs were often quite important in the development of new policy initiatives. This often seemed to be of particular importance in situations in which the legislature itself was operating on a very limited basis and in contexts in which the executive branch had been slow to develop its expertise.

The results of the fifty-state statistical analyses, particularly in terms of correlations, also underscore the importance of legislative roles. In the correlation analyses, legislative professionalism was quite persistently associated with many of the stronger policy efforts. Among the regression analyses, legislative professionalism emerged as a major predictor of state responses in areas such as Title XX utilization, the income maintenance factor, and aspects of Medicaid spending levels.

The case studies, and to some extent the statistical analyses, thus point to an important legislative role. Particularly where expertise may be lacking elsewhere, the development of professional staffs can make an important contribution to the overall legislative role. It should also be emphasized that the increasing competence and specialization of legislators in the more full-time legislatures also reinforce the importance of legislative professionalism. An expansion in legislative capacity thus clearly emerges as an important general characteristic of the overall developments in the states in recent years.

Administrative Agencies

The roles of key administrators and major agencies also constitute an important aspect of political capacity in the states. In particular, we have been interested in assessing the roles of the SUAs and, to a lesser extent, administrative departments involved with programs that also affect the elderly. A number of departmental roles have clearly been important in policy development in areas such as social services and health departments. This frequently has involved issues such as the development of proposals for changes in SSI benefits and regulations for long-term care facilities. Because the administratively focused aspects of the interviewing process drew more heavily upon the aging network than other areas, and in view of the absence of statistical measures of other departmental characteristics, the following analysis does not specifically seek to evaluate the roles of the related departments and agencies.

The Department Level. It was often difficult to find indications of department heads who were responsible for strong policy initiatives in the area of aging, particularly as they pertained to the social services programs being conducted by the SUAs. In the departments that had gone through a substantial integration, there tended to be a concern with the degree of autonomy that was granted to the SUA. This was an issue particularly in Florida, in which the regional offices of the SUA had been reduced to components within the regional offices of the parent department. In a similar case, in Washington, there was some concern initially with the implications of the fairly low hierarchical position of the Bureau of Aging in the newly organized department. Interestingly, however, in the views of some observers, a subordinate hierarchical position can also be potentially helpful in the development of new initiatives from within a state unit itself, since potentially there can be greater autonomy than occurs where one is organizationally closer to the top political appointees.

The most frequently given descriptions of department secretaries varied between "uninterested but generally supportive" to "only concerned when there is a possible troublesome issue within our agency." The maintenance of effective secretaries in these positions proved to be a problem, with frequency in turnover and fairly substantial use of interim appointees. Lack of continuity in departmental leadership appeared to be a particularly acute problem in the integrated departments, perhaps most notably in Iowa, which experienced a rapid turnover of directors in the early 1970s. Although there was undoubtedly some behind-the-scenes activity in support of some programs on the part of department secretaries, they were frequently seen as taking limited promotive roles.

The SUAs. The variation in SUAs that emerged from the case study states includes not only formal structure but also leadership styles and organizational activity. Perhaps not surprisingly, the formal structural arrangement did not emerge as a major factor in molding the nature of the SUA's operations or of its apparent success. This interpretation, it should be noted, parallels the tendency for formal hierarchical arrangements not to correlate with differences in policy outcomes.

In terms of approaches to the coordinating and policy-promoting roles across policy areas in the state capitals, all the SUAs manifested significant problems. With modest-sized staffs and budgets in relationship to other departments, there was often considerable difficulty in achieving the probably unrealistic goals that were initially associated with the Older Americans Act. Some educating of those in other departments could take place, and joint ventures did emerge in a few instances. Overall, however, the coordinating role appeared to involve considerable difficulty in each of the eight state governments.

There were marked differences in the advocacy and program promotion roles in the state legislatures. In several instances, the state directors and their staffs tended to keep the state legislature at arm's length and to focus on their program operations. In some instances, there were important efforts behind the scenes to facilitate lobbying activities by outside groups. Less frequent were the situations in which legislative strategies (including the political significance of project locations) would become a part of the considerations and interactions within the SUAs. There are obvious advantages and disadvantages, it should be noted, with each of these strategies. If other actors are able to push for aging programs, then an emphasis on technically competent and well-run programs can help by giving those advocates a good agency to promote, one which has the confidence of the governor and key state legislators. This strategy is less viable, however, where few other forces are promoting program development. Conversely, the paradox for the politically active SUAs is that greater political involvement can also mean that electoral defeat of key supporters can substantially alter one's position. Even the establishment of stable legislative coalitions can be politically dangerous if promoted legislation contradicts other parts of the governor's program.

The advisory councils to the SUAs also displayed varying levels of overall effectiveness. On balance, the constraints on the advisory councils seem to have been quite substantial. The strong emphasis on representation, along with the rapid turnover in personnel, meant that it was often difficult to develop a sustained organization with significant policy promotion roles. In many respects, the councils would seem to have constituted a useful first step in the development of political representation for the aging rather than a final organizational form. In states in which aging has been a relatively new issue, some of the educational activities associated with the advisory councils seem to have fostered greater involvement than in other states on the part of the aging in program development. As vehicles for mobilizing support for Older Americans Act programs, the advisory committees on occasion have also had some impact, particularly where few other organizations are willing to pursue aging advocacy.

As aging-based advocacy interests begin to develop in a state, however, there is a tendency for separate organizations to emerge. Such organizations can at points pursue electoral-politics interests more aggressively and may be able to develop stabler leadership groups. There can be effective relationships between some of these groups and the advisory councils, although initially conflicts over organizational turf are apt to occur. Ultimately, then, one of the important consequences of the advisory councils may be their ability to facilitate the development of additional interest group activity.

It is important to stress, in a broader sense, that a substantial amount of organizational capacity building has been taking place throughout the 1970s. Accounts of problems in the early 1970s such as lack of continuity in leadership and inadequate ability to attract trained professionals were all too prevalent. By 1980, however, the SUAs we visited could point to a variety of improvements in the management of basic programs and promotion of advocacy. This development ultimately will be extremely important since, in the era of limits in which so many states now seem to find themselves, the development of programs that can withstand tough scrutiny will be an extremely important contribution.

Summary

From a variety of perspectives, then, the growth of political capacity has been an important aspect of state government development in recent years, a development that has significant implications for the manner in which states develop policies for the aging. The gubernatorial, legislative, and administrative areas have all seen changes that enhance the capacity for states to design their own policies and to carry out policy implementation effectively. In the search for sources of policy, at the same time, there have been indications that factors such as ambitious and effective governors, well-staffed legislatures, and administrators with strong political skills can make a clear difference in the nature of a state's policy response for the aging.

Aging-Based Advocacy

The nature of interest group activity in a state takes on considerable importance in this assessment regarding not only the conclusions that can be drawn about influence patterns directly but also in terms of the factors that are contributing to greater interest group activity and their implications for future developments in the states. Because the eight case study states differ on a wide variety of socioeconomic and political characteristics, it is useful to consider at the outset the nature of the differences in levels of activity one finds among those eight states. The role of interest groups has clearly been growing, but with major differences among the eight states. Levels of interest group activity during the 1950s and early 1960s in all states except California were characterized by an absence of lobbying by the aging and a limited promotive role by professionals on behalf of the aging. California, with its unique old-age movement (see Putnam 1970), was an exception to a pattern in which the advocacy that did take place for the aging was done normally by others. Where advocacy did occur, individuals with backgrounds in social work, religious organizations, or liberal policy organizations were the primary spokespersons. The depression-spawned Townsend movement was basically dead by the mid-1950s, and not much new activity had taken its place.

By the 1970s, lobbying on the part of the aging, as well as interest group activity in general, was a growing phenomenon in state politics. As the separate state discussions have emphasized, Minnesota and Washington produced two relatively strong efforts, while Maine produced an effective effort (primarily in the late 1960s and early 1970s) that was geared to the informal and localized nature of politics in that state. Florida, by the end of the decade in particular, was presenting a stronger set of organizations, as well as a rather vocal Silver-Haired Legislature, which began in 1978. In general, the case studies suggested that the states were moving from patterns of limited participation and political lobbying being done for the aging (insofar as it took place at all) to situations in which the aging themselves constitute both the key leadership group and the rank-and-file membership of the overall interest group.

The level of interest group development can also be related in a number of ways to our basic conceptual model. The two states that had the most distinct organizations were Minnesota and Washington. Those developments took place in the context of states that had a relatively high level of political openness and capacity and of general policy liberalism. Although Washington's fiscal capacity has been constrained by the absence of an income tax, both states, as of the 1970s, also had relatively well-developed economies and high personal income levels. Groups in these states thus had definite advantages in terms of factors that would facilitate effective interest group development. The evolution in California, a third state that had those resources, instead took a curious turn. Because a number of other factors were nudging

California toward strong efforts in most other areas, there was less of a necessity for the development of strong interest groups in the 1970s. The lack of lobbying probably curtailed social services policy development but did not detract from the development of strong commitments in other areas.

The remaining states also fit our conceptual model in a number of respects. Interest group activity in Florida was handicapped by the absence of a liberal tradition and by a low level of fiscal capacity while it was aided to some extent by the growth in political capacity in the administrative branch and within the state legislature. For Iowa, the relatively rural nature of the state may have slowed development somewhat, as did its average position in terms of general policy liberalism. In Ohio, fairly strong lobbying activities did emerge at points, with open political conflict on issues like nursing home reform. This probably reflected at least in part the size of the stakes that were involved. Ohio has been handicapped, however, by a time-honored tendency to try to avoid spending commitments, which is reflected in its relatively low score on general policy liberalism and by its unusually low tax effort. While lobbying activity might be seen as necessary, it could also be viewed by potential participants as having little chance of success. Finally, Maine and North Carolina, as less economically developed states, also illustrate the manner in which different factors can intervene. In Maine, localized groups could at points develop a fair degree of access to the state legislature, and the relatively small size of the state seems to have facilitated that development. In addition, Maine could build upon fairly substantial traditions as a liberal state. In North Carolina, however, despite some tendencies toward a liberal tradition but perhaps reflecting a low overall tendency toward political participation, activity until well into the 1970s manifested little tendency for the aging to mobilize to speak on their own behalf. The overall direction in the level of interest group activity in the eight states was thus clearly toward greater involvement—but with major differences among the eight states.

The search for indications of influence on the part of the aging-based interest groups produces, in turn, a rather mixed result. The states in which the clearest direct role on significant issues appears to have emerged are Minnesota and Washington. In aspects of policy development in these two states, specific commitments such as a continuation of threatened Medicaid benefits and an expanded dental plan would emerge with specific and fairly forceful roles being filled by the aging-based interest groups. In some instances in other states as well, there was fairly forceful advocacy around specific issues like the level of funding for social services. Often, however, the aging-based interest groups were not pivotal in the building of support for major new policies or in the specific bargaining processes that produced those final results. Interest groups might be able to raise issues but would not have a major role in other aspects of policy development.

The results from the fifty-state statistical analysis are also sobering for those who hope to see an increasingly efficacious interest group role emerging at the state level. In part, the available measures clearly do not tap all aspects of interest group activity. Nonetheless, in both the correlation and the regression analyses, the measures of AARP size and of NCSC lobby effort did not have an appreciable impact. It is interesting to note that the measure of general activity drawn from frequency of legislative testimony by aging-based organizations did suggest the importance of actions that promote a general interest in aging-related issues in a state.

Ultimately, both the case studies and the statistical analyses point to a useful role for interest groups, but one that can be effective only when other key factors promoting state policy development are also present. If a state lacks interested leaders, tax capacity, political institutions familiar with handling comparable issues, and a tradition of governmental responsiveness, then the role of interest groups becomes extremely difficult. Aging-based interest groups appear able, in short, to play a supportive, but not a pivotal, policy development role.

Underlying Factors

A full exploration of the factors that influence state policy for the aging, as developed throughout this book, requires a consideration of several dimensions that underlie the specific concepts of political capacity and advocacy activities for the elderly. In this section, we reconsider the other major factors in that design, including political openness, fiscal capacity, general policy liberalism, overall socioeconomic characteristics of the states, and characteristics of the aging population.

Political Openness

The measures of political openness employed in this book show a decidedly marginal ability to help explain major policy outcomes. Furthermore, their degree of explanatory power appears to have been declining over time. This seems to reflect the growing importance of subgovernment politics in specific policy areas. The degree of openness probably helped the amount of advocacy activity and may have contributed to the development of expanded political capacity in some states. The extent to which influences from political openness have to be seen as operating indirectly is most apparent as one reflects on the specific results of our regression analyses. The two measures in this area, one should recall, were voter turnout and party competition. These two measures did enter some of the regression equations but primarily for the early period. For the 1970s, party competition entered a few of the regression equations in the opposite (negatively associated) manner from what one would have expected. Overall, one has to conclude that, on the basis of the statistical analyses, political openness measures as of the 1970s provide little explanatory power in seeking to determine the sources of state policy effort.

Fiscal Capacity

Fiscal capacity, as reflected particularly in the extent of a state's tax effort relative to tax capacity, served as a key factor in the development of many important programs. The process was not automatic, with some states showing an apparent lag in their ability to develop new programs through tax effort as capacity grew. The related dimensions of political capacity and general policy liberalism often supplanted fiscal capacity in the regression results. Nonetheless, fiscal capacity served as an extremely important factor that contributed directly to policy effort. The repeated appearance of the tax effort measure and tax percentage of revenue in the regression analyses is an impressive indication that policies do not emerge in some automatic response to general patterns of socioeconomic development.

General Policy Liberalism

The general policy liberalism factor also occupies an important position in shaping state policy responses for the aging. This factor, which taps a state's general willingness to use the public sector, had very strong correlations with a number of our major policy measures and at least periodically entered some of the regression equations. Programs for the aging are clearly related to that underlying variation in the willingness of a state to use its public sector aggressively for social purposes.

Socioeconomic Characteristics

Several of the socioeconomic influences have been important in shaping state policy efforts. In the correlation and regression analyses, a fairly persistent impact comes from the level of industrialization-urbanization. In addition, the magnitude of advantaged groups (the status factor) and disadvantaged groups (the need factor) in a state's population was persistently associated with the stronger policy efforts (particularly in relationship to health policy) and entered the regression equations in several instances. It is perhaps not unexpected that they were also less extensively correlated with regulatory policies.

It is nonetheless apparent from this analysis that socioeconomic factors often serve as facilitators of policy responses. This emphasis, it should be noted, parallels the interpretation by Stonecash (1980), which stressed the importance of socioeconomic factors in determining the boundaries within which political action can take place rather than the specific directions in which those policy efforts evolve. Supportive of this view in our study is the extent to which the socioeconomic variables produce strong correlations but still do not enter the regression equations quite as often as some of the indicators of more proximate factors, especially fiscal capacity, plus measures of political capacity.

In relating socioeconomic variables with other sources of state policy, it is also essential to emphasize the extent to which political factors (including political culture and past levels of spending effort) serve as forces shaping those overall policy responses. On measures of change in income, and simply on the basis of an examination of more rapidly growing states, it is apparent that new wealth does not translate directly into policy responses. Furthermore, there also seems to be some delay in the extent to which states with developed programs will reduce those efforts as their economic bases begin to decline. Thus, it may well be that political factors will be especially important in shaping the speed of a state's response to changes in its socioeconomic conditions.

Characteristics of the Aging Population

The characteristics of the aging population, with some exceptions, have not emerged in either the statistical analyses or the case studies as strong influences on policy development. In the case studies, even Florida, which had the highest percentage of aging persons of any state, did not show a particularly strong response to that factor. Increases in consumer protection efforts could be partly attributed to the impact of sheer numbers of aging persons, and some social services program initiatives might reflect the magnitude of that state's aging population. Overall, however, the impact of sheer size was not strong in areas such as health care and income maintenance in any of our case study states. Where there were pockets of large elderly population within sections of a state—the southern counties in Iowa, for example—a clear tendency existed for those concentrations not to produce an extensive policy response.

The statistical analyses produced a limited indication that characteristics of the aging were a significant factor in shaping state policy responses. For regulatory policy, there were some indications that the size of the older population was related to the extent of funeral industry regulation and that the percentage of older persons living in poverty was related to the extent of hearing aid reform. However, other regulatory relationships were inverse, such as the negative correlation between the size of the older population and the development of consumer-oriented public guardianship laws.

The absence of major relationships was also apparent for the expenditure-based policies. On income maintenance policies—tax relief and the more general income maintenance factor—efforts were correlated positively with higher levels of median income for those households headed by an individual age 65 and over but not with larger numbers of needy older persons. On Medicaid program development, the characteristics of the older population did not have a strong or consistent relationship. Furthermore, the correlation between the health and welfare factor and the size of the aging population was virtually zero. In terms of social services, there were fairly clear indications that large percentages of older persons in a state accompany tendencies to spend a smaller portion of available Title XX funds on the elderly. Similarly, regarding the percentage of older persons in a state and overall social services efforts, the correlation between our social services factor and the percentage of the aging in a state was $-.327$. Rather than large numbers of aging persons contributing to greater responses, there was some tendency for the states to try to spread their social services dollars more thinly among the potential recipients.

The impact of migration patterns also needs to be considered in evaluating the lack of relationship between aspects of the aging population and policy responses. Net migration for the aging has been operating rather strikingly to increase the number of older persons in states that are not making extensive policy efforts. Most notably, migration of the elderly was slightly negatively correlated with both the health and welfare factor and the income maintenance factor. For social services, the relationship was not inverse, but there was also little indication that large numbers of migrants were prompting a significant increase in social services efforts. Clearly, what has happened in recent years is that elderly migrants have been locating in states with lower tax levels and that absence of tax effort has reduced the potential policy response for the aging. Ironically, then, the elderly seem to be congregating in the very states that are least likely to serve their public sector needs. The reasons for this obviously involve the characteristics of a state's private sector, especially the cost of living, and the natural environment, notably the weather. Of course, one major factor helping to keep the cost of living low in the sunbelt states is low taxes. Thus, it could be that one of the major attractions of those states for the elderly is their smaller public sectors, although it is not entirely clear how extensively the migrants tend initially to comprehend the relative absence of services in those states. The extent to which this pattern persists in future years has obvious policy implications.

Both demographic and political factors are involved in the absence of a strong state response to the characteristics of the aging. To some extent, the states with high percentages of older persons are not states in which either the levels of economic resources or the tendency to use the public sector are likely to lead to strong policy efforts for the aging. That list of states with the highest percentage of aged persons in their population, one should recall, includes several states with low levels of economic development and/or traditions of governmental response, such as Florida, Arkansas, Missouri, South Dakota, Nebraska, and Kansas. There is no common underlying need dimension among the aged in the states, at least insofar as statistical attempts to produce a composite factor can detect. The percentage of elderly persons in a state does not reflect any common dimensions in areas such as proportion of widows or the percentage of elderly who are over age 75. In addition, it should be emphasized that the variation among the states on the percentage of the population age 65 and over has consistently been relatively small. In 1980, for example, the highest percentage other than for Florida was just over 13 percent, and only 15 states had less than 10 percent. The range of variation is thus quite small and not one that would be expected to enter a large number of statistical analyses seeking to explain policy outcomes with a large number of independent variables.

Finally, it is also worth noting that there are some tendencies for states with very small older populations (in numbers and in percentages) to have rather high benefit levels. It is not difficult to sense one interpretation: State governments may be more willing to grant extensive benefits when the number of potential recipients is quite low. While this is quite possibly a part of the answer, there is also an interesting tendency in some of the western states—Alaska and Arizona (primarily in its early days), for example—to adopt relatively generous programs on the basis of the view that the elderly in their states were often pioneers and thus deserve to be assisted.

Part of the reason for the absence of any strong findings on the characteristics of the aging may also be more directly political. In several of the states with particularly high percentages, such as Iowa and Missouri, those older persons are geographically dispersed and therefore difficult to organize politically, and in the Iowa case study the elderly were regarded as relatively voiceless in that state's politics. Conversely, in Minneapolis, although the numbers for the entire state were not uniquely high, the geographic concentration of individuals in older neighborhoods and in senior housing projects was judged to increase significantly the amount of political mobilization that took place. This suggests that the extent to which the aging may be able to mobilize politically is conditioned not only by numbers but also by the effect of geographic considerations on possibilities for collective action.

After considering all the necessary qualifications, the basic finding of this study regarding demographic impacts on policy warrants serious consideration among students of public policy and the aging. It has often been suggested that the growing percentage of older persons in the U.S. population in the coming years, along with likely increases in political activity, will lead to an increased level of political response to the needs and political desires of the elderly (Cutler 1977). The demographic shift may well be an important influence, but overall policy responses are likely to depend upon a variety of other factors such as economic conditions, societal attitudes, and specific lobbying activities. Insofar as states can create models illustrating developments that may also occur at the national level, a sense of caution is in order regarding the extent to which a demographic shift, in and of itself, will lead to increased policy responses.

Summary

In general, our combined analyses indicate that the states that exert substantial effort on behalf of the aging tend to be those with the fiscal and political capacity to do so and those that traditionally have produced liberal policies in a variety of areas. Such states have, in turn, tended to be more socioeconomically developed than others. These traits have, in the past, distinguished what are now called the snowbelt states from those now known as the sunbelt states. The characteristics of a state's aging population, the extent of its visible advocacy on behalf of that population, and the openness of its political system in general have apparently had relatively little impact on state policy efforts for the aging. This pattern does vary somewhat from one policy area to another, especially between expenditure-based and regulatory policies, and it appears to be weakening over time as the economic and political capacities of the states become more similar and as subgovernment processes gain importance. Chief among these processes is the fairly recent development of more extensive behind-the-scenes advocacy, not necessarily in more open political systems and not necessarily representative of all segments of the elderly population. The future thus seems to portend the decline of influences on policymaking that can be identified through aggregate analysis but the rise of influences that are potentially more manipulable.

9

The States, Federalism, and the Future

The states seem destined to continue—and possibly to expand—their roles in policy development for the aging. When considering the debate over federal and state roles, it is essential to recognize that the once often lamented use of subnational governments for policy development is now receiving widespread interest from a variety of political perspectives (see Hawkins 1982; Schechter 1983). It is nonetheless often unclear just how those roles might evolve and what positions should be taken by those who are sympathetic to an enhanced public sector role in response to the needs of the aging in the United States.

Controversies over the role of the states often reflect a disagreement over the proper scope of government in the contemporary United States. In other contexts, disagreements stem from differing views as to the importance of goals such as equalization and targeting within policies for the aging and the appropriateness of in-kind programs versus income assistance. Our findings suggest a number of conclusions that are considered appropriately as part of that larger debate over state government roles. We thus conclude by looking at questions such as the capacities of state governments, levels of responsiveness to the elderly, equalization and targeting issues, possible federal roles, and prospective strategies for the states.

Capacities for State Action

The states have shown both major increases and areas of continuing limitations in their generation of capacities for developing and implementing policies for the aging. On a general level, growth is apparent in the development of more professional legislatures, governors with longer periods of service and better staffs, and administrative units with more effectively trained personnel. Several developments are also important quite specifically for policies relating to the elderly.

One clear indication of the enhanced capacity for state governments to act has come in the area of Medicaid reform. Writers looking at the responses in recent years have, in particular, often stressed the willingness of the states to redesign their Medicaid programs on a more cost-conscious basis than before (Feder and Holahan 1980; Bovbjerg and Holahan 1982). The importance of greater fiscal and political capacity for dealing with Medicaid policies was also apparent in our analyses. Capacity measures were related to outcome differences in a number of the Medicaid regressions, and in the case studies there were repeated instances in which a legislative committee, health department, or staff group within a governor's office worked quite extensively on Medicaid reform. Medicaid policy thus stands as an area in which the states increasingly do have the political capacity to address fairly complex questions of public policy.

Regarding the capacities of the network that was established as part of the Older Americans Act, the results are unfortunately quite mixed. It is evident from our findings that the initial hopes for a major coordinating and promoting role have not been realized (see also Estes 1979). In a few instances, such as the strong developments in the state of Washington, there were indications that the development of capacities for policy implementation through case management approaches could be quite extensive. It should also be noted in considering issues of political and fiscal capacity that the increasing concentration of the elderly in a few populous states means that the creation of a few strong units in those large states can quickly affect the lives of a substantial segment of older Americans. Specifically, as of 1980, approximately 45 percent of all older persons age 65 and over lived in just six states (Lammers 1983). Nonetheless, despite the real progress that has been made in many states in recent years, the organizational capacity of SUAs and AAAs is often quite modest. A stretching of financial and personnel resources across a broad range of programs has too often retarded the development of capacities either for dealing with complex policy development questions or implementing a broad range of policies.

The question of state fiscal capacities also raises continuing uncertainties. There has been a fairly substantial equalizing of tax capacity among the states, with the southern states now much closer to the national average in tax capacity. There are also indications that the states with declining economies have often been surprisingly willing to maintain program commitments even in the face of economic adversity. Tax increases, for example, occurred in some 37 states between 1981 and 1983, and the largest increases came in the economically depressed midwestern states (Stanfield 1983, p. 1320).

The willingness of the states to expand their tax efforts to allow an expansion in programs for the aging is nonetheless quite uncertain. When one compares degrees of support for different levels of government (federal, state, and local), the states have partially closed the gap in the extent to which the federal government is seen as being more apt to spend funds effectively. Nonetheless, the respective percentages still find the state government trailing the federal government in citizen perceptions regarding overall effectiveness by approximately 11 percent (U.S. Advisory Commission on Intergovernmental Relations 1983, p. 3).

The states must also continually deal with questions of their business climate as an extensively debated issue in the modification of their tax policies. It needs to be recognized, of course, that a large percentage of the new jobs that are created in each of the states comes from the growth of existing firms and not the attraction of new industries and jobs on the basis of favorable taxes (see Liner and Lynch 1977; Weinstein and Firestine 1978). Nonetheless, the widely held attitude that lower taxes can help create jobs often operates as a constraint on possible increases in state taxes. There are also some indications, most notably for Florida, that the desire for population growth can contribute to a reluctance to increase taxes. This development has a direct impact on policies for the aging since the motivation of keeping taxes low to attract retirees also has the longer-term effect of placing individuals who often ultimately find themselves in need of public services in states in which those lower tax levels reduce the potential for extensive program development. The states, in short, have been sustaining their tax efforts to a substantial degree and undertaking some increases in the face of economic adversity. The underlying constraints on state tax efforts, however, seem likely to continue in the foreseeable future. The states thus have sharply enhanced their capacities for aging-related policy development when compared with earlier decades. Their willingness to use their tax capacity, however, is open to continuing question.

Responsiveness to the Elderly

It is also essential to consider the relative degree of emphasis that may be given to the needs of the elderly as a proportion of general state policy commitments. On this issue, the evidence is again quite mixed. The area of major growth clearly has been Medicaid. This growth has occurred, however, in the context of a program design that has made it difficult for states directly to curtail their programs. Thus, rather than voting on a change in budgetary expenditures, the state legislatures have had to deal with reimbursement issues, optional service requirements, and eligibility standards. It should also be recalled that while Medicaid expenditures have grown quite rapidly, educational expenditures and not Medicaid costs have shown the greatest increase in the past several decades (Davidson 1980, p. 22). In the area of social services, the total dollar commitments on the part of the states have been quite modest, and they have not been linked to the factors that have led to major program development in other areas of state spending.

It is also dramatically apparent from our analyses that an expansion in the number of older persons in a state, especially persons for whom aid seems increasingly appropriate, does not necessarily lead to enhanced policy efforts. As emphasized in the previous chapter, the characteristics of the aging in a state have simply not been a major force contributing to more generous policies. The percentage of older persons, and their needs, certainly on some occasions can be a factor in state responses. This requires, however, that other factors—principally political and fiscal capacity—be built upon if the states are to engage in expanded policy responses.

When issues of responsiveness are raised for existing programs, it appears that the aging have usually been able to get a reasonable share of state assistance when they are competing with other specific recipient groups. As reviewed in chapter 5, the distribution of Title XX funds, for example, has found the aging receiving what observers like Gilbert and Specht (1982) have judged to be a fair share. It remains to be seen whether some of the issues of the 1980s, like utility rate relief formulas, will produce a similar fair share for the elderly. In part, these questions raise issues of eligibility requirements and targeting strategies—a set of issues to which we now turn.

Equalization and Targeting Issues

Policy questions involving targeting and equity issues are now receiving substantially greater attention (see Garfinkel 1982; Neugarten 1982; Hale and Palley 1981). For some observers, a key problem in the development of policies at all levels of government is the absence of sufficient attention to the economic and social conditions of potential recipients of governmental assistance. A concern with the frail elderly and minorities of various kinds leads many observers to prefer having assistance provided on some basis other than general eligibility (Federal Council on Aging 1978). Indeed, the 1978 amendments to the Older Americans Act mandated that SUAs direct more Title III Funds to those elderly "in greatest economic and social need." State governments, from this perspective, are a frequent focal point for ciriticism. Several of our findings need to be considered in light of that debate.

First, it is not clear that states view the development of targeted and general eligibility programs on an either-or basis; that is, states that tend to do more for the elderly overall are also more apt than others to develop extensive programs that are targeted for the low income elderly. Circuit-breaker legislation, for example, was strong in states that were also making greater efforts in less income-sensitive policy commitments. Obviously, one might argue in favor of a different mix of general assistance and targeted assistance within a given state. Nonetheless, the simultaneous growth of both universal and targeted programs suggests that, at least under some conditions, it may be possible to build strong programs involving both targeted and general eligibility programs. In addition, this finding is at least congruent with the view that it is easier to build political support for targeted programs when there is also program development taking place for a broader segment of the elderly. In contrast, it can of course be argued that, in an era of limits, it is ethically preferable to target scarce program resources where they are most needed.

Second, there are historical indications that the states have been willing to apply eligibility requirements to assistance programs that involve aspects of targeting. Specifically, during the 1950s, requirements for relative responsibility laws were established in some 35 states. In 14 of those states, the requirements also mandated that the financial contributions of the younger family member be deducted from what the older person would receive from the state even if the money from the family member was not forthcoming (Schorr 1960). On the basis of an analysis of family responsibility laws in our project, it is also apparent that the states with the most stringent requirements were doing relatively less, overall, in their policy efforts. On the basis of simple correlations, these states were smaller, growing more slowly, possessed a smaller-than-average population age 65 and over, and made a lower average monthly payment for AFDC recipients than other states. In terms of the general lack of progressiveness in these states, they also displayed low scores on Walker's innovation index. From both these correlations and evaluations of those laws prior to their abandonment in 1965 (with the advent of Medicaid), it is clear that the states that used relative responsibility requirements were not particularly anxious to expand the overall size of their state welfare programs. Given the administrative problems those laws presented, it is certainly also debatable whether or not such efforts should be reinstated. (As of 1984, the major such experiment was emerging in Idaho.) Nonetheless, there are definite precedents for state action involving targeting of programs.

On programs specifically designated for the aging, it should also be emphasized that the states are developing more interest in, and capacity for, various forms of targeted assistance. In part because of the discretion that is granted with existing regulations, the states are really invited to develop their own formulas. Research by Cutler and Harris (1983) has shown rather strikingly that the widespread variation among states in targeting formulas in Title III programs produces a situation in which no two states use both the same factors and the same weights in their allocation formulas. Clearly, the states have been, and are, willing to confront targeting issues.

The question of state approaches to targeting is also often raised in the context of differences between likely federal and state responses. According to Hudson (1981), an expansion in the scope of decision making at the federal level is apt to enhance the position of the have-not groups because of the greater tendency for subnational governments to be dominated by a few well-organized interests. From this perspective, a concern with assistance being directed increasingly toward the more disadvantaged segment of the older population would not be enhanced by a greater reliance upon state governments. It may be, however, that conditions that are emerging in the 1980s will increasingly call into question that association between targeting commitments and federal rather than state government roles.

Conditions are clearly changing at both the state and federal levels. As we have seen, the states are developing increased capacities for dealing with targeting issues. At the same time, the likelihood that the federal government will develop programs focused on those in greatest need has come into greater question. Historically, the national commitment to programs that focused on those in greatest need was closely tied to the association between liberal ideologies and the political power of its spokespersons in both Congress and the presidency. What the liberal ideology actually produced was a situation in which legislators from the prosperous parts of the country (the industrial heartland and the East) were willing to support programs that aided areas with the largest number of individuals in greatest need in other regions. Thus, support for SSI, for example, emerged from a coalition that included southern leaders such as Russell Long and Wilbur Mills along with strong support from northern liberals (Burke 1974). Even in the 1950s and 1960s, it should be emphasized, the overall operation of the federal government did not have a strong impact on the redistribution of economic resources in the nation (Echols 1980). Nonetheless, within specific programs such as Medicaid and OAA, there was a willingness on the part of some legislators to support programs that did not give their relatively more prosperous states an average per capita share of program dollars or, in many instances, revenues commensurate with the level of federal taxes being extracted from those states.

It is less clear in the 1980s that the federal commitment to income-sensitive programs can be either maintained or enhanced. In part, the past decade witnessed the growth of much greater awareness among members of Congress regarding their constituents' share in various federal programs. The rise of regionally based organizations, including the Northeast-Midwest Economic Advancement Coalition and the Southern Growth Policies Board, was just one manifestation of the increased interest in regional allocation issues. Major figures in domestic policy debates, like Senator Patrick Moynihan from New York, would write extensively on the appropriateness of greater federal attention to the needs of the older sections of the nation (see Moynihan 1980). Along with the greater sensitivity to grant-in-aid formulas in Congress, there is also the open question as to what ideologies will hold sway at the White House and how they will influence the evolution of federal policies. One possibility, it should be emphasized, is that a Republican president would be in favor of both targeting and a contraction in overall program benefits. Aspects of Reagan's housing policies, as reviewed by Zias, Struyk, and Thibodeau (1982, pp. 65–83), for example, show President Reagan proposing changes in housing assistance with program formulas giving more aid to those in greatest need while also cutting the size of total programs.

In sum, our evidence certainly does not suggest that the states are likely suddenly to become the focal point for targeting strategies in programs for the aging. It does seem important to take a cautious view, however, toward the suggestion that a continued and perhaps increased reliance upon state governments is likely to constitute a restraint on the development of greater need sensitivity in programs for the aging.

As a related policy question, the degree of equity that is achieved in the operation of programs across the states also deserves consideration. To what extent are individuals in similar situations likely to have their cases handled in similar ways in various parts of the country? In confronting this question, one can consider the underlying conditions that may influence degrees of equity, the trends over the past two decades, and the levels of equity now being achieved.

There is clearly an opportunity for increasingly uniform handling of similar cases throughout the country in future years. This occurs as the range of variation in economic resources, and particularly per capita income, continues to narrow. As we emphasized in the previous chapter, however, there have not been clear indications that those with newly developed wealth will be willing to undertake the political steps needed to develop stronger public sector commitments. In addition, the tendency for the elderly population to grow in areas with weak policy efforts (in part through migration) needs to be recognized. From a personal choice perspective, one might argue that individuals are simply choosing their preferences for lower taxes rather than additional services. One suspects, however, that many persons are not entirely aware of the public assistance differences as they make choices based upon ratings of tax burdens in the respective states. In any event, while overall changes toward greater uniformity in state economic resources are increasing the opportunity for greater equity, the increase in the number of older persons in states with poor economies and/or a limited tax effort seems likely to continue.

Regarding trends, the one clear indication that states are achieving greater equalization occurs with Medicaid. As emphasized in chapter 4, there has been a sharp decline in the variation of spending levels for the aging as the program has matured. In other policy areas, however, there has not been a comparable indication of equalization. In part because of the growth in the nature of Social Security policies, the range of state spending on income maintenance programs was actually showing greater variation by 1975 than in earlier decades. As reviewed by Klingman (1982), the coefficient of variation (standard deviation divided by the mean) for state OAA/SSI average payments reversed its trend toward greater uniformity between 1955 and 1965 and increased even beyond the 1955 levels as of 1975. While it is important to emphasize that the degree of uniformity in program spending has been going up on the most costly state program for the aging, the overall picture is clearly not one in which the states have been moving forcefully toward greater uniformity of effort.

The prevailing distribution of state policy efforts for the aging thus continues to find those residing in the poor states confronting average payment and expenditure levels that lag behind those states in which there are greater concentrations of economic resources and/or fewer older persons who are in need. While that correlation between the larger number of needy persons in a state's population and weaker policy efforts has itself declined, the present situation is still one in which an individual residing in California, Washington, or Wisconsin is apt to receive more generous public sector responses than a person residing in Florida, Texas, or Utah.

To resolve equity issues fully, it would be necessary to carry out regional transfers of funds for which support seems difficult to build in the context of present sensitivities over state and regional relationships to the federal government. Thus, while some social changes seem destined to reduce aspects of the inequity issues, other changes—and political resistances in states with increasing wealth—suggest that equity questions are likely to remain difficult in the years ahead.

The Federal Role

The early 1980s produced a major round of bargaining, and ultimately a substantial stalemate, in proposals for rapidly transforming several federal and state programs for the aging. The most dramatic proposal was in 1982 when the states were asked by the Reagan administration to accept a swap in which the federal government would assume all costs for Medicaid while the state governments took over responsibility for AFDC and food stamps. In the initially proposed swap, there was also to be a short-term trust fund through which federal funds would be dispensed to cushion the fiscal impact on the states.

The resulting negotiations were unusually extensive. As reviewed by a key administration spokesman (see Williamson 1983), the negotiations seemed to resemble more closely some of the lengthy deliberations that have taken place in Canada between the provinces and the federal government than some of the earlier efforts in the United States (for the Canadian experiences on similar issues, see Simeon 1972). For a variety of reasons, but perhaps most centrally a concern with fiscal impacts, those proposals ultimately died and the Reagan administration retreated to a more modest agenda. Nonetheless, the basic question remained. Should some programs, like Medicaid, be federalized, and were there grounds for returning some programs more substantially to the states?

From our vantage point, a federalizing of Medicaid constitutes no easy or obvious solution to the problems that have long surrounded that program. For the elderly, several key questions remain: What will be the eligibility requirements for assistance in nursing homes, and how effectively will they be operated? From the standpoint of governmental decision makers, the same agenda must be confronted at any level of government: How can one insure that additional money is in fact producing improved care, and what level of expenditure is appropriate? The question thus seems to be more appropriately focused on the type of program package being proposed and not a general issue of federal or state government roles.

Turning to social services, the primary thrust of recent proposals has been toward an expanded state role through block grants. There is again nothing automatic about the likelihood that greater state discretion will produce less emphasis on institutional care and greater emphasis on programs that seek to prevent institutionalization [for a similar view, see Hudson (1981)]. The interest in community care waivers on the part of the states is, however, quite encouraging for those seeking less emphasis on institutionalization as a basic policy response. Once waivers became available, over half of the states requested such enhanced flexibility for the development of social services.

From a more general perspective, several basic points need to be stressed regarding the federal role. First, one should seek to avoid situations in which federal standards become maximums, either literally or in terms of the politics they are likely to produce. Second, there is greater justification in awarding discretion to the states than in earlier decades. The development of state capacity and the uncertain nature of future policy responses at all levels of government suggest the appropriateness of a more flexible stance on the part of the federal government. Third, the states should be encouraged to develop innovations that relate to local needs and conditions. From this perspective, several points emerge regarding state strategies and policy options.

State Strategies

Clearly, major potentials exist for expanded state action for the aging in the coming years. First, there is considerable opportunity for an expansion in regulatory efforts and off-budget transactions. These approaches are important, given the fiscal constraints the states seem destined to face. Housing policies, for example, offer opportunities for both state and local governments to experiment with granny-flat policies that may expand the range of available housing options. Second, the possibility of state regulations that allow for home equity to be utilized before actual sale, as is proposed with RAMs, deserves careful consideration. Given the size of the potential savings involved, questions surrounding the design of utility rates for not only heating and electricity but also telephone use deserve extensive state action. For some of the major regulatory issues of the coming years, the dollars actually saved by elderly consumers can be substantially greater than those being spent directly on state-funded programs. While all types of programs need to be considered carefully, it is especially important not to ignore regulatory issues simply because they do not involve potential for political victories through direct increases in state appropriations.

In approaches to overall health and social services costs, it is obvious that the states will have to give greater attention to cost control strategies. Although the actions that have emerged in the early 1980s are quite substantial, the sorting out of reimbursement formulas and the various uses of contracting plans deserve more extensive consideration. In this regard, it will be particularly important for state officials effectively to monitor actions in other states that they may borrow. In a time of considerable uncertainty in both health and social services policies, the diffusion of innovations needs to be strengthened wherever possible.

The states also need to undertake more careful examination of the relative program costs and differing impacts on various social and economic groups among the aging. In terms of comparisons across policy areas, there has been a surprisingly limited amount of attention to relative costs. It is rare to find states like Iowa in recent years, in which expenditures for the aging are systematically compiled for an extensive range of state programs. Similarly, greater attention needs to be directed toward the characteristics of recipient groups across the full range of aging-related programs. Greater information on program costs and clientele characteristics will obviously not insure easier, or more effectively designed, programs for the aging, but without such efforts, opportunities will be lost for some potential improvements in the design of state policies.

Ultimately, state responses in the future will also require extensive attention to political support issues. In some states, it seems likely that more political action will have to be undertaken simply to maintain the programs that have been developed. We admittedly have not seen lobbying alone as a factor that can easily alter state responses. However, it is also clear that socioeconomic conditions, including the conditions of the aging, will not be sufficient to assure that policy directions will change in a state, even when they might be sufficient to allow an enhanced policy effort. When advocacy occurs along with the support of steps designed to achieve greater political capacity in a state and the nurturing of a political culture that is conducive to enhanced state action, political activity can contribute to the extent and quality of state policy efforts for the aging.

Appendix: Variable List

AARP Members. State AARP membership as a percentage of state population age 60 and over. *Source:* AARP organizational records.

ADEA Age. Number of years since adoption of state age discrimination program. *Source:* Illinois Department of Aging, *Age Discrimination in Employment of Older Persons: A Review of Federal and State Legislation and Enforcement* (Urbana: University of Illinois, 1977), table 14, pp. 77–79.

ADEA Scope. Scope of coverage and enforcement provisions in state age discrimination in employment programs. Total number of points accumulated in five statutory areas, including organizations covered, exemptions, age limits, penalties, and nature of enforcement. *Source:* Illinois Department of Aging, *Age Discrimination in Employment of Older Persons: A Review of Federal and State Legislation and Enforcement* (Urbana: University of Illinois, 1977), table 14, pp.77–79.

AFDC Payment. Average monthly payment per recipient of Aid to Families with Dependent Children, state and local portion. *Sources:* U.S. Bureau of the Census, *Statistical Abstract of the United States,* various years, and U.S. Department of Health, Education, and Welfare, Social Security Administration, *Social Security Bulletin,* April 1966; *Public Assistance Statistics,* various years.

Aged Income. Median family income for families whose head is 65 years of age or older. *Sources:* U.S. Bureau of the Census, *Census of Population: 1970;* U.S. Bureau of the Census, *Current Population Reports,* Series P-20, no. 334.

Aged Migration. In-migration of persons aged 65 and over as a percentage of total population aged 65 and over. *Sources:* U.S. Bureau of the Census, *Census of Population, 1960;* U.S. Bureau of the Census, *Current Population Reports,* Series P-25, no. 701.

Aged Pct. Change. Percentage change in the age 65 and over population over the past five years. *Source:* computed from census data. (See Aged Pct. Pop.)

Aged Pct. Pop. Percentage of population age 65 and over. *Sources:*

U.S. Bureau of the Census, *Census of Population: 1960, 1970;* U.S. Bureau of the Census, *Current Population Reports,* Series P-20, no. 334.

Aged Poor.   Aged poor as a percentage of total population. *Source:* Neil Gilbert, Harry Specht, and Gary Nelson, "Social Services to the Elderly: Title XX and the Aging Network," Final report submitted under Grant 90-A-945/01 from AoA, DHEW (San Francisco: Institute for Scientific Analysis, February 1979), table 8.4, pp. 155–156.

Aged Pov. Pct.   Percentage of population aged 65 and over living in poverty. *Source:* U.S. Bureau of the Census, *Current Population Reports,* Series P-20, no. 334.

CASP Aged Pct.   Percentage of CASP social services allocated to the elderly. *Source:* Neil Gilbert, Harry Specht, and Gary Nelson, "Social Services to the Elderly: Title XX and the Aging Network," Final report submitted under Grant 90-A-945/01 from AoA, DHEW (San Francisco: Institute for Scientific Analysis, February 1979), table 8.1, pp. 148–149.

Centralization.   State government revenue as a percentage of state and local government revenue. *Source:* U.S. Bureau of the Census, *Statistical Abstract of the United States,* various years.

Circuit-Breaker.   Number of years since enactment of state circuit-breaker program. *Source:* U.S. Advisory Commission on Intergovernmental Relations, Significant Features of Fiscal Federalism: 1976–77 Edition, Vol. 2, Revenue and Debt, pp. 117–120.

CON Age.   Number of years since adoption of state Certificate of Need program. *Source:* Medicine in the Public Interest, Inc., *Certificate of Need: An Expanding Regulatory Concept* (Washington, D.C.: Chayet and Sonnenreich, 1978).

CON Home Health.   Scope of home health agency coverage under the state Certificate of Need program. *Source:* Medicine in the Public Interest, Inc., *Certificate of Need: An Expanding Regulatory Concept* (Washington, D.C.: Chayet and Sonnenreich, 1978).

Consumer Laws.   Number of consumer-oriented enactments as of the mid-1970s. *Source:* Lee Sigelman and Roland Smith, "Consumer

Legislation in the American States: An Attempt at Explanation,"
Social Science Quarterly 61 (June 1980):58–70.

Cost Control.   Establishment of reform provisions in Medicaid nursing
home reimbursement policies as of 1975. Factor score components
include: prospective reimbursement plans, reimbursement on the
basis of experiences for similar facilities, and occupancy requirements. Proportion of variance = .709. *Source:* U.S. Department
of Health, Education, and Welfare, Public Health Service, Health
Resources Administration. *Characteristics of State Health Facility
Licensing Practices: A Comparative Review.* May 1978.

Development.   Index of socioeconomic development derived from a
cluster analysis of the following three factors for 1975: industrialization-urbanization, need, and status.

Diversity.   Sullivan's index of cultural diversity. *Source:* John L. Sullivan, "Political Correlates of Social, Economic, and Religious Diversity in the American States," *Journal of Politics,* February 1973,
p. 73.

Early Health.   Early aging health policy factor. Composite factor measuring extensiveness of state health policy efforts for the elderly
prior to Medicaid (early 1960s). Variables:

1.   State and local expenditures for Medical Assistance to the Aged
     (MAA) per elderly person, 1964. *Source:* Council of State
     Governments, *Book of the States, 1966–67,* table 7, p. 365.

2.   Total number of dental services available to recipients of Old
     Age Assistance (OAA), 1960. *Source:* U.S. Department of
     Health, Education, and Welfare, *Medical Resources Available
     to Meet the Needs of Public Assistance Recipients: Report to
     the U.S. House Committee on Ways and Means, 1961,* pp. 12–
     13.

3.   Medical expenditures as a percentage of total Old Age Assis-
     tance (combined state and federal expenditures), 1960. *Source:*
     same as (2).

4.   Average monthly medical payment per recipient of Old Age
     Assistance, 1960 (combined state and federal payment). *Source:*
     same as (2).

5. Number of years since first participation in a medical vendor payment program for nursing home patients. *Source:* same as (2), plus U.S. Department of Health, Education, and Welfare, Social and Rehabilitation Service, National Center for Social Statistics, *Public Assistance Statistics,* various years.

6. Number of years since adoption of state Medicaid program. *Source:* U.S. Department of Health, Education, and Welfare, Social and Rehabilitation Service, National Center for Health Statistics, *Medicaid Selected Statistics, 1951–1969* (1970), p. 35.

Proportion of variance = .537

ERA Age. Number of years since ratification of the Equal Rights Amendment for women. *Source:* Janet K. Boles, *The Politics of the Equal Rights Amendment* (New York: Longman, 1979), table 1.1, pp. 2–3.

ERA Ease. Ease of ratification of the Equal Rights Amendment. *Source:* same as ERA Age.

Fire Regs. Number of fire safety regulations for nursing homes. *Source:* Jordan Braverman, *Nursing Home Standards* (Washington, D.C.: American Pharmaceutical Association, 1969), pp. 66–69.

Funeral Board. Percentage of membership of state funeral home regulatory body that is not industry related. *Source:* "Analysis of State Statutes, Rules, and Regulations Affecting the Funeral Practices Industry" (private study conducted for the Consumer Federation of America, 1976), Federal Trade Commission staff paper supplied by Mike Rodemeyer, May 1980.

Funeral Scope. Number of consumer-oriented regulations for the funeral home industry. *Source:* "Analysis of State Statutes, Rules, and Regulations Affecting the Funeral Practices Industry" (private study conducted for the Consumer Federation of America, 1976), Federal Trade Commission staff paper supplied by Mike Rodemeyer, May 1980.

General Lib. Composite factor measuring the propensity of state government to use the public sector for social purposes. Variables: McCrone-Cnudde scale of anti-discrimination provisions as of 1961. *Source:* Donald J. McCrone and Charles F. Cnudde, "On Measuring Public Policy," pp. 523–530, in Robert E. Crew, Jr., ed., *State Politics: A Reader.* Belmont, Calif.: Wadsworth, 1968. Also, the following variables listed herein: Innovation, AFDC Payment (1965), ERA Age, Consumer Laws, and T20 Utilization.

Proportion of variance = .615

Generic Age.   Number of years since adoption of generic drug substitution legislation. *Source:* American Pharmaceutical Council, "Legislative Report," 15 January 1980 (flyer).

Generic Scope.   Scope of state legislation supporting generic drug substitution. Total number of points accumulated for various statutory requirements and limitations (0 = no law). *Source:* American Pharmaceutical Council, "Legislative Report," 15 January 1980 (flyer).

Gov. Ambition.   Governor's extent of office holding and frequency of election victory. This score was designed to measure the extent to which governors had long-term and electorally successful careers. For each governor, one point was awarded for: a political role prior to age 35; office holding of eight or more years prior to first service as governor; each successful reelection; service for more than four years; service for more than eight years; election to national office following service as governor; and post-governorship service in a statewide office. Scores were averaged when more than one individual served in a five-year period. *Source:* Robert Sobel and John Raimo (eds.), *Biographical Directory of the Governors of the United States, 1798–1978,* 4 vols. (Westport, Conn.: Meckler Books, 1978).

Gov. Power.   Index of formal power of the governor as developed by Joseph Schlesinger. *Sources:* Herbert Jacobs and Kenneth Vines, *Politics in the American States: A Comparative Analysis* (Boston: Little, Brown, 1965), p. 229; 2nd ed. (1971), p. 232: Council of State Governments, *The Book of the States, 1976–77.*

Gov. Reputation.   Governor's reputational rating as developed by Larry Sabato. *Source:* Larry Sabato, *Goodbye to Good-Time Charlie: The American Governor Transformed, 1950–1975* (Lexington, Mass.: D.C. Heath, Lexington Books, 1978), pp. 223–232.

Guardianship.   Scope of state public guardianship laws for the elderly.

Total number of points accumulated for various statutory procedures and requirements. *Source:* Winsor C. Schmidt et al., *Public Guardianship for the Elderly: A National Study,* Final report to AoA, Grant 90-A-1680(01) (Tallahassee: Florida State University, Institute for Social Research, December 1979), table 3–1, pp. 45–47.

Health/Welfare. Composite factor measuring the extensiveness of state health and welfare policy effort for the aging as of 1975. Variables:

1. State expenditure for aged Medicaid recipients per elderly person, 1975. *Source:* U.S. Department of Health, Education, and Welfare, Health Care Financing Administration, *State Tables, Fiscal Year 1975, Medicaid: Recipients, Payments, and Services* (1976), table 23, pp. 62–63.

2. State Medicaid expenditure for home health-care services per elderly person, (1975). *Source:* same as (1).

3. State Medicaid expenditures for dental-care services per elderly person, 1975. *Source:* same as (1).

4. State Medicaid expenditure for skilled nursing-care services per elderly person, 1975. *Source:* same as (1).

Also, all variables comprising the composite factor, Income Maint., listed herein.

Proportion of variance = .675.

Hearing Age. Number of years since adoption of hearing aid regulations. *Source:* "A Review of State Hearing Aid Dealer Licensing Laws," *Hearing Aid Journal,* 1977 (flyer).

Hearing Board. Percentage of hearing aid board members who are not dealers. *Source:* same as Hearing Age.

Hearing Scope. Scope of state hearing aid regulations. Total number of points accumulated for various statutory requirements and restrictions. *Source:* Public Citizen's Retired Professional Action Group, *Paying Through the Ear: A Report on Hearing Health Care Problems* (Washington, D.C.: Public Citizen, Inc., 1973).

Hospital Beds.   Total number of hospital beds per 1,000 population. *Source:* U.S. Bureau of the Census, *Statistical Abstract of the United States,* various years.

Hospital Bed Change.   Change in number of hospital beds per 1,000 persons over previous five years. *Source:* same as Hospital Beds.

Income Change.   Percentage change in per capita income over the previous five years. *Source:* computed from U.S. Bureau of the Census, *Historical Statistics of the United States;* U.S. Bureau of the Census, *Statistical Abstract of the United States, 1976.*

Income Maint.   Composite factor measuring the extensiveness of state income maintenance policy effort for the aging as of 1975. Variables (all listed herein): SSI Limits-C, SSI Limits-I, SSI Pct. Poor, SSI Ratio, Tax Relief.

Proportion of variance = .789.

Indust.-Urban.   Composite factor measuring the extensiveness of industrialization and urbanization in the state. Variables:

1.   Population density. *Source:* U.S. Bureau of the Census, *Historical Statistics of the United States;* U.S. Bureau of the Census, *Statistical Abstract of the United States,* various years; U.S. Bureau of the Census, *Current Population Report,* Series P-20, no. 307.

2.   Percentage of population residing in urban places. *Source:* U.S. Bureau of the Census, *Historical Statistics of the United States.*

3.   Percentage of population residing in Standard Metropolitan Statistical Areas. *Sources:* U.S. Bureau of the Census, *Census of the Population: 1950, 1960;* U.S. Bureau of the Census, *Statistical Abstract of the United States,* various years.

4.   Percentage of labor force not employed in agriculture. *Sources:* U.S. Bureau of the Census, *Census of Population: 1960;* U.S. Bureau of the Census, *Current Population Reports,* Series P-20:, no. 334.

5.   Value added by manufacture. *Source:* U.S. Bureau of the Census, *County and City Data Book,* various years.

6. Union Membership as a percentage of the nonagricultural population. *Source:* U.S. Bureau of the Census, *Statistical Abstract of the United States: 1978,* table 699, p. 430.

Proportion of variance: ranges from .574 to .719 for various years.

Innovation. Walker index of overall policy innovativeness in the state prior to 1965. *Source:* Jack L. Walker, "The Diffusion of Innovations among the American States," *American Political Science Review* 63 (September, 1969):880–899.

Legis. Apport. Composite factor measuring the degree of legislative apportionment in the state, using the methodology developed in the following: William Anderson et al., *Government in the Fifty States* (New York: Holt, Rinehart and Winston, 1960) p. 224; and Glendon Schubert, *Reapportionment* (New York: Charles Scribner and Sons, 1965), pp. 66–67. The measure employs the following variables (drawn from Council of State Governments, *Book of the States,* Lexington, Ky., various years), first reflected (reversed) to measure positive apportionment rather than malapportionment:

1. Percentage below the state average of the least populous legislative district in the lower house.

2. Percentage above the state average of the most populous legislative district in the lower house.

3. Percentage below the state average of the least populous legislative district in the upper house.

4. Percentage above the state average of the most populous legislative district in the upper house.

Percentage of variance: ranges from .401 to .788 for various years.

Legis. Profess. Composite factor measuring the degree of legislative professionalism in the state, using the methodology developed in John G. Grumm, "The Effect of Legislative Structure on Legislative Performance," pp. 298–322 in Richard I. Hofferbert and Ira Sharkansky, eds., *State and Urban Politics: Readings in Comparative Public Policy* (Boston: Little, Brown, 1971). Variables:

1. Length of regular and extra legislative sessions in calendar

days. *Source:* Council of State Governments. *Book of the States,* various years.

2. Number of legislative enactments per biennium. *Source:* same as (1).

3. Estimated biennial compensation of legislators. *Source:* same as (1).

4. Total legislative control expenditures in thousands of dollars (fiscal years). *Source:* U.S. Bureau of the Census, *State Government Finance,* various years.

5. Legislature's approach to program review (1975 only): 0 = no concerted effort; 1 = limited effort; 2 = intensive effort. *Source:* Edgar D. Crane, Jr., *Legislative Review of Government Programs: Tools of Accountability* (New York: Praeger, 1977), p. 92.

Proportion of variance: ranges from .548 to .672 for various years.

Life Expectancy. Life expectancy at birth for total population. *Source:* Gladys K. Bowles and James D. Tarver, *Net Migration of the Population, 1950–60 by Age, Sex and Color* (Washington, D.C.: U.S. Economic Research Service, 1965); and Gladys K. Bowles et al., *Net Migration of the Population, 1960–70 by Age, Sex and Color* (Athens: University of Georgia, 1975).

MAA Expend. State and local expenditure for Medical Assistance to the Aged (MAA), 1964. *Source:* Council of State Governments, *Book of the States, 1966–67,* table 7, p. 365.

Migration. Net migration rates for the total population. *Source:* Gladys K. Bowles and James D. Tarver, *Net Migration of the Population, 1950–60 by Age, Sex and Color* (Washington, D.C.: U.S. Economic Research Service, 1965); and Gladys K. Bowles et al., *Net Migration of the Population, 1960–70 by Age, Sex and Color* (Athens: University of Georgia, 1975).

Need. Composite factor measuring the magnitude of disadvantaged groups in the state. Variables:

1. Percent of population black. *Sources:* U.S. Bureau of the Cen-

sus, *Census of Population: 1970;* U.S. Bureau of the Census, *Current Population Reports,* Series P-23, no. 67.

2.   Percent of population nonwhite. *Source:* same as (1).

3.   Ratio of nonworking to working population. *Sources:* U.S. Bureau of the Census, *Census of Population: 1960, 1970;* U.S. Bureau of the Census, *Current Population Reports,* Series P-20, no. 334.

4.   Gini index of income inequality. *Source:* James E. Jonish and James B. Kau, "State Differentials in Income Inequality," *Review of Social Economy* 31 (October, 1973), table 1, pp. 181–182.

5.   Percentage of families below the poverty level. *Source:* U.S. Bureau of the Census, *Current Population Reports,* Series P-20, no. 334.

Proportion of variance: ranges from .644 to .759 for various years.

NCSC Effort.   Lobbying effort by the state chapter of the National Council of Senior Citizens, rated by a knowledgeable member of its national staff.

N.H. Beds.   Nursing home beds per 1,000 elderly persons. *Source:* John Holahan, *Financing Health Care of the Poor: The Medicaid Experience* (Lexington, Mass.: D.C. Heath, Lexington Books, 1975), pp. 19–20.

N.H. Reimburs.   Medicaid program reimbursement procedures. *Source:* Stephen M. Davidson, "Variations in State Medicaid Programs," *Journal of Health Politics, Policy, and Law 3* (Spring 1978):60–61, table 3.

OAA Payment.   State and local portion of average payment per recipient for Old Age Assistance (OAA). *Source:* Council of State Governments, *Book of the States,* various years.

Party Compet.   Index of competitiveness for state elections. *Source:* Herbert Jacob and Kenneth Vines, *Politics in the American States: A Comparative Analysis* (Boston: Little, Brown, 1965), p. 65; 2nd ed. (1971), p. 87; 3rd ed. (1976), p. 61.

Patient Care. Total number of patient care regulations for nursing homes. *Source:* Jordan Braverman, *Nursing Home Standards* (Washington, D.C.: American Pharmaceutical Association, 1969), pp. 66–69.

Pol. Culture. Index of Elazar's classification of dominant culture. *Source:* Daniel J. Elazar, *American Federalism: A View from the States* (New York: Thomas Y. Crowell, 1966), p. 108.

Pop. Change. Percentage change in total population over the past five years. *Source:* Computed from census data. (See Total Pop.)

Property Tax. Property taxes as a percentage of total state and local government revenue from taxes. *Source:* U.S. Advisory Commission on Intergovernmental Relations, *Significant Features of Fiscal Federalism, 1976–77 Edition,* Vol. II, Revenue and Debt, pp. 126–129.

Scope of Govt. Composite factor measuring the relative size of state and local government in the state. Variables:

1. State and local tax revenue per $1,000 of personal income. *Sources:* U.S. Bureau of the Census, *U.S. Census of Governments: 1957;* U.S. Bureau of the Census, *Governmental Finances,* various years.

2. State and local revenue from own sources per million population. *Sources:* U.S. Bureau of the Census, *U.S. Census of Governments: 1957;* U.S. Bureau of the Census, *Governmental Finances,* various years.

3. State and local revenue from own sources per $1,000 of personal income. *Sources:* same as (2).

4. State and local government employees (full-time equivalent) as a percentage of the labor force. *Source:* U.S. Bureau of the Census, *Statistical Abstract of the United States,* various years.

5. State and local government employees (full-time equivalent) per million population. *Source:* same as (4).

Proportion of variance: ranges from .642 to .784 for various years.

Senior Orgs.   Number of senior organizations represented by witnesses before the Senate Special Committee on Aging. *Source:* U.S., Congress, Senate, Special Committee on Aging, *Witness Index and Research Reference,* 86th–94th Cong., 1959–1975 (1976).

Social Services.   Composite factor measuring the extensiveness of state social services policy effort, 1977. Variables:

1.   Percentage of Title III (Older Americans Act) funds allocated to actual social services rather than administration, etc. *Source:* National Association of State Units on Aging, internal survey.

2.   Amount of state funds in State Unit on Aging budget per capita. *Source:* same as (1).

3.   Amount of state funds in State Unit on Aging administrative budget per capita. *Source:* same as (1).

Proportion of variance = .601

SSI Aged Pay.   Total average monthly payment per recipient of Aid to the Aged. *Source:* Council of State Governments, *The Book of the States,* various years.

SSI Blind Pay.   Total average monthly payment per recipient of Aid to the Blind. *Source:* Council of State Governments, *The Book of the States,* various years.

SSI Disab. Pay.   Total average monthly payment per recipient of Aid to the Disabled. *Source:* Council of State Governments, *The Book of the States,* various years.

SSI Limits-C.   Monthly dollar limit on state supplemental payments under Supplemental Security Income to aged couples. *Source: SSI Advocates Handbook,* (New York: Center on Social Welfare Policy and Law, 1975), chart A, p. 166 ff.

SSI Limits-I.   Monthly dollar limit on state supplemental payments under Supplemental Security Income to aged individuals living independently. *Source: SSI Advocates Handbook,* (New York: Center on Social Welfare Policy and Law, 1975), chart A, p. 166 ff.

SSI Pct. Aged.   Recipients of SSI-Aged state supplement as a percentage of all elderly. *Source:* Neil Gilbert, Harry Specht, and Gary Nelson, "Social Services to the Elderly: Title XX and the Aging Network," Final report submitted under Grant 90-A-945/01 from AoA, DHEW (San Francisco: Institute for Scientific Analysis, February 1979).

SSI Pct. Poor. Recipients of SSI-Aged as a percentage of elderly poor. *Source:* computed from project data. (See SSI-Aged.)

SSI Ratio. Ratio of SSI-Aged state supplement recipients to federal SSI recipients. *Source:* computed from project data. (See SSI-Aged.)

Status. Composite factor measuring the magnitude of advantaged groups in the state. Variables:

1. Percentage of the employed population in professional and managerial occupations. *Source:* U.S. Bureau of the Census, *Current Population Reports,* Series P-20, no. 334.

2. Percentage of the population age 25 and over that finished high school. *Source:* U.S. Bureau of the Census, *County and City Data Book,* various years.

3. Median number of years of schooling completed among the population age 25 and over. *Source:* same as (2).

4. Personal income per capita. *Source:* U.S. Bureau of the Census, *Historical Statistics of the United States;* U.S. Bureau of the Census, *Statistical Abstract of the United States; 1976.*

5. Median family income. *Source:* U.S. Bureau of the Census, Historical Statistics of the United States; U.S. Bureau of the Census, *Current Population Reports,* Series P-20, no. 334.

Proportion of variance: ranges from .707 to .813 for various years.

SUA Budget. Total budget of the State Unit on Aging, divided by the number of elderly persons in the state. *Source:* National Association of State Units on Aging, internal survey.

SUA Size. Composite factor measuring the size of the State Unit on Aging, as of 1977. Variables:

1. Total budget of the State Unit on Aging. *Source:* National
    Association of State Units on Aging, internal survey.

2. Total administrative budget of the State Unit on Aging. *Source:*
    same as (1).

3. Number of professional staff in the State Unit on Aging. *Source:*
    same as (1).

4. Number of Area Agencies on Aging in the state. *Source:* same
    as (1).

Proportion of variance = .514 (SUA Size and SUA Status together).

SUA Status. Composite factor measuring the status of the State Unit
on Aging within the state hierarchy of agencies as of 1977. Variables:

1. State Unit on Aging level within state government: 1 = office,
    bureau, or division; 2 = commission, council, or board; 3 =
    governor's office; 4 = cabinet department. *Source:* National
    Association of State Units on Aging, internal survey.

2. Location of State Unit on Aging in an "umbrella" agency: 0
    = yes; 1 = no. *Source:* Same as (1).

3. Status of Director of State Unit on Aging: 0 = appointed; 1 =
    merit. *Source:* Same as (1).

Proportion of variance = .271 (SUA Size and SUA Status together).

Tax Effort. Tax effort relative to capacity, for state and local government. *Source:* Kent D. Halstead, *Tax Wealth in Fifty States* (Washington, D.C.: National Institute of Education, DHEW, 1978), table
7, pp. 36–37.

Tax Pct. Percentage of state-local general revenue from taxes. *Source:*
U.S. Advisory Commission on Intergovernmental Relations, *Sig-
nificant Features of Fiscal Federalism,* 1976–77 Edition, vol. 2,
Revenue and Debt.

Tax Regress. Index of tax regressivity. *Sources:* Stephen E. Lile,
"Family Tax Burden Differences among the States," *State Government* 49 (Winter 1976):17; and Stephen E. Lile and Don M.

Soule, "Interstate Differences in Family Tax Burdens," *National Tax Journal* 22 (December 1969):445.

Tax Relief. Average dollar amount of tax relief for the elderly, including property and income tax provisions. *Source:* U.S. Department of Housing and Urban Development, Office of Policy Development and Research, *Property Tax Relief for the Elderly: A Compendium Report,* April 1975.

T19 Aged Exp. State expenditure for aged Medicaid recipients as a percentage of all persons aged 65 and above. *Source:* U.S. Department of Health, Education, and Welfare, Health Care Financing Administration, *State Tables, Fiscal Year 1975, Medicaid: Recipients, Payments, and Services (1976),* table 23, pp. 62–63.

T19 ICF Exp. State Medicaid expenditures for intermediate care services per elderly person, 1975. *Source:* U.S. Department of Health, Education, and Welfare, Health Care Financing Administration, *State Tables, Fiscal Year 1975, Medicaid: Recipients, Payments, and Services (1976),* table 23, pp. 62–63.

T19 Needy Elig. Availability of Medicaid services to medically needy persons. *Sources:* Stephen M. Davidson, "Variations in State Medicaid Programs," *Journal of Health Politics, Policy, and Law* 3 (Spring 1978):60–61, table 3.

T19 Opt. Serv. Extensiveness of optional services covered under Medicaid. *Source:* same as above.

T19 SNF Exp. State Medicaid expenditure for skilled nursing care services per elderly person. *Source:* U.S. Department of Health, Education and Welfare, Health Care Financing Administration, *State Tables, Fiscal Year 1975, Medicaid: Recipients, Payments, and Services* (1976), table 23, pp. 62–63.

T19 Total Exp. State expenditure for all Medicaid recipients per capita. *Source:* U.S. Department of Health, Education and Welfare, Health Care Financing Administration, *State Tables, Fiscal Year 1975, Medicaid: Recipients, Payments, and Services (1976):*62–63, table 23.

Total Pop. Total state population. *Sources:* U.S. Bureau of the Census, *Historical Statistics of the United States;* U.S. Bureau of the

Census, *Statistical Abstract of the United States,* various years; U.S. Bureau of the Census, *Current Population Reports,* Series P-20, no. 307.

T20 Pct. SSI. Percentage of Title XX expenditures for the aged going to aged persons receiving SSI. *Source:* Neil Gilbert, Harry Specht, and Gary Nelson, "Social Services to the Elderly: Title XX and the Aging Network," Final report submitted under Grant 90-A-945/01 from AoA, DHEW (San Francisco: Institute for Scientific Analysis, February 1979), table 8.4, pp. 155–156.

T20 Utilization. Extensiveness of the use of state funds to obtain the maximum amount of federal assistance in Title XX. *Source:* Neil Gilbert, Harry Specht, and Gary Nelson, "Social Services to the Elderly: Title XX and the Aging Network," Final report submitted under Grant 90-A-945/01 from AoA, DHEW (San Francisco: Institute for Scientific Analysis, February 1979).

Union Members. Union members as percentage of labor force. *Source:* U.S. Bureau of the Census, *Statistical Abstract of the United States: 1978,* table 699, p. 430.

Unemployment. Percentage of economically active persons unemployed. *Source:* U.S. Bureau of the Census, *Current Population Reports,* Series P-20, no. 334.

Voter Turnout. Percentage of voting-age population voting for president. *Sources:* U.S. Bureau of the Census, *Historical Statistics of the United States;* U.S. Bureau of the Census, *Statistical Abstract of the United States: 1979.*

References

Aaron, Henry J. 1975. *Who Pays the Property Tax?* Washington, D.C.: The Brookings Institution.

Abernethy, David S., and David A. Pearson. 1979. *Regulating Hospital Care.* Ann Arbor, Mich.: AUPHA Press.

Advisory Commission on Intergovernmental Relations, 1982. *Federalism in 1982: Renewing the Debate.* Washington, D.C.

Alfaro, Jose, and Monica Holmes. 1981. "Caveats and Cautions: Title XX Group Eligibility for the Elderly." *The Gerontologist* 21 (August):374–381.

Anderson, Douglas D. 1981. *Regulatory Politics and Electric Utilities.* Boston: Auburn House.

Bass, Jack, and Walter De Vries. 1976. *The Transformation of Southern Politics: Social Change and Political Consequences Since 1945.* New York: New American Library.

Beyle, Thad L., and Merle Black. 1975. *Politics and Policy in North Carolina.* New York: MSS Information Corporation.

Bingham, Richard D. 1977. "The Diffusion of Innovation among Local Governments." *Urban Affairs Quarterly* 13 (December):223–232.

Bone, Hugh. 1978. "The Political Setting." In Frank Mullen et al., eds., *The Government and Politics of Washington State.* Pullman: Washington State University Press, pp. 1–17.

Bovbjerg, Randall R., and John Holahan. 1982. *Medicaid in the Reagan Era: Federal Policy and State Choices.* Washington, D.C.: Urban Institute Press.

Brown, David K. 1983. "Administering Aging Programs in a Federal System." In William P. Browne and Laura Katz Olson, eds., *Aging and Public Policy: The Politics of Growing Old in America.* Westport, Conn.: Greenwood Press, pp. 201–219.

Bruner, Charles H. 1978. "Representation by Surrogate: The Politics of Aging in a State Legislative Setting." Ph.D. dissertation, Department of Political Science, Stanford University.

Bryan, Frank M. 1981. *Politics in the Rural States: People, Parties, and Processes.* Boulder, Colo.: Westview Press.

Buchanan, Robert J. 1981. *Health-Care Finance.* Lexington, Mass.: D.C. Heath and Company, Lexington Books.

Burke, Vincent J. 1974. *Nixon's Good Deed: Welfare Reform.* New York: Columbia University Press.

Cady, John F. 1975. *Drugs on the Market.* Lexington, Mass.: D.C. Heath and Company, Lexington Books.

Canon, Bradley C., and Lawrence Baum. 1981. "Patterns of Adoption of Tort Law Innovations: An Application of Diffusion Theory to Judicial Doctrines." *American Political Science Review* 75 (December):975–987.

Citizens Conference on State Legislatures. 1971. *State Legislatures: An Evaluation of their Effectiveness.* New York: Praeger.

Cobb, Roger, and Charles Elder. 1972. *Participation in American Politics: The Dynamics of Agenda-Building.* Boston: Allyn and Bacon.

Colburn, David R., and Richard K. Scher. 1980. *Florida's Gubernatorial Politics in the Twentieth Century.* Tallahassee: University Presses of Florida.

Congressional Quarterly. 1983. "The New Face of State Politics." *Congressional Quarterly* 41 (September 3):1767–1871.

Council of State Governments. Biennial. *Book of the States.* Lexington, Ky.

Crane, Edgar G., Jr. 1977. *Legislative Review of Government Programs: Tools of Accountability.* New York: Praeger.

Cronin, Thomas E. 1980. *The State of the Presidency.* Boston: Little, Brown.

Cutler, Neal E. 1977. "Demographic, Socio-economic, and Political Factors in the Politics of Aging: A Foundation for Research in Political Gerontology." *American Political Science Review* 71 (March):1011–1025.

Cutler, Neal E., and Charles S. Harris. 1983. *Approaches to Best Practices in the Use of Intrastate Funding Formulas for Targeting Services to Older Americans.* Washington, D.C.: Bureau of Social Science Research, Inc.

Davidson, Stephen M. 1978. "Variations in State Medicaid Programs." *Journal of Health Politics, Policy, and Law* 3 (Spring):60–61, table 3.

———. 1980. *Medicaid Decisions: A Systematic Analysis of the Cost Problem.* Cambridge, Mass.: Ballinger.

Derthick, Martha. 1970. *The Influence of Federal Grants: Public Assistance in Massachusetts.* Cambridge: Harvard University Press.

———. 1975. *Uncontrollable Spending for Social Services.* Washington, D.C.: The Brookings Institution.

Dobson, Douglas, and David A. Karns. 1979. "Public Policy and Senior Citizens: Policy Formation in the American States." Final Report to the Administration on Aging, no. 90-A-1055. DeKalb: Northern Illinois University.

Drake, David F. 1980. "The Cost of Hospital Regulation." In Arthur Levin, ed., *Regulating Health Care.* New York: Proceedings of the Academy of Political Science, pp. 45–59.

Dunlop, Burton D. 1979. *The Growth of Nursing Home Care.* Lexington, Mass.: D.C. Heath and Company, Lexington Books.

Dunn, William. 1981. *Public Policy Analysis: An Introduction.* Englewood Cliffs, N.J.: Prentice-Hall.

Dye, Thomas. 1966. *Politics, Economics and the Public: Policy Outcomes in the American States.* Chicago: Rand McNally.

Dye, Thomas R., and Virginia Gray. 1980. *The Determinants of Public Policy.* Lexington, Mass.: D.C. Heath and Company.

Echols, John M., III. 1980. "Fiscal Redistribution and State Spending Differentials: The United States in Comparative Perspective." In Barry S. Rundquist, ed., *Political Benefits: Empirical Studies of American Public Programs.* Lexington, Mass.: D.C. Heath and Company, chapter 7.

Elazar, Daniel J. 1972. *American Federalism: A View from the States,* 2nd ed. New York: Harper & Row.

Ellul, Jacques. 1967. *The Technological Society.* New York: Knopf.

Ellwood, John W. 1982. *Reductions in U.S. Domestic Spending: How They Affect State and Local Governments.* New Brunswick, N.J. Transaction Books.

Estes, Carroll L. 1979. *The Aging Enterprise.* San Francisco: Jossey-Bass.

Estes, Carroll L.; Robert J. Newcomer; and associates. 1983. *Fiscal Austerity and Aging: Shifting Government Responsibility for the Elderly.* Beverly Hills, Calif.: Sage.

Fairholm, Gilbert W. 1978. *Property Tax Relief Programs for the Elderly: A Review of Current Literature and Policy Implications for Virginia.* Charlottesville: Virginia Center on Aging, Virginia Commonwealth University.

Feder, Judith, and John Holahan. 1980. "Administrative Choices." In Theodore R. Marmor, Judith Feder, and John Holahan, eds., *National Health Insurance: Conflicting Goals and Policy Choices.* Washington, D.C.: The Urban Institute, pp. 21–71.

Feder, Judith, and William Scanlon. 1980. "Regulating Bed Supply in Nursing Homes." *Milbank Memorial Fund Quarterly: Health and Society* 58 (Spring):54–88.

Federal Council on Aging. 1978. *Public Policy and the Frail Elderly.* Washington, D.C.: U.S. Department of Health, Education, and Welfare.

Federal Trade Commission. Bureau of Consumer Protection. 1978a. *Funeral Industry Practices: Final Staff Report and Proposed Trade Regulation Rule.* Washington, D.C.: U.S. Government Printing Office.

———. 1978b. *Hearing Aid Industry: Final Report to the Federal*

Trade Commission and Proposed Trade Regulation Rule. Washington, D.C.: U.S. Government Printing Office.

Feldstein, Paul J. 1977. *Health Associations and the Demand for Legislation.* Cambridge, Mass.: Ballinger Publishing Company.

——. 1980. "The Political Environment of Regulation." In Arthur Levin, ed., *Regulating Health Care.* New York: Proceedings of the Academy of Political Science, pp. 6–20.

Fenton, John H. 1966. *Midwest Politics.* New York: Holt, Rinehart & Winston.

Foster, John L. 1978. "Regionalism and Innovation in the American States." *Journal of Politics* 40 (February):179–187.

Fry, Brian, and Richard Winters. 1970. "The Politics of Redistribution." *American Political Science Review* 64 (June):508–522.

Garfinkel, Irwin, ed. 1982. *Income-Tested Transfer Programs: The Case For and Against.* New York: The Academic Press.

Garfinkel, Irwin, and Felicity Skidmore. 1978. *Income Support Policy: Where We've Come and Where We Should Be Going.* Madison: Institute for Research on Poverty, University of Wisconsin.

Gieske, Millard L. 1979. *Minnesota Farmer-Laborism: The Third Party Alternative.* Minneapolis: University of Minnesota Press.

Gilbert, Neil. 1981. "The Transformation of Social Services." In Neil Gilbert and Harry Specht, eds., *The Emergence of Social Welfare and Social Work.* Itasca, Ill.: F.E. Peacock, pp. 101–118.

Gilbert, Neil, and Harry Specht. 1979. "Title XX Planning By Area Agencies on Aging: Efforts, Outcomes and Policy Implications." *The Gerontologist* 19 (June):264–274.

——. 1981. *Social Services to the Elderly Under Title XX: National Trends, 1976–1980.* Berkeley, Calif.: Institute for Scientific Analysis.

——. (1982). "A 'Fair Share' for the Aged: Title XX Allocation Patterns, 1976–1980." *Research on Aging* 4 (March):71–86.

Glick, Henry R. 1981. "Innovation in State Judicial Administration: Effects on Court Management and Organization." *American Politics Quarterly* 9 (January):49–69.

Gold, Steven David. 1979. *Property Tax Relief.* Lexington, Mass.: D.C. Heath and Company, Lexington Books.

Gormley, William T., Jr. 1983. *The Politics of Public Utility Regulation.* Pittsburgh: University of Pittsburgh Press.

Gray, Virginia. 1973. "Innovation in the States: A Diffusion Study." *American Political Science Review* 67 (December):1174–1185.

Grimaldi, Paul L. 1980. *Supplemental Security Income: The New Federal Program for the Aged, Blind and Disabled.* Washington, D.C.: American Enterprise Institute.

Grumm, John G. 1971. "The Effects of Legislative Structure on Legislative Performance." In Richard I. Hofferbert and Ira Sharkansky, eds., *State and Urban Politics: Readings in Comparative Public Policy*. Boston: Little, Brown, pp. 298–322.

Gutowski, Michael F., and Jeffrey L. Koshel. 1982. "Social Services." In John L. Palmer and Isabel V. Sawhill, eds., *The Reagan Experiment*. Washington, D.C.: Urban Institute Press, pp. 307–328.

Hale, George E., and Marian Lief Palley. 1981. *The Politics of Federal Grants*. Washington, D.C.: Congressional Quarterly Press.

Halstead, Kent D. 1978. *Tax Wealth in Fifty States*. Washington, D.C.: National Institute of Education.

Harbert, Anita S. 1976. *Federal Grants in Aid: Maximizing Benefits to the States*. New York: Praeger.

Hawkins, Robert B., Jr. 1982. *American Federalism: A New Partnership for the Republic*. San Francisco: Institute for Contemporary Studies.

Herzog, Barbara. 1978. *Aging and Income: Programs and Prospects for the Elderly*. New York: Human Sciences Press.

Holahan, John. 1975. *Financing Health Care for the Poor: The Medicaid Experience*. Lexington, Mass.: D.C. Heath and Company, Lexington Books.

Holtzman, Abraham. 1963. *The Townsend Movement*. New York: Bookman Associates, Inc.

Hopkins, William S. 1961. *Aging in the State of Washington*. Seattle: University of Washington Press.

Hudson, Robert B. 1981. "A Block Grant to the States for Long-Term Care." *Journal of Health Politics, Policy and Law* 6 (Spring):9–28.

Jones, Charles O. 1975. *Clean Air: The Policies and Politics of Pollution Control*. Pittsburgh: University of Pittsburgh Press.

Kasschau, Patricia L. 1978. *Aging and Social Policy: Leadership Planning*. New York: Praeger.

Kemp, Kathleen A. 1978. "Nationalization of the American States: A Test of the Thesis." *American Politics Quarterly* 6 (April):237–247.

Kincaid, John E. 1982. *Political Culture, Public Policy and the American States*. Philadelphia: Institute for the Study of Human Issues.

Klingman, David. 1982. "The Impact of Changing Intergovernmental Relations on State and Local Expenditures and Revenues." Paper presented at the Annual Convention of the American Political Science Association, Denver, 1–5 September.

Klingman, David, and William W. Lammers. 1984. "The 'General Policy Liberalism' Factor in American State Politics." *American Journal of Political Science* 28 (August), forthcoming.

Koff, Sondra Z. 1981. "The Delivery of Health Care and Political Culture." *Policy Studies Journal,* Special Issue no. 1, pp. 294–300.

Lammers, William W. 1982. "Governors as Policy Leaders: A Quantitative Assessment." Paper presented at the Annual Convention of the American Political Science Association, Denver, 1–5 September.

———. 1983. *Public Policy and the Aging.* Washington, D.C.: Congressional Quarterly Press.

Leach, Robert H. 1983. Intergovernmental Relations in the 1980's. New York: Marcel and Dekker, Inc.

Lee, Philip R., and A.E. Benjamin. 1983. "Intergovernmental Relations: Historical and Comparative Perspectives." In Carroll L. Estes, et al., *Fiscal Austerity and Aging: Shifting Government Responsibility for the Elderly.* Beverly Hills, Calif.: Sage, pp. 59–81.

Lindeman, David A., and Alan Pardini. 1983. "Social Services: The Impact of Fiscal Austerity." In Carroll L. Estes et al., *Fiscal Austerity and Aging.* Beverly Hills, Calif.: Sage, pp. 133–155.

Liner, E. Blaine, and Lawrence K. Lynch. 1977. *The Economics of Southern Growth.* Durham, N.C.: Southern Growth Policies Board.

Lockard, Duane. 1959. *New England State Politics.* Princeton, N.J.: Princeton University Press.

Lovell, Catherine H. 1983. "Some Thoughts on Hyperintergovernmentalization." In Richard H. Leach, ed., *Intergovernmental Relations in the 1980s.* New York: Marcel and Dekker, Inc., pp. 86–95.

Lowy, Louis. 1980. *Social Policies and Programs on Aging.* Lexington, Mass.: D.C. Heath and Company, Lexington Books.

Marmor, Theodore R. 1970. *The Politics of Medicare.* Chicago: Aldine Publishing Co.

Matura, Raymond C. 1981. "Self Advocacy by the Elderly: A Case Study." Paper presented at the Annual Convention of the Gerontological Society, Toronto, 11 November.

Mendleson, Mary A. 1974. *Tender Loving Greed.* New York: Alfred A. Knopf.

Merritt, Richard E. 1982. *Recent and Proposed Changes in State Medicaid Programs: A Fifty State Survey.* Washington, D.C.: Intergovernmental Health Policy Project, George Washington University.

Mitford, Jessica. 1963. *The American Way of Death.* New York: Simon & Schuster.

Moon, Marilyn. 1977. "The Economic Welfare of the Aged and Income Security Programs." In Moon and Eugene Smolensky, eds., *Improving Measures of Economic Well-Being.* New York: Academic Press, pp. 87–110.

Morehouse, Sara McCally. 1980. *State Politics, Parties and Policy.* New York: Holt, Rinehart & Winston.

Mosher, Frederick C., and Orville F. Poland. 1964. *The Costs of American Governments: Facts, Trends, and Myths.* New York: Dodd, Mead and Company.

Moynihan, Daniel P. 1980. *Count Our Blessings.* Boston: Little, Brown.

Myrtle, Robert; William W. Lammers; and David Klingman. 1982. "Long Term Care Regulation in the States: A Systemic Perspective." Paper delivered at the Annual Convention of the American Public Health Association, Montreal, 14–18 November.

Nelson, Gary. 1980. "Contrasting Services for the Aged." *Social Service Review* 54 (September):376–389.

Neugarten, Bernice L., ed. 1982. *Age or Need?: Public Policies for Older People.* Beverly Hills, Calif.: Sage.

Olson, Mancur, Jr. 1971. *The Logic of Collective Action: Public Goods and the Theory of Groups.* New York: Schocken.

Perry, Charles S. 1981. "Energy Conservation Policy in the American States: An Attempt at Explanation." *Social Science Quarterly* 62 (September):540–546.

Perry, James. 1976. "Strikes in State Government Employment." *State Government,* Autumn, pp. 255–264.

Pertschuk, Michael. 1982. *Revolt Against Regulation: The Rise and Pause of The Consumer Movement.* Berkeley: University of California Press.

Peterson, George E. 1982. "The State and Local Sector." In John L. Palmer and Isabel V. Sawhill, ed., *The Reagan Experiment.* Washington, D.C.: Urban Institute Press, chapter 6.

Plotnick, Robert B., and Felicity Skidmore. 1975. *Progress Against Poverty: A Review of the 1964–1974 Decade.* New York: Academic Press.

Pratt, Henry J. 1976. *The Gray Lobby.* Chicago: University of Chicago Press.

Public Citizen's Retired Professional Action Group. 1973. *Paying Through the Ear: A Report on Hearing Health Care Problems.* Washington, D.C.: Public Citizen, Inc.

Putnam, Jackson K. 1970. *Old-Age Politics in California.* Stanford, Calif.: Stanford University Press.

Ranney, Austin. 1976. "Parties in State Politics." In Herbert Jacob and Kenneth N. Vines, eds., *Politics in the American States: A Comparative Analysis,* 3rd edition. Boston: Little, Brown, pp. 51–91.

Ransone, Coleman B., Jr. 1982. *The American Governorship.* Westport, Conn.: Greenwood Press.

Reagan, Michael D., and John G. Sanzone. 1981. *The New Federalism.* New York: Oxford University Press.

Redford, Emmette S. 1969. *Democracy in the Administrative State.* New York: Oxford University Press.

Riley, Dennis D. 1975. *Specialized Policy Making: A System-Subsystem Model.* Phoenix: Center for Public Affairs, Arizona State University.

Rose, Arnold. 1963. *The Aging in Minnesota.* Minneapolis: University of Minnesota Press.

Rose, Douglas D. 1973. "National and Local Forces in State Politics: The Implications of Multi-Level Policy Analysis." *American Political Science Review* 67 (December):1162–1173.

Rosenbaum, Walter. 1981. *Energy, Politics and Public Policy.* Washington, D.C.: Congressional Quarterly Press.

Rosenthal, Alan. 1981. *Legislative Life: People, Process, and Performance in the States.* New York: Harper & Row.

Ruchlin, Hirsch S. 1977. "A New Strategy for Regulating Long Term Care Facilities." *Journal of Health Politics, Policy and Law* 2 (Summer):190–211.

Sabato, Larry. 1978. *Goodbye to Goodtime Charlie: The American Governor Transformed,* 1950–1975. Lexington, Mass.: D.C. Heath and Company, Lexington Books.

———. 1983. *Goodbye to Goodtime Charlie: The American Governorship Transformed,* 2nd ed. Washington, D.C.: Congressional Quarterly Press.

Salkever, David S., and Thomas W. Bice. 1979. *Hospital Certificate of Need Controls.* Washington, D.C.: American Public Enterprise Institute in Health Policy.

Savage, Robert L. 1978. "Policy Innovativeness as a Trait of American States." *Journal of Politics* 40 (February):212–224.

———. 1981. "Looking for Political Subcultures: A Critique of the Rummage-Sale Approach." *Western Political Quarterly* 34 (June):331–336.

Scanlon, William. 1978. *A Theory of the Nursing Home Market.* Working Paper 5057-1A. Washington, D.C.: Urban Institute.

Schechter, Stephen L. 1983. "The State of American Federalism: 1982." *Publius* 13 (Spring):1–11.

Schlesinger, Joseph. 1971. "The Politics of the Executives." In Herbert Jacob and Kenneth N. Vines, eds., *Politics in the American States: A Comparative Analysis,* 2nd ed. Boston: Little, Brown, pp. 207–238.

Schmidt, Winsor D.; Kent S. Miller; William G. Bell; and B. Elaine New. 1979. *Public Guardianship and the Elderly.* U.S. DHEW,

Final Report to Administration on Aging, Grant no. 90-A-1680(01). Washington, D.C.: U.S. Government Printing Office.

Schorr, Alvin. 1960. *Filial Responsibility in the Modern American Family*. Washington, D.C.: Department of Health, Education and Welfare.

Schram, Sanford E. 1981. "Politics, Professionalism, and the Changing Federalism." *Social Service Review* 55 (March):78–92.

Schubert, Glendon. 1965. *Reapportionment*. New York: Scribners.

Schulz, James H. 1980. *The Economics of Aging*, 2nd ed. Belmont, Calif.: Wadsworth Publishing.

Sharkansky, Ira. 1968. *Spending in the American States*. Chicago: Rand McNally.

———. 1969. "The Utility of Elazar's Political Culture: A Research Note." *Polity*, Fall, pp. 66–83.

———. 1972. *The Maligned States: Policy Accomplishments, Problems, and Opportunities*. New York: McGraw-Hill.

Sharkansky, Ira, and Richard I. Hofferbert. 1969. "Dimensions of State Politics, Economics, and Public Policy." *American Political Science Review* 63 (September):867–879.

Sigelman, Lee, and Roland E. Smith, 1980. "Consumer Legislation in the American States: An Attempt at Explanation." *Social Science Quarterly* 61 (June):58–70.

———. 1981. "Personal, Office and State Characteristics as Predictors of Gubernatorial Performance." *Journal of Politics* 43 (February):169–180.

Silverman, Milton, and Philip R. Lee. 1974. *Pills, Profits and Politics*. Berkeley: University of California Press.

Silverman, Milton; Philip R. Lee; and Mia Lydecker. 1981. *Pills and the Public Purse*. Berkeley: University of California Press.

Simeon, Richard. 1972. *Federal-Provincial Diplomacy*. Toronto: University of Toronto Press.

Smith, David B. 1981. *Long Term Care in Transition: The Regulation of Nursing Homes*. Washington, D.C.: AUPHA Press.

Spiegel, Allen D. 1979. *Medicaid Experience*. Rockville, Md.: Aspen Systems.

Stanfield, Rochelle. 1983. "Federalism Report." *National Journal* 15 (June 26):1320–1326.

Steinberg, Raymond M. 1977. *A Longitudinal Analysis of 97 Area Agencies on Aging*. Los Angeles: University of Southern California, Social Policy Laboratory.

Stevens, Robert, and Rosemary Stevens. 1974. *Welfare Medicine in America: A Study of Medicaid*. New York: Free Press.

Stonecash, Jeff. 1980. "Sources of State Policy." In Thomas R. Dye and Virginia Gray, eds., *The Determinants of Public Policy.* Lexington, Mass.: D.C. Heath and Company, chapter 2.

———. 1983. "Comparative State Political Analysis." Paper delivered at 1983 American Political Science Association Meetings, Chicago, September.

Struyk, Raymond J., and Beth J. Soldo. 1980. *Improving the Elderly's Housing.* Cambridge, Mass.: Ballinger Publishing Company.

Sullivan, John L. 1972. "A Note on Redistributive Politics." *American Political Science Review* 66 (December):1301–1305.

———. 1973. "Political Correlates of Social, Economic, and Religious Diversity in the American States." *Journal of Politics* 37 (May):392–416.

Surrey, Stanley. 1973. *Pathways to Tax Reform—The Concept of Tax Expenditures.* Cambridge: Harvard University Press.

Underwood, James E., and William J. Daniels. 1982. *Governor Rockefeller in New York: The Apex of Pragmatic Liberalism in the U.S.* Westport, Conn.: Greenwood Press.

U.S. Bureau of the Census. 1981. *Statistical Abstract of the United States.* Washington, D.C.: U.S. Government Printing Office.

U.S. Department of Housing and Urban Development. 1975. *Property Tax Relief Programs for the Elderly: An Evaluation.* Washington, D.C.

U.S. General Accounting Office. 1982. *Preliminary Findings on Patient Characteristics and State Medicaid Expenditures for Nursing Home Care.* Washington, D.C.: U.S. Government Printing Office.

———. 1983. *Medicaid and Nursing Home Care: Cost Increases and the Need for Services Are Creating Problems for the States and the Elderly.* Washington, D.C.

U.S. Office of Management and Budget. 1983. *Special Analyses: Budget of the United States Government FY 1984.* Washington, D.C.: U.S. Government Printing Office.

Uslaner, Eric M. 1978. "Comparative State Policy Formation, Interparty Competition, and Malapportionment: A New Look at 'V.O. Key's Hypothesis'." *Journal of Politics* 40 (May):409–432.

Uslaner, Eric M., and Ronald E. Weber. 1977. *Patterns of Decision Making in State Legislatures.* New York: Praeger.

Viscusi, W. Kip. 1979. *Welfare of the Elderly: An Economic Analysis and Policy Prescription.* New York: John Wiley & Sons.

Vladeck, Bruce C. 1980. *Unloving Care: The Nursing Home Tragedy.* New York: Basic Books.

Walker, David B. 1981. *Toward a Functioning Federalism.* Cambridge, Mass.: Winthrop.

Walker, Jack L. 1969. "The Diffusion of Innovations Among the American States." *American Political Science Review* 63 (September):880–899.

————. 1971. "Innovation in State Politics." In Herbert Jacob and Kenneth N. Vines, eds., *Politics in the American States: A Comparative Analysis.* Boston: Little, Brown, pp. 354–387.

Walker, James W., and Harriet L. Lazer. 1978. *The End of Mandatory Retirement: Implications for Management.* New York: John Wiley & Sons.

Weinstein, Bernard L., and Robert E. Firestine. 1978. *Regional Growth and Decline in the United States.* New York: Praeger.

Weiss, Leonard W. 1981. "State Regulation of Public Utilities and Marginal-Cost Pricing." In Leonard W. Weiss and Michael W. Klass, eds., *Case Studies in Regulation.* Boston: Little, Brown, pp. 262–292.

Welch, Susan, and Kay Thompson. 1980. "Impact of Federal Incentives on State Policy Innovation." *American Journal of Political Science* 24 (November):715–729.

Williamson, Homer. 1976. Personal communication. St. Cloud, Minnesota.

Williamson, John B.; Linda Evans; and Lawrence Powell. 1982. *The Politics of Aging: Power and Policy.* Springfield, Ill.: C.C. Thomas.

Williamson, Richard S. 1983. "The 1982 New Federalism Negotiations." *Publius* 13 (Spring):11–32.

Wing, Kenneth R., and Burton Craige. 1979. "Health Care Regulation: Dilemma of a Partially Developed Public Policy." *North Carolina Law Review,* August, pp. 1165–1195.

Zias, James P.; Raymond J. Struyk; and Thomas Thibodeau. 1982. *Housing Assistance for Older Americans: The Reagan Prescription.* Washington, D.C.: The Urban Institute Press.

Index

About the Authors

William W. Lammers is a professor of political science and a research associate in the Andrus Gerontology Center at the University of Southern California. His previous books include *Public Policy and the Aging* and contributions to *Aging: Prospects and Issues* and *Work and Retirement: Policy Issues*. Specialized analyses and discussions of aging-related issues and executive behavior have appeared in such journals as: *American Journal of Political Science, Canadian Journal of Political Science, Political Science Quarterly, Polity, Presidential Studies Quarterly, Public Administration Review,* and *Research on Aging*. In his state research, he has conducted extensive interviews of legislators, lobbyists, and members of the aging network in all sections of the country.

David Klingman is an associate professor of political science at The George Washington University, specializing in public policy analysis. His previous studies of public policy and of electoral patterns have appeared in such journals as: *American Journal of Political Science, American Political Science Review, British Journal of Political Science, Political Studies, Sage Professional Papers,* and the *Western Political Quarterly*. His research activities have included extensive analyses of policy change over time and, in his joint research with William Lammers, the integration of case studies and systematic measures of change in aging-related policies.

253